PRAISE FOR
CAROL GURN

D0401727

"I took a workshop with Carol Gurney many years ago, and it totally turned around how I relate to animals. In this wonderful, warm book, Carol will teach you the skills of communication and you will be forever grateful."
—Louise L. Hay, author of *You Can Heal Your Life*

"Carol Gurney can really express herself when it comes to teaching the art of communicating with animals. And believe me, it works! Carol's HeartTalk Program℠ goes beyond talking with animals. It is a marvelous way to expand our relationships with the animals in our lives."
—Arthur Myers, author of *Communicating with Animals*

"I first met Carol Gurney about ten years ago when I attended a talk she gave on animal communication. . . . I was definitely impressed. She struck me as a person 'with both feet on the ground,' and I really liked how she approached her work. I decided to have her do a reading on my own eight pets, in part to further test her skills. She came through again with flying colors. She came up with things that she could not have known by ordinary means. The rest is history. I have referred many clients to her over the years and have been happy with the results. . . . Carol has had a profound effect on the way I view—and the way I experience—my relationship with our furry, feathery, scaly companions and other fellow earth beings. She is a very special lady!"
—Kathleen M. Carson, D.V.M.

"[Carol] has the ability to obtain precise information directly 'from the horse's mouth' concerning the sources of its pains and diseases. If I have a horse patient that is not improving with either conventional or alternative medicine, I might ask Carol to try to obtain some more information using her skill. Occasionally, her input has been more helpful than X rays or blood tests in arriving at a diagnosis."
—Greg Ugarte, D.V.M.

Please turn the page for more extraordinary acclaim. . . .

"*The Language of Animals* offers us great possibilities in deepening our connections with our kindred spirits. Carol's program can help us get in touch with levels of connection beyond our normal recognition."
—Allen M. Schoen, D.V.M., MS, author of *Kindred Spirits* and Director, Veterinary Institute for Therapeutic Alternatives

"Carol has done a wonderful job of opening us up to the magic of communication with the animals in our lives. I particularly like the exercises she outlines throughout the book. They provide the reader with the key to open the door into a new way of seeing the animals around us and coming to understand them better."
—Faith Maloney, Director, Best Friends Animal Sanctuary

"Carol has not only been a liaison to my clients in helping them communicate with their animal friends, but she has also helped me to hear that voice within that speaks to us all."
—Karen S. Martin, D.V.M.

"[Carol has] certainly brought the awareness about animal communication to many more thousands of pet owners and veterinarians. [Her] skill will save lives and provide the understanding for the pet owners, helping them to make the best decision."
—Roger W. Valentine, D.V.M.

"Carol's style of teaching is simple, clear, and down-to-earth. She is a gifted teacher with a gentle and caring soul, and she makes it easy to learn how to communicate with animals in a safe, supportive, and loving environment. Her workshops are incredible to experience. It was so much more than I ever would have expected from any workshop. . . . It was truly a heart-opening experience."
—Linda Gray (actress)

"The work that Carol Gurney does, helps connect people to their pets, thus making the bond stronger and more meaningful."
—Alice Villalobos, D.V.M.

Julian & Susan,
Keep your hearts open!
Carol Gurney

the
Language
of
Animals

Steps to

Communicating

with Animals

CAROL GURNEY

A DELL TRADE PAPERBACK

A DELL TRADE PAPERBACK

Published by
Bantam-Dell Publishing
a division of
Random House, Inc.
1540 Broadway
New York, New York 10036

The quoted passage on page 236 is *The Bridge* by
Rachelle Hasnas, copyright 1987. Reprinted by permission of
Rachelle Hasnas.

Copyright © 2001 by Carol Gurney

Cover design by Beverly Leung
Book Design by Lynn Newmark

All rights reserved. No part of this book may be reproduced or
transmitted in any form or by any means, electronic or
mechanical, including photocopying, recording, or by any
information storage and retrieval system, without the written
permission of the publisher, except where permitted by law.

Dell books may be purchased for business or promotional use or
for special sales. For information please write to: Special
Markets Department, Random House, Inc., 1540 Broadway,
New York, New York 10036.

DTP and the colophon are trademarks of Random House, Inc.

Library of Congress Cataloging-in-Publication Data
Gurney, Carol.
The language of animals : 7 steps to communicating with
animals / by Carol Gurney.
    p. cm.
Includes bibliographical references (p. 237).
ISBN 0-440-50912-2
1. Human-animal communication. 2. Extrasensory perception
in animals. 3. Telepathy. I. Title.
QL776 .G87 2001
591.59—dc21   00-065743

Printed in the United States of America

Published simultaneously in Canada

August 2001

10 9 8 7 6 5

I dedicate this book to my beloved animals, Soleil, Tallanny, Dudley, Scooter, Joy Boy, and Jessie, who have taught me the most important lessons of my life.

My journey with animal communication began with my first cat, Soleil, who was in my life for sixteen years. Through our relationship, I came to have a true understanding of cats and the important lesson of learning to accept an animal's true nature. Her special light guided me to investigate concepts and beliefs that I had not previously been open to.

I thank my horses, Dudley and Tallanny. Dudley taught me about strength and self-confidence. He knew exactly what he wanted in life and he achieved his dreams. Tallanny, who has been with me for eighteen years, taught me the meaning of love. Upon meeting him it was love at first sight, and by looking into his beautiful brown eyes I recognized a connection I had never felt before. It was because of his quiet strength, spirit, and wisdom that I could begin my journey of personal growth. He was, truly, the first individual who unlocked the doors to my heart. He is the best friend I have ever had and has given me the courage to believe in and trust my dream—to listen to animals heart to heart.

I thank my cat Scooter for being the orchestrator of harmony in my life for the past twenty-one years. He magically appears on my lap, knowing when I most need his grounding. In my busy life, his presence filled me with a profound sense of peace, silence, and contentment. The depth of his wisdom has been a precious jewel to me and to thousands of my students over the years.

I thank my fourteen-year-old cat, Joy Boy, whose courage, strength, and confidence has been an anchor for all of us. He was the irresistible personification of joy. The lightness of his presence brought a smile to everyone's face. With his lion's heart, he taught me how to set priorities and simplify my life, allowing me to let go of things that no longer serve me. I thank him for his courage and strength to be my teacher on so many levels.

I am grateful to my dog, Jessie, for her never-ending patience and loving persistence in trying to balance the elements of work and play within my life for the last nine years. Her golden qualities—her enthusiasm and willingness to share her experiences and open her heart—have been invaluable to my students and me. Her sweet and welcoming nature brings a sense of tremendous comfort and ease to everyone she meets and teaches.

From my heart, I thank them all for the tender healing they have brought to my life over the years. They are my shining light revealing the way back home. This book would not have been possible without them.

ACKNOWLEDGMENTS

Writing this book was a journey of discovery, and along the way I was blessed with the guidance of many helpful, loving, wise, and talented people. I wish to graciously thank them all for their effort and support, which made this book possible.

My first steps began with the encouragement of my consultant, Judith Pynn. She lovingly led and guided me through the process of writing a book. There was never a time she wasn't there for me with graciousness and professionalism.

I thank my assistant at the time, Sheri Davidson, for her encouragement to write this book. As she got to know my work firsthand through my workshops, her enthusiasm moved me forward in my goal of sharing the HeartTalk Program^{SM} with everyone.

And this book would not be possible without the help of Sheri's mother, Stella Davidson, who sat with me for countless hours critiquing my preliminary material. Where would I be without you, Stella?

I thank my agent, Jody Rein, for her speed in pulling the project together and finding me such a reputable publisher as Bantam Dell.

I thank my assistant, Karrel Christopher, for the unbelievable patience, insight, and overwhelming love she shared with all of us during such a transitional time. She is one of the most loving souls I have had the pleasure of knowing, and worked tirelessly to assure the thoroughness of this project. She has been my anchor and kept me connected at a heart level when times got tough.

Thanks to my editor, Jennie Shortridge, who did a fantastic editing job on such a difficult time schedule, creating continuity throughout the book from start to finish. It was a pleasure working with her easy and friendly style of communication. Thanks also to my editor at Bantam Dell, Danielle Perez, for knowing and believing in my talents.

This book could not have been written without the overwhelming patience and direction I received from Ellen Novak, who guided me through the pitfalls of communicating with a computer. I much prefer communicating with animals. She was a godsend. There is absolutely no way I could have accomplished this task without her.

My thanks to Art Myers, the author of *Communicating with Animals,* who has made such a fine contribution to the field of animal communication by sharing so many insights from animal communicators throughout the country.

I thank Leigh Taylor-Young for the opportunity to communicate with her animals when they were in need. From that experience sprang her interest in developing her own communication skills. I am blessed to have her introduce the HeartTalk Program[SM]. She is a great role model for me since she truly lives her life from her heart. Few people could cross her path without recognizing her strong spiritual essence, her sense of truth and integrity, and her deep sense of compassion for all beings. Thank you, Leigh, for being you!

And, finally, I thank all my clients and their animals for sharing their lives with me and, through their stories, making this book possible.

CONTENTS

part III
lessons of the heart

chapter 11

FOREWORD

I first met Carol Gurney when I was having trouble with my beautiful white Persian cat, Quan. Quan was unhappy with my choice of boyfriend and let me know by urinating on his clothing! I had heard of Carol through a friend, so I called her for a consultation. That first meeting was extraordinary. Carol sat quietly with Quan, who remained very peaceful, looking almost as if she were sleeping. Amazingly, Carol communicated a stream of accurate information, things she had no way of knowing, and helped us find a solution to the problem. I knew right then that Carol had a special gift, and she sparked in me my own quest for heightened awareness and communication with animals.

Every relationship I've had with an animal since childhood has been a primary relationship for me. I am a lover of animals. They enchant me, delight me, entertain me, mystify me, and, most important, they open my heart. In my darker hours, I have often been deeply comforted by their empathic expression of concern through a look, a cuddle, or a sound. In my greatest joys, they will leap with me in the sharing and endure my waltzing them around a room, as I sing to them my happiness. They have added the greatest quality to my life, and I feel honored and blessed by their presence. After working with Carol, learning her HeartTalk Program^{SM}, and now reading this book, *The Language of Animals*, my relationships with animals have deepened. I always knew at some level that animals and humans shared some type of communication, but I didn't realize the depth of animals' perceptions. After Carol's first session with Quan, I began to deal with my cat with more awareness and respect. It wasn't that I hadn't respected her before, but now I was beginning to understand just how much animals have to give us in their own kind of wisdom.

A word I take deeply to heart from Carol and her work is *intention*. It's a word I've used often in my awakening to communication with animals. I'd always "talked" with Quan, even before the issue with my gentleman friend, but I now added my intention of openness, the intention that she actually did understand me. This helped me move forward in my journey. Quan also helped me in ways I did not realize at the time. I thought I was experiencing my own epiphany; however, I became aware that she was actually showing me that if I surrendered judgment and closed-mindedness and approached her with willingness and humility, then assuredly we would communicate. It worked. I actually felt that I entered her frequency, like finding a wavelength on a radio. We are wired differently, animals and humans, but there is a place you can find this frequency, where there is pure communication.

Carol has worked with my animals and me many times since that first meeting, and every experience continues to amaze me. Developing my own intuitive "languaging" with animals has intensified my awareness of how these relationships can play a bigger and more fulfilling role in life. We tend to take them so for granted, yet they can be teachers and healers. For me, my cats (I have since added my beloved Lucky to the family) have always offered me the opportunity to slow down and quiet my world so I can listen to their wisdom and perceptions. If I get busy at my desk for too many hours, Lucky will walk across my computer keyboard, plop himself in front of me, or paw at my pen, and say it's time to stop. I do always listen but, to be perfectly honest, I don't always follow their advice. The biggest gift we humans can give ourselves is to listen to animals and not assume they are limited in the ways we've been taught. They are boundless in what they have to give, in the richness of their communication, if we would but stop and listen and commune in return.

As for animals being healers, let me tell you about my "adopted" palomino draft horse, Charlie, who pulled carts full of children at Disneyland for twenty years. When he became too old to do his work anymore, he went to live at Windermere Ranch in the Santa Barbara Mountains. Here he was lovingly cared for by the staff and many visitors. I "adopted" him by participating in his care.

Unfortunately, I never had a strong emotional relationship with my father. I never had a sense of being cherished or safe in ways that stabilized my emotional development. I tell you this about myself because one day, when I went to the ranch to groom Charlie, I received the greatest gift from him. As I stroked and brushed him, Charlie just stood there good-naturedly, eyes halfway closed, and I felt a profound, enduring sense of patience and love emanating from him. This shouldn't be surprising, given that this horse pulled children in carts for twenty years, but I was struck by this warm, loving energy that entered the core of my being. All of a sudden, I felt as if I'd found the qualities of the father I had missed. Everything I'd wished for in my life from my father was manifest at this very moment. I'd never known these feelings or that I could experience them. Charlie's energy enveloped me and offered such unconditional safety and love that it was palpable.

I leaned into Charlie, weeping, and he just stood and held me for the longest time as I cried on his shoulder. It was a most amazing experience and revelation. When I left him that day, I asked if I could hold his head in my arms, and as I gently put my head to his, I whispered to him that he was the father I had never known. I thanked him for this beautiful gift of love and reminded him that he would forever be with me.

I stayed connected with my dear friend Charlie until the day he couldn't get up anymore. All the horses on the ranch came around him and held for him as he had for me. They circled Charlie as he gently left this life. Although he may be gone, this wise, patient teacher left a legacy of love and healing.

If you ever wished for a deeper connection with your animals, you have come to the right place by reading *The Language of Animals*. In this book, Carol awakens us to a greater awareness of our connection with animals. She gives guidance and provides practical, easy-to-do, and confidence-building exercises. She covers every base of animal communication, from choosing a new companion to the death of an animal.

The special chapter on death and dying explains every step of this painful process: how to tackle the practicalities, what your options are, what you can do to treasure your animals during the dying process and after, and, of course, how to communicate along the way (and afterward). The gift she gives in this chapter is an opportunity to be with each emotion during the dying process rather than just be overwhelmed. The hands-on advice, the enlightening information, and the stories are so profound they truly move you to tears.

I buy a lot of books about animals; I love them. *The Language of Animals* is the first book that tells animal lovers in the simplest way how they can work with the love they have for their animals and how they can benefit. Nobody else I'm aware of has ever done this.

I have implemented every aspect of the book into my relationships with animals and with humans. Every single exercise, every anecdote, every lesson she teaches can be applied across the board to enriching our relationships with all living beings. I think of *The Language of Animals* as a manual for living, because by reading it we learn to know and love ourselves better as we learn to communicate with animals. I believe God has given Carol a unique gift, but she'll tell you she's simply reintroducing us to the language of the heart—our own intuition.

As you read and learn from this book, let your heart guide you. Let the animals teach and inspire you, and let yourself be open to all possibilities!

—Leigh Taylor-Young, actress

INTRODUCTION

Believe it or not, my veterinarian introduced me to the world of animal communication. It was 1980, and I was a corporate executive at a major advertising agency. I took my cat Soleil to the vet because she had suddenly stopped using her litter box. Because the vet could find no physical cause, he told me it was probably an emotional problem and suggested I see an animal communicator. After checking around, I called well-known animal communicator Penelope Smith.

She spent a short time with Soleil and found her to be stressed and feeling insecure about my imminent separation from my husband. Soleil was consoled and given a better understanding of the situation. Within a few days of Penelope's visit, my cat was not only using her litter box but actually looked different, carrying herself with more confidence.

The dramatic turnaround prompted me to enroll in one of Smith's workshops, which, unfortunately, was devastating. I felt like a failure; while the other students were establishing real connections to animals, I couldn't seem to break through. I kept thinking, "What's wrong with me?" I learned a great deal at the workshop, but came away with a sense of frustration with myself.

After the workshop, I didn't even try to practice animal communication. I was too scared. I wasn't sure I would know if I was really doing it or just making it up. Yet I discovered something surprising about myself: It was what I wanted to do more than any-thing in the world. But it felt like a fantasy or unattainable dream—not something that I would ever be able to do.

My whole life I have been very determined and worked hard to achieve my goals. I began my career as a secretary. Through self-determination and focus, I built a successful advertising ca-reer. I was promoted often, won accolades, dealt with high-ranking officials in major corporations. In 1983, however, after having been with the advertising agency for ten years and being promoted to the first female vice president in that office, I knew I needed more, something more fulfilling.

I started my own business as a consultant, helping corporations handle the growth and relocation of their businesses. I had man-aged to carefully oversee the physical growth of the advertising agency, and I knew that other businesses could benefit from my experience and be saved from the pitfalls and mistakes often made during the expansion process. I developed not only a new business but an entirely new concept in the marketplace.

During this time, a prospective client told me about Charlotte Podrat, who taught people to ride horses at her ranch in Malibu. Because this was also one of my greatest pleasures, I called her and started taking riding lessons. I was still in the midst of starting the new company when I met a remarkable horse at her stable: Tallanny. I learned to ride with him, and when his guardian de-cided to sell him, I didn't want to lose him. In spite of the fact that I had no business buying a horse, because I needed to devote my time and energy and finances to a new business, nothing could stop me. I felt compelled to be with him and decided to follow my heart. I bought my first horse ever.

I continued to board Tallanny at Charlotte's Purple Hills Ranch and went there as often as I could, every evening after work and on weekends. Spending time with Tallanny made me think about my frustrating experience at the animal-communication workshop. I knew he was a special horse and that at some level we had a special connection. I spent hours just sitting with him, hop-ing I would be able to connect with him in some way, hoping that one day I would be able to hear his thoughts and know they were not mine. I found myself wanting to be with him more than I did my clients.

After many months of spending quiet time together, I finally learned to just "be" with Tallanny, and that's when I felt my first connection. To my surprise, it came from my heart, not my mind. That's what was different from the experience I'd had at the workshop. It was as though I could actually feel a slight sensation in my heart and then a feeling of tremendous love and acceptance. It was not a mental connection; it was like looking into the eyes of the soul and heart. Only then, when I connected at a heart level, did I begin to communicate successfully with my beloved Tallanny. When other boarders at the ranch saw the special connection I had developed with my horse, they asked me to help them with their animals.

One day while at a client's office, I shared photos of Tallanny and me at the ranch. As she pointed to the picture, my client said, "*This* is you." Then she looked straight into my eyes as I sat dressed in my corporate attire and said, "This is *not* you." Looking at the photo again, she said, "This is where you belong." I was shocked at her proclamation. I felt very happy with my business, but I was willing to listen; after all, she was my client. Then I tucked that experience away and didn't think about it again until some time later.

Near the end of the third year of my business, I decided to have a session with a highly recommended spiritual counselor, Sanda Fraser (now Jasper). I had successfully consulted a psychic once before, and it seemed the right time to again hear some words of wisdom. The moment I sat down with Sanda, she said, "It's so nice to know that you're an interspecies communicator." I did a double take. How did she know that's what my fantasy, my dream was? My client's words—"*This* is you. . . . This is where you belong"—came back to me. I suddenly understood that it was only a dream or fantasy until I decided to make it a reality. That's all I needed—validation to give myself permission to move forward with my life.

Within those three years, my business had become a major success. I realized I felt complete with it—I had done what I needed to do. Needless to say, friends and business associates thought I was crazy to let go of a thriving business to enter the field of animal communication, where there were only three other people known to be doing this in the entire country. But I knew it was time to move on.

I sold my business and moved to a ranch in the country where I could have Tallanny, as well as my three cats, with me. I spent the next year putting my business acumen to work, doing research and development and figuring out what my new career was going to look like. I asked myself many questions: What was I supposed to do with this ability? How was I to start this new and different career? What did it really mean to be an interspecies communicator? How could I help make a difference in the world?

Most important, I talked with as many animals as I could. I spent the year offering my time free of charge to people who needed help with their animals, to convince myself, for sure, that I truly had a connection with animals and could really do this and be of service.

During this time, I made a stunning discovery and realized I had found my purpose in life. As I worked with animals and their humans, I began to see the bigger picture, the roles that animals play in our lives. I saw that animals are a reflection of us, mirroring our own internal imbalances, and will often act out things that are unresolved within us, things that need to be nurtured and healed. This was what I needed to help people understand about animals; this was the healing that needed to take place.

Once I was confident that I had something to offer both humans and animals, it was time to go "public." I began my business by doing long-distance consultations, because I was most comfortable connecting with the animals that way. As I felt more secure about my abilities, I started doing house calls, eventually progressing to all-day consultations at a ranch or someone's home. After just a few years in animal communication, I enjoyed success as I had in the advertising industry. As word about my unique business spread, newspapers and magazines wrote about me, television networks became interested in sharing my stories, and national organizations asked me to lecture and give workshops around the country.

My clients also showed an overwhelming interest in learning to communicate with animals. They were hungry to hear their animals, and I was hungry to teach them. I decided to sit down and pull together a down-to-earth program that taught animal communication simply and step-by-step. Although I was nervous about teaching people I didn't even know, I knew my communication and connection came from my heart. So I would teach the way it happened for me—a heart to heart connection. As my teaching evolved, so did the structure of the workshops.

I started by teaching a one-day Animal Communication Workshop, locally at first, and then clients of mine from around the country wanted to learn. I turned it into a two-day workshop and took it on the road.

As time went on, clients asked for more advanced workshops. I developed the Advanced Workshop for people to learn long-distance communication and started the Body Balancing Workshop for people wanting to understand how to help their animals' physical bodies. When certain students expressed an interest in learning to do animal communication professionally, I developed the Comprehensive Training Program, the first of its kind in the country. This program provides a format for people to perfect communication skills and learn a variety of specialties, including problem-solving techniques, the death and dying process, communication with animals who have passed on, finding lost animals, handling sensitive situations, psychological aspects of the business, and even marketing skills. The program evolved into the 7-Step HeartTalk Program℠ you will read about in this book.

People from all walks of life now come to my workshops or call me for consultations and tutoring, including breeders, trainers, veterinarians, chiropractors, and people who simply want to know more about their animals. My clients even include major racetracks, such as Tampa Bay Downs, and celebrities such as Patrick

Stewart, Linda Gray, Lesley Ann Warren, and Leigh Taylor-Young, who wrote the Foreword for this book. You, too, should feel free to call me about consultations or training (see the Resources section at the back of the book for my contact information).

Just as I faced challenges early on, my students sometimes struggle in learning to be effective animal communicators; it's a natural part of the process. One such student was Nanci Shapiro of Minneapolis. She had attended some animal communication classes before she came to her first workshop with me. She complained that she was able to get snippets of information from animals, but nothing substantial. When we talked about it, she realized she could feel her heart shutting down as she worked with an animal. She decided to telepathically invite both of her dogs to help her with this problem and imagined them standing like guards at either side of the doors of her heart. Once she did that, she felt safe and secure and immediately received a free flow of information from the next animal she worked with. Nanci is now a professional animal communicator.

Another student, Lucy Roberts of Milwaukee, came to my workshop disillusioned about animal communication. She'd always heard that once you tap into an animal's psyche, the floodgates of information open, but she never experienced this. She was heartened to hear that neither had I. Lucy relaxed, and the next day, as we did an exercise called Quick Word Association (which you'll learn to do as well), she felt her first telepathic connection. Near the end of the week, I found her crying. I was surprised, because she'd been doing so well. When I asked what was wrong, she said, "Oh, no, these are tears of joy! I'm finally getting it!"

Animal communication is nothing new or controversial. The question is not "When did we begin to be able to communicate with other species?" but "When did we stop?" Although there has been a resurgence in interest in the subject recently, consider the indigenous peoples, such as Native Americans and Aborigines, who were in total harmony with the spirits of animals and with all of nature. Consider St. Francis of Assisi and his connection to animals. In her book *Animals: Our Return to Wholeness*, Penelope Smith says, *Since about 1987, it's as if a moratorium on recognizing animals as intelligent beings has been lifted.*

Just as the public's awareness of animal communications grows, my HeartTalk Program℠ continues to evolve and expand. I've added audio- and videotapes and now this book. I can only imagine what will be next!

As you read the book and begin to practice the exercises, remember: This is not something that will happen for you overnight. It's like learning any new language or starting any new business. It takes time, determination, practice, desire, commitment, compassion, and more compassion. For me, it evolved over many years. Becoming an animal communicator was absolutely the hardest thing I've ever done. But every day that I do my work now is a new day for me, a continuing journey of self-discovery.

If I could do it, anyone can! It takes practice, but I am happy to say that of the thousands of people who have attended my workshops, not one has been unable to make a connection with animals. In learning to bridge the communication gap with animals, many of them have also discovered new intuitive and empathetic skills that improve their human relationships as well as aid in their own personal growth. Best of all, they open their hearts to accept the love their animals give so freely.

I wish you joy and success in your new journey!

Soleil, who introduced Carol to the world of animal communication.

Carol with Tallanny, the master of the HeartTalk Program[SM].

CHRISTIAN PEACOCK

1

hearttalk

1

Straight from the Heart

When we are babies, we see animals as being no different from ourselves. They are simply big furry beings full of love and generosity. We share the same language, communicating telepathically until we learn to communicate verbally, and then we are pulled farther and farther away from our connection to them.

Telepathic communication is like a heartbeat—it's happening within us all the time without our conscious awareness. Like breathing, our intuition carries on just fine in our daily lives without our acknowledgment or appreciation. But unlike the rhythmic beating that sustains our physical bodies, our spiritual hearts thrive only after we begin to recognize, validate, and nourish our inner lives. As adults, this part of us may lie dormant until we make a conscious effort and nurture this subtle and remarkable part of our being.

We seldom recognize the heart's language, which is our intuition. We telepath to each other; we empathetically connect with our animals and significant others. The thought of a friend fills our mind moments before she calls, a person meets another for the first time and experiences a sort of recognition or immediate connection, or occasionally a person knows what another is going to say before the words are spoken. Perhaps you or someone you know has experienced one or more of these connections. We often label these occurrences as something coincidental—as a thought, an extrasensory perception, an accident, common sense, or simple compassion toward another.

I invite you to journey with me as we explore the notion that we can learn to distinguish our own thoughts and feelings from those originating elsewhere. We pick up others' thoughts and feelings all the time and mistake them for our own, because heart intelligence is shared by all sentient beings. We can reclaim a language that goes beyond our five physical senses, one we enjoyed as infants and spontaneously used to communicate as children.

In her book, *The Healing of Emotion*, Chris Griscom writes:

> *When we focus on a tree, a plant, a bird, or other animals such as horses, dogs, cats . . . the language we speak with them is the language of the heart—that is, the universal means by which all forms of consciousness can communicate with each other.*

Happily, we can learn to recognize, validate, and develop this language of the heart and soul to nourish our inner lives; we can learn to recognize the ways we communicate with all creatures that share this earth. They have much to tell us!

Of all the communications I have ever received from a living being—human or otherwise—perhaps the most heartrending came from a horse named Star. His guardian asked me to look into a chronic stiffness Star had in his neck. As I began to stroke his neck and gently lay my hands on him, he radiated an energy so intense it was tangible, even catching the attention of the ranch hands working in the barn. I could feel his pulse throbbing as he told me, in a flood of emotion, how profoundly grateful he was to his new guardian, who he believed had saved his life. With his pre-

vious person, he had been a competition horse, a hard-driven jumper who had begun to lose his edge as his youth faded. He had heard his people say that if he didn't fetch a decent price at auction, he would be sent to the slaughterhouse. As a result, he was terrified. Afraid to sleep, he stood listening, every day and night, to the sounds of trucks coming and going from the ranch, filled with dread that one of them would be coming to take him away. Overwhelmed with stress and fear, his neck had frozen up from the strain of listening. Still strong and vital, he wasn't ready to die.

By that point in the story, a few of the ranch hands stopped working altogether and came over, drawn by the strong feeling of longing emanating from the horse.

Star said that in his new life he was being retrained for dressage, balletic exhibition riding in which a horse and a person closely synchronize their movements to execute an elegant dance. The work was challenging but mentally satisfying and, above all, he loved being so attuned to a human being that they could move together as one. He had never felt such kinship, such union. He wanted the woman to know how much he loved her, both for giving him the chance to live and for the tremendous gift of the closeness and affection he had come to feel with her.

But even in his new environment, he could not sleep. Star feared that his new guardian had no idea of the depth of his gratitude and love for her and that one day she, too, would choose to let him go.

I couldn't help but weep at his heartfelt declaration, and I could see tears in the eyes of the ranch hands looking on. Not wanting to break the connection, I signaled to one of them to get his guardian. She hadn't known what was on Star's mind, she said, but she had noticed that he seemed distracted. I asked her to close her eyes, take some deep breaths, and allow him to connect with her. When she did, she was almost bowled over by the depth of his emotion, his overwhelming devotion and gratitude. Stroking him, she promised that he would never again wait in terror, listening for the dreaded trucks. She assured him he had a permanent home under her protection and love.

I asked Star what else he needed. His answer was simple: "I want to go to sleep." We accompanied him to his stall, ranch hands and all, and watched in amazement as he gently and peacefully lay down and slept, finally getting the rest he so desperately needed.

Everyday miracles such as this one moved me to write this book, to share the gift of animal communication. The animals in our lives are constantly "talking" to us, but until we learn how to listen, we miss all but the most obvious messages—the cat plopping on the computer keyboard to make us stop working, the dog standing at the door with the leash in his mouth or, sensing that we've had a hard day, comforting us with a nuzzle and a lick. In turn, we are hard-pressed to make them understand us, with a vocabulary that doesn't go much further than a shout or a cuddle or a swat. These limited expressions prevent us from resolving conflicts about issues such as housebreaking, determining if an animal is ill, helping an animal become reoriented in a new home, or conveying any other message that requires a higher degree of articulation than a handful of words and actions. What's more, it prevents us from participating fully in what can be some of the most loving and fulfilling relationships in our lives.

Animal communication is not hocus-pocus; it involves no psychic ability. Don't be intimidated by the term *telepathy*. All it means is a heightened ability to use the intuition we already have—recovering the language we knew as children. Even now, we glance at a friend across a crowded room at a party and sense that she needs to be rescued from a bore. As parents we communicate intuitively with our infants and can often sense, even from another room with the door closed, that our baby needs us. It is as natural as breathing, as automatic as the beating of our hearts. I call it talking "heart to heart," and I have taught this universal language to nearly six thousand people over the past fourteen years.

Humans are born communicators; we don't have to wait until we acquire language skills to get our point across. We have awareness before we have spoken language. This kind of communication is not just limited to parents and infants. It happens between animals, and between animals and people when there is an empathetic bond—a heart connection.

Wordless communications happen all the time, quietly and unobtrusively, so subtly that they often go unnoticed while the constant noise of conscious thoughts and emotions claim our attention. But intuition is no less real for its subtlety. We don't need words to hear what our hearts are saying.

We must realize that we are much more than our conscious minds. We are physical, mental, emotional, and spiritual beings, as are the animals. We have come to depend on our verbal language and our conscious mind so much that it separates us from our connection to our whole selves, our intuitive selves, our receptive, feeling selves. Our conscious minds speak to us the most loudly; in fact, they shout at us all day long, drowning out the subtle cues of intuition. Intuition is like a muscle that needs exercise. And, like a muscle, intuitive strength takes time to develop, sometimes even years. As Neale Donald Walsch aptly notes in *Conversations with God: An Uncommon Dialogue, Book 3*:

> *To develop your psychic "muscle," you must exercise it. Use it. Every day. Right now the muscle is there, but it's small. It's weak. It's under-used. So you'll get an intuitive "hit" now and then, but you won't act on it. You'll get a "hunch" about something, but you'll ignore it. You'll have a dream, or an "inspiration," but you'll let it pass, paying it scant attention.*

To communicate with animals, you need to strengthen that muscle, and that is what I designed the HeartTalk Program℠ to do.

Part I of this book, "HeartTalk," is the instructional portion, explaining the HeartTalk Program℠, the actual step-by-step process of connecting with an animal, in two sections. The first section teaches seven steps for preparation to help you focus your mental energies, get centered, and clarify your thoughts. We will review easily grasped techniques for making connections, and practice three powerful guided exercises to heighten your natural empathetic/intuitive capacities. The second section provides seven steps to begin the process of reaching out to any animal in your life. You will telepathically share the thoughts, ideas, and sensations you want to express to your animal and learn to understand his or her response to you.

Part II, "Matters of the Heart," applies these communication techniques to real-life situations. I will discuss and suggest solutions for common problems such as upheavals from adding new animals to your household, difficulties in housetraining, and aggressive behavior between animals. You will learn how to relocate successfully with your animals, how to find them if they become lost, how to comfort sick and injured animals, and, most important, how to know when it is time for them to leave and how to say good-bye.

Part III, "Lessons of the Heart," will show what animals have to teach us. They help us learn about ourselves by mirroring our actions through their behaviors. They teach us to reconnect with the natural world. And one of the most important lessons we receive from them is learning how to love ourselves the way they love us—unconditionally.

My hope is that by reading this book you will experience not only a deeper connection with your beloved animal companions but also a newfound respect for all living creatures, for the environment, and for life in general.

Let's begin our adventure!

2

The HeartTalk Program^{SM}

Through the ages, people have referred to a language of the heart—not to the language of the intellect or even the language of the emotions, but of the heart. Let's imagine that each human being is a wheel and that the components of who we are—mental, emotional, spiritual, and physical—are spokes of the wheel. At the center of the wheel, unifying all these components, is our heart. The heart is the core, the foundation of our physical, emotional, mental, and spiritual lives—the essence of who we are. I call my program HeartTalk because, in communicating with animals, I find that I tap into that center and use all aspects of myself.

Here's how I experience connecting with an animal: First, I focus my attention on the animal (mental). I feel a strong sensation in my heart (physical), and I feel warm and full of love (emotional). It's as if the doors of my heart begin to open (spiritual), and once they do, I feel that the animal engages with me in the same way. We connect—heart to heart.

After the heart connection is made, more specific two-way communications can be made through feelings, thoughts, or even a knowingness, that state of simply understanding something without necessarily knowing how or why. But where the communication begins is with the heart opening—creating within myself a state of receptivity.

I devised this method for myself, and it is the method that comes most naturally to me, but it seems to be just as effective for the thousands of people I teach. Why? Because it involves connecting to the heart and soul. It allows us to be in that open and receptive state we would be in if we stopped trying to act consciously, if we stopped rushing and allowed ourselves to slow down. It is the state of just "being," instead of thinking or doing. It will be this quality of just being that you'll attempt to cultivate as you learn the HeartTalk Program℠.

Remember, your heart accepts everything. Your heart holds no judgment or criticism. It is the center, the core of who you are. Its language, what we call intuition, is a powerful form of communication.

When we meet people for the first time, we decide on what level we are going to communicate with them. If we do not feel safe, we will stay on a guarded, intellectual level and not share our feelings. However, when we meet people whose hearts are open, who are truly interested in knowing who we are, and who do not judge or criticize us, we feel more at home. We spontaneously begin to share all of who we are: our emotional, intellectual, physical, and spiritual selves. We do this because they have provided a safe and inviting space by opening themselves to us on a heart level.

When we open our hearts to animals, it allows them to express all of who they are. If we only project ourselves mentally to them, we may experience an intellectual conversation with them. In order to go to deeper levels of communication and trust, they need also to feel safe with us. If we trust our own feelings and accept all of who we are, that openheartedness creates an atmosphere for a greater intimacy with all of life.

Because we all lead such busy lives, however, we have all but forgotten how to just "be." Our society generally measures the rate of our success by what we do and not who we are. In addition, we are accustomed to giving *out* information rather than being receptive. When we learn to communicate telepathically, we focus less on what we tell animals and more on what we hear from them. The essence of this program is receptivity, expanding our awareness on all levels—physically, mentally, emotionally, spiritually—to listen with our hearts. Listening, not reasoning, is the foundation of intuition.

Generally speaking, in today's society we allow the conscious mind to overanalyze and override intuition; we trust reason and logic because they are more familiar and more valued by society and therefore more comfortable. However, reason and logic are limiting. Every time we ignore what our hearts are trying to tell us, we limit ourselves and our connections to others. We limit ourselves when we feel we have to act or react, to move forward. By residing in our center, by letting go and just being, we learn to balance ourselves.

You'll find that learning to slow down and just be will not only improve your relationships with animals, it will enhance your entire life. You will be relearning how to ground and center yourself.

Pam, a client of mine from Mesa, Arizona, had an experience with animals that helped her with this very issue. A very bright accountant, Pam had a gregarious personality. She liked loud music, spoke in a very loud tone, and moved very quickly.

At a workshop one day, the subject of rabbits came up. I asked Pam, who had recently acquired two rabbits, to tell us about her experience with them.

She told us a phenomenal story about how her rabbits had changed her life. She said that during most of her life, she had not been aware of having a soul. During recent therapy, however, she came to the realization that she indeed had a soul, a major breakthrough in her personal development. At that moment, she had a strong urge to get a rabbit or two. She had never before had that interest.

Being an accountant, she researched the subject thoroughly: What kind of rabbit did she want, what color, what size, what breed. She then bought two rabbits and her life changed dramatically for the better. She began to consider the needs and sensitivities of the rabbits. She realized that she needed to quiet everything down—her voice, the way she moved around the house, the music she played—because the rabbits were so fearful of her loud noises and quick movements.

In slowing herself down, she was able to still her mind and body so dramatically that her whole way of expressing herself was different. She was able to feel centered and calm for the first time in her life. It is interesting that once Pam discovered her soul—her heart center—she was able to identify what she needed in her life. The wise part of her decided she needed rabbits, and if it weren't for them, she would still be moving at 150 mph.

GETTING STARTED

We're now ready to begin the journey, to learn the first part of the HeartTalk Program℠. These seven steps will prepare you for your communication with animals. They include meditation, exercises, and several connection techniques. They are designed to help you learn to slow down and get centered, open your heart, and clarify and expand your thought processes. You will learn to develop your innate intuitive abilities to the point that it is possible for you to communicate telepathically. You'll benefit most by approaching this with an open mind, self-confidence, and a sense of fun as you learn how to make the connection, not only with animals, but also with yourself.

7-STEP HEARTTALK PROGRAM℠—PREPARATION
Step 1: **Find your still point**
Step 2: **Open your heart**
Step 3: **Understand the lines of communication**
Step 4: **Experiment with connection techniques**
Step 5: **Learn to focus**

Step 6: **Recognize your style of connection**
Step 7: **Exercise your telepathic muscle**

Step 1: **Find Your Still Point**

The first and most critical step in developing your intuition is to learn to relax, both physically and mentally. If our bodies are gripped with tension and our minds constantly busy with thoughts, our listening abilities are drastically diminished. To center yourself and concentrate your attention fully, you will need to "get still"—to control and shut down the distracting clutter of everyday thoughts.

I realize how challenging getting still can seem. It is said that we humans generate about forty thousand thoughts a day. That's a lot of thinking and self-talk. Imagine your mind as a telephone (pre-voice mail, that is!). Most of the time our lines are busy—in order for anyone to get through, we have to hang up, decrease the number of thoughts we process, and become receptive and ready to listen. We need to open the line to receive others' communications. A number of relaxation and centering techniques can help us do this, including yoga, tai chi, and meditation. Of these, meditation is the easiest, for it requires no special training. I encourage people in my workshops to meditate every day.

BEGINNING TO MEDITATE

When you first attempt to meditate, you might feel some agitation. We are so comfortable using our conscious minds that this slowed-down feeling actually makes some people uncomfortable. When we begin to bring that silence to our minds, we can become antsy, nervous, and resist the silence. We may choose to run away, to get busy again, to distract ourselves. This resistance keeps our feelings from emerging.

In order to open your heart to yourself and others, you must first be willing to experience the range of your feelings. If meditation is too uncomfortable for you, then simply sit and allow yourself to listen to your breath. That's all—just do that for five to ten minutes. Or get a piece of paper and give yourself permission to draw for five to ten minutes. You don't need to draw anything specific; simply let your hand move in a free-form manner, allowing the crayon, the paintbrush, the pen or pencil to go anywhere and do anything it wants. Let your body and mind know what it feels like to do nothing. It's important to begin to incorporate some downtime for yourself so that your body and mind can rest and your spirit can awaken.

Meditation gives us the ability to listen to our inner selves. This is where it all begins—within us. How well do we know ourselves? Do we listen to our bodies when they are trying to communicate with us? Do we acknowledge our emotional needs? Our spiritual needs? The more in touch we are with ourselves, the easier the communication will be with others.

Start your meditation by creating a peaceful environment in your home, with a comfortable chair, where you can be alone and undistracted. If you wish, you can light a candle or have some flowers around to offer beauty and fragrance. Create your own special atmosphere.

When you are comfortable with this downtime, try adding some simple breathing exercises. Close your eyes and allow yourself to take deep breaths. As you breathe, mentally scan your body for any parts that feel tense. Concentrate on sending your breath into those spots as you inhale. On the exhale, allow all the tension to release and dissipate into the air. Gradually your body will be filled with a feeling of love and acceptance. Once you grow accustomed to this routine, you will find that you hunger for these islands of stillness in your day. Over time you may benefit by increasing your meditation periods by five minutes or so each day, eventually allowing yourself thirty to sixty minutes.

Step 2: Open Your Heart

If you have never meditated before and you just spent five minutes getting quiet, congratulations! It is extremely challenging to change your habits and your lifestyle to incorporate quiet time. Keep adding as much time as you possibly can. Remember, this is your life, and you deserve to be loved—especially by yourself—to the fullest.

Once you have learned to find your still point, you are ready to practice opening your heart through a deep relaxation exercise and a powerful guided meditation. Women are particularly challenged to find time for themselves, because they are so busy being caretakers. This is the time to embark on a new journey and take the time to nurture and appreciate yourself. In every workshop I teach, this is where we start. Many people who come to my workshops have practiced meditation for years, and they say this meditation is one of the best they have ever experienced.

You might want to tape-record yourself reading this entire section so you can sit with your eyes closed and leave your mind free to follow along. If you don't feel comfortable recording it for yourself, have a friend whose voice you like record it for you. Or, if you prefer, you can order the audiotape or videotape of all the exercises in this book from my office.

Before you begin the meditation, select a quiet environment with a supportive and nurturing ambiance, and sit in a comfortable chair.

RELAXATION AND MEDITATION

This exercise will help you relax your body, quiet your mind, and open your heart. The following meditation is designed to open your senses to information and to allow you to find that place within your heart where your love and compassion lie—and, most important, to bathe yourself in that love. You will use this meditation often while reading and practicing the exercises in this book, and it's a great tool for quieting yourself whenever you work telepathically with animals. It enables you to see how magnificent and wonderful you are, to see yourself as animals see you—with unconditional love.

♥ Close your eyes and place your feet flat on the floor. Take a few deep breaths. With each breath, scan your body for any tension you are holding. Breathe into those areas one by one, and on each exhale allow all of that tension to be released. *(Pause approximately 30 seconds.)*

♥ Now imagine that you have roots growing from the bottoms of your feet. These roots come from a very old and wise tree and extend deep into the earth. These roots will help keep you connected to the earth and grounded throughout the entire day. *(Pause approximately 30 seconds.)*

♥ Now imagine a most wondrous white light above your head. This light comes to you from the highest spiritual plane. Imagine two doors at the top of your head, and allow these doors to slowly open. As they open, allow this white light to gently and easily enter your body and move all the way down into your ankles and the balls of your feet and your toes. *(Pause approximately 15 seconds.)*

♥ Allow the light to rise, filling your calves, all the way up to your knees. Know that with each breath you take, your body becomes more and more relaxed and your mind more and more quiet. *(Pause approximately 15 seconds.)*

♥ Let the light continue to rise, filling your thighs, your buttocks, and your pelvic area, all the way up to your waist. Let all of the thoughts of today, tomorrow, and yesterday drift on by. *(Pause approximately 15 seconds.)*

♥ Allow the light to continue to rise to fill your stomach and chest area, lungs, heart, and back. Let every cell, every atom, and every molecule in your body be nurtured and supported by this light. *(Pause approximately 15 seconds.)*

♥ Allow the light to flow down your arms into your wrists, the palms of your hands, and your fingers. You may even feel a slight tingling sensation or a sense of heat or warmth in your hands. Feel the light as it rises back up your arms, all the way up to your shoulders and neck area. Know that with each breath you take, your body becomes more and more relaxed and your mind more and more quiet. *(Pause approximately 15 seconds.)*

♥ Feel the light as it continues to rise into your jaw, your mouth, and your ears, and let it relax every muscle in your body. Now let the light fill your nose and cheeks, your eyes and your forehead, your entire skull. *(Pause approximately 15 seconds.)*

♥ How wonderful it feels to let all of your thoughts and concerns just drift by! Now allow yourself to grow with this light and become as big as you possibly can, expanding yourself outward. *(Pause approximately 15 seconds.)*

♥ From this place, see yourself walking down a path, a path that leads to an environment that represents peace and tranquillity for you. This could be the mountains, a meadow, the forest, or the ocean. And as you walk upon the earth, allow yourself to feel its rhythms beneath your feet. *(Pause approximately 20 seconds.)*

♥ Feel the sun as it warms your body and the wind as it caresses your face. *(Pause approximately 20 seconds.)*

♥ Smell all the earthy odors and fragrances that surround you. *(Pause approximately 20 seconds.)*

♥ See all the colors and beauty that surround you, knowing that what you see is but a mere reflection of your own inner beauty. *(Pause approximately 20 seconds.)*

♥ Now allow yourself to continue to walk down the path. And as you continue walking, you see a most magnificent waterfall in the distance, a waterfall with a great sense of strength and yet a gentleness to it. *(Pause approximately 15 seconds.)*

♥ As you get closer and closer, walk beneath the waterfall, allowing it to embrace you and support you. Sink deeper and deeper into yourself, into your heart center. *(Pause approximately 15 seconds.)*

♥ Let yourself find that place within your heart where all of your love and compassion lie. You are allowing yourself to come back home to who you really are. What do you feel like? Sense and feel how magnificent and beautiful you are. This is the part of yourself that the animals see and feel all the time. Allow yourself to feel that love that the animals feel for you. *(Pause approximately 5–7 minutes.)*

♥ When you feel complete, easily and effortlessly walk out from under the waterfall and continue to walk along the path. And as you walk down the path, be aware of any animals that might be around

you or might want to make themselves known to you. Look around
and see who they might be. *(Pause approximately 1 minute.)*

💟 Take a few deep breaths, knowing that each breath you take allows you to become more and more aware of your physical body
and more and more aware of your current environment. *(Pause approximately 20 seconds.)*

💟 And when you feel complete and comfortable, open your eyes.

After doing this exercise, most people feel relaxed and experience a deep sense of peace and tranquillity. This is the place from
which we communicate with animals and with people—from the
center of our heart. Many people like to do this meditation every
day, for several reasons: to get centered so they can start their day
from a loving place, to help them relax, and to focus when they sit
down with their animals. You can do this as often as it pleases you.

Step 3: **Understand the Lines of Communication**
Now that you have learned the foundation of all communication—to just be—you can begin to think about how you actually
communicate with animals. We are ready to learn how to receive
and send communication. The next two steps are designed to help
you decipher how the information is being exchanged and experiment with some of the various methods. You'll see what actually
happens "behind the scenes" of your own communication style.
We often do things so naturally that we don't stop to think about
how we are doing them.

How do we get our thoughts across in the hundreds of wordless messages we send every day? The process seems almost automatic when we communicate with other human beings who are
already programmed to understand our whole complex set of signals and cues. But those signals and cues are less well known for
the more universal language of intuition. To communicate with animals, it's helpful to break down that automatic process into
smaller, more easily recognized steps. Imagine trying to describe a
Spanish omelette to someone who's never had one—it's difficult

unless you speak in terms of its ingredients: eggs, peppers, cheese, and so on, which the person will understand and easily fit together. In the same way, you will begin to transmit your ideas to animals (and vice versa) by concentrating on each "ingredient" of the communication separately.

Thoughts. You receive thoughts from your animal all the time, but you may not be aware of them. For example, you may know that your dog wants to go out before he scratches at the door, or that he's ready for his meal although it's not dinnertime, or that he isn't feeling well. You send your thoughts to your animals all the time without consciously being aware that they are indeed hearing and acting on them.

Consider, for instance, what you are thinking when you're training your dog to stay off the furniture. The thought you want him to receive is the command "Off!" But as you're saying it, you're also thinking, "I bet that just as soon as I turn my back, that dog is going to jump back on the sofa." And so he does, because you are sending him a mixed message—the word *Off!* but also your own mental image of his body landing on the couch, a picture that is much stronger than a mere word. You will learn to send the messages you want, but be aware that it will take practice to keep your mind centered on one clear thought at a time.

Emotions. You receive your animal's feelings and emotions as well. You may sense your dog's sadness when you leave the house or go on vacation, his apprehensiveness about being around a particular person or going to the vet's office. Therefore, when you want to convey your feelings to the animal, you need to feel those feelings clearly to get the message to the animal successfully.

For example, if you want your dog to know how unhappy you are when he chases after bicyclists or joggers, you have to summon up strong feelings of dismay and worry to emanate to him. When you let the animal feel the emotions his actions arouse in you, he will usually curtail his objectionable behavior, for it will pain him to sense your distress.

Images and Pictures. You also receive images and pictures from animals. You may see an image of a leash in your mind when the dog wants to go for a walk, or a picture of his water bowl when he is thirsty and his water bowl is empty. A picture of your car may flash through your mind; perhaps your dog wants to go for a long-overdue ride. You may see an image of your cat's best friend, whom he wants to play with but can't because you just moved to a new neighborhood. These are not just images made up by your own imagination but images that are being sent directly by your animal. They try to get through to us in any way they can.

For example, to communicate by sending images when house-breaking a puppy, you can visualize him pushing through the dog door, running outside, squatting, and relieving himself. As you learn to send this full sequence of pictures, he will better grasp what you expect him to do.

Physical Sensations. You may also receive physical sensations from animals. You might feel a sudden headache that comes and goes in a flash. Again, this is not your imagination. Your dog is most likely experiencing a headache, and because you are sensitive, you are picking it up. You may feel a sudden upset in your stomach that passes within seconds. Your cat might have an upset tummy and want some relief.

When you want to send a message through a physical sensation, then you will learn to bring that feeling up in your body and send it to the animal. For instance, you might want to send a frightened animal a sense of safety. You could begin by taking some deep breaths until you feel very relaxed and comfortable in the animal's presence. By creating and setting this example of peace within yourself, the animal will sense it and begin to calm down himself.

Spiritual. You see how we can receive communication on a mental level through animals' thoughts, on an emotional level through their feelings, images, and pictures, and on a physical level through their physical sensations. You can also receive communication from animals on a spiritual level. This communication may come through any of the above means, but the content will be of a spiritual nature and much more profound than everyday things such as what they like to do or what they like to eat. They may share with us a lesson or an eye-opening observation about ourselves or life in general.

If you are a very spiritually oriented person and you focus on that level, then you most likely will have a spiritual conversation. Be aware of the depth and possibilities of the communication that can be received and exchanged between humans and animals.

You can see the need for clarification in your thought processes in sending information and the quietness required to receive it. Clarifying your thought processes can make you more aware of the message you are already receiving from the animals. It can also help you break down the messages you want to send into more transmittable and recognizable forms.

Step 4: Experiment with Connection Techniques

You will use the "ingredients" of communication described above in practicing the connection techniques that I teach in my workshops. One of these may feel more natural to you than others, so experiment to find the technique that feels most compatible with your own intuitive style.

If you are a person who is an artist or in a creative field, then the following creative-visualization technique may be comfortable for you, since this is how you see the world—in images. If you are a person who is comfortable with your feelings, then the gestalt technique outlined below might fit nicely with your personality. Find what works best for you. That's what makes intuitive communication so much fun to learn: You have choices.

CREATIVE VISUALIZATION

Animals very often send us images representing the concept, emotion, or sensation they want us to understand. We can reach out to them effectively using the same visualizations. Say, for example, you want to ask an animal what he most likes to eat. You might start by projecting in your mind, as if on a movie screen, a picture of his empty bowl. Then, with practice, you can mentally watch as a particular kind of food appears in the bowl. At first you may think your thoughts are filling that bowl, but it's more likely that your dog is communicating with you. This kind of creative visualization is like a back-and-forth slide show between you and the animal, in which you send out an image in your mind and then wait to see what image you receive in return. If you have trouble "seeing" the images when you first try, remember, as with any new skill, creative visualization requires practice for most people.

For many of my students, this technique seems as natural as breathing, but it was a challenge at first for me. I couldn't stop using my conscious mind. I was afraid that I wouldn't have the right color bowl or the right size bowl—there was no way I could conjure up such an image so spontaneously. However, visualization became easier when I recognized that if I expressed a thought to an animal, my subconscious mind would automatically imprint that thought as an image. I didn't actually have to sketch out the picture myself. Now that I'm more proficient in and comfortable with telepathy, I've grown more relaxed and can even use images playfully to emphasize the points I'm trying to get across in emotions and thoughts.

A *client of mine, Scott from Santa Barbara, California, called me in a panic after finding his beagle Bernard nose-to-nose with a coyote. He had yelled at the top of his lungs for Bernard to run, but with typical beagle stubbornness, Bernard refused to back off. Scott eventually rescued Bernard, but he was terrified to think what could have happened. He asked me to warn Bernard to stay far away from the coyote den. Hard as I tried to convince him, the strong-willed Bernard just wouldn't understand that coyotes were more dangerous than the horses, goats, and big dogs he had confronted in the past. Finally, because I wasn't getting through, I decided to get visual. In my mind, I formed a picture of a big coyote opening his jaws and taking Bernard's body into his mouth. Now, instead of stonewalling, all I got from Bernard was a loud "Wow!" The next day Scott called to report that whatever I'd said had worked. Bernard wouldn't even walk in the direction of the coyote den!*

Try this simple exercise to help develop your own visualization skills. Imagine a ball bouncing from where you are sitting to a specific spot across the room. Keep practicing until you almost believe you can actually see the ball. Once you have that down, try sending mental images of other objects to different spots in the room. It can take a little time, but with practice you'll develop a sense of real control.

GESTALT TECHNIQUE

The gestalt method is a psychotherapeutic technique designed to help you re-create and come to understand another person's view of reality through role-playing. If, for example, you were having a problem with your mother, a gestalt therapist would ask you to pretend that your mother was sitting in a particular chair in the room. You would face her and tell her how you felt. Then you would move over to the chair where you had imagined your mother sitting and switch roles, pretending to be your mother and responding to what you, the child, had just said. This is a profound method of communication, for in playing the role of another person you must perceive and interpret events through his or her eyes and are compelled to feel empathy.

In my work, this technique is used to help you experience being an animal. Standing in your own shoes, you ask an animal a question and then, reversing roles, answer the question from his or her point of view. Gestalt is an especially useful technique for people who have trouble in their early attempts to connect with animals. If they have to try to become the animal, they can often forget themselves and lose the self-consciousness that stands in the way of communication.

I tried this technique when I was unable to establish a clear connection with a goose. It was my first attempt at this, so I wasn't quite sure what I was going to experience. First I felt the smoothness of his feathers, his fast heart rate, and a sensation of being low to the ground. Once I got used to how it felt physically to be a goose, I was then able to connect with his thoughts and feelings. He was absolutely thrilled that someone was taking the time to say hello and get to know him. He said no one had ever tried to connect with him or understand him before.

Try this exercise for yourself. Sit in a quiet room with your animal and simply feel what it is to be him. Imagine being his size, weight, what it feels like to have fur. What does he like to do, and why? What makes him tick? By putting yourself in his paws, you will be on the path to empathetic and intuitive communication.

Many of my students find these techniques helpful, especially in the beginning. Like anything new, we all need to start somewhere. Many of them go on to find their own communication styles. Again, what is most important is finding what works for you. We have a tendency in the beginning to compare ourselves to others. One person envies the fact that another person in the workshop receives pictures and images, where she receives feelings. The other person, however, is just as envious that that woman receives feelings. Accept and trust your natural gifts. You will eventually get it all. Be happy with your connection and the fact that it is happening for you. How exciting to know that you are in the midst of tremendous growth for yourself! This is just the beginning.

Step 5: **Learn to Focus**

Now you're ready to put your sending and receiving abilities into practice, in a sort of dry run. I encourage you throughout all the exercises to have as light an attitude as possible. The harder you try, the harder the exercises will be. Make this fun for yourself. Trust that you can do it, and it will happen for you easily and effortlessly.

The following exercise allows you to practice sending information to imaginary animals. Then, by moving into the receptive mode, you allow the information to come back to you. The first time I did this exercise, I imagined sending a deep sense of appreciation to a beloved dog. It was a very powerful exercise for me.

SENDING-AND-RECEIVING EXERCISE

Begin by first reading through this exercise without attempting it. Then move on to the guided exercise that follows to actually put it into practice. You will choose a feeling (joy, love, surprise), a thought ("Let's play," "You're beautiful," "Find your bone"), and an image (a tree, a red ball, the park) to practice sending telepathically from your heart. First, you will pretend that a dog is sitting on the floor next to your feet; then send the feeling to the dog. Have confidence that the feeling is being sent to the dog. The intention of wanting that feeling to be there is all that is necessary. Then you will imagine how happy the dog is to receive your feeling and will allow the feeling to return to you, with no effort necessary. The intention of wanting it back is all that is required. This will give you a sense of what it is like to send and receive information telepathically.

This exercise allows you to have a focus. When you put it into practice with a real animal, you will focus on that animal wherever he is in the room. Suppose you want to communicate with your springer spaniel, Buffy, but your two other dogs are also in the room with you. In order to make sure your connection is with Buffy and that you won't receive messages from all three dogs at one time, you will need to consciously direct your attention to Buffy only. If you simply put your question out without directing it to a specific animal in the room, you won't know who is answering you. Since they will all want to talk with you, it might be best, in the beginning, to have only one animal in the room with you at a time. But if that is impossible, let your animals know they will each have a turn and let them know with whom you will be starting.

Next, you will pretend a cat with whom you want to make contact is lying on the table. You will send a thought to the cat.

Again, you will imagine how happy the cat is to receive the thought; then have the thought come back to you. Finally, you will send the image onto the ceiling, pretending there is a bird there you want to contact. And, again, imagine the bird's delight in receiving it, and let the image return to you.

Let's begin. You might want to tape-record this portion for yourself so you can just sit back, relax, and follow the instructions or order the audio- or videotape from my office.

❤ Close your eyes and take a few deep breaths, knowing that each breath you take allows you to find that place within your heart where all your love and wisdom lie. Now focus on the feeling you would like to work with. Let this feeling rest within your heart center. Feel and sense it as best you can. *(Pause approximately 30 seconds.)*

❤ Allow that feeling to go onto the floor in front of you, to a dog you imagine waiting there. Your wanting that feeling to be there is all that is necessary. Just visualize the dog receiving the feeling. *(Pause approximately 30 seconds.)*

❤ Now imagine how happy the dog is to receive your feeling and to feel so connected to you. When you can sense his happiness, allow the feeling to return to you and let it rest in your heart center. Your intention of wanting it back is all that is required. No pulling or struggle is necessary. See it resting once again in your heart center. *(Pause approximately 30 seconds.)*

❤ Concentrate on the thought you want to send, and let it rest in your heart center. When you're ready, allow the thought to go onto a table in the room, pretending that there is a cat resting there. Visualize the cat receiving the thought; that's all that is necessary. *(Pause approximately 30 seconds.)*

❤ Imagine how happy the cat is to receive your thought, to feel a connection with you. When you've sensed that happiness, allow the thought to return to you. Let it come back to you and rest in your heart center. Just visualize it back. *(Pause approximately 30 seconds.)*

❤ Now focus on the image you want to send, letting it rest in your heart center. Then allow the image to go to the ceiling, pretending there is a bird above that you want to contact. *(Pause approximately 30 seconds.)*

♥ Feel the bird's happiness at receiving your image and at feeling so connected to you. Allow the image to return to you and once again rest in your heart center. Simply visualize it there. *(Pause approximately 30 seconds.)*

This exercise helps you learn to focus your attention to a specific area or location. It teaches you to concentrate your energy rather than letting your thoughts scatter in all different directions. It also lets you begin to work with sending and receiving feelings, thoughts, and images.

If you found the exercise difficult, ask yourself where the difficulty was. Was it easier for you to send than to receive? Or vice versa? Sometimes it will show you where your problem is within your own verbal communication. For instance, if you have difficulty in receiving the information back, then you might find it hard to listen to people. If you had difficulty in sending the information out, then you might find it hard to express yourself. The solution is to practice the exercise to develop your listening and communication skills. Keep doing the exercise until it becomes very comfortable and easy for you. Practice makes perfect.

Step 6: **Recognize Your Style of Connection**

In the exercise above, you experienced sending information in a variety of ways. Think about it for a moment. Was it easier for you to send a picture than a feeling? Or did you drift from the picture and send more of a thought about the image? Or was it easier to send the feeling associated with the object rather than the actual image of the object? Keep thinking about how all of these exercises happen for you, so you can become familiar with your own style. Figure out what happens for you behind the scenes. By becoming conscious of how you are doing it, you will be much more comfortable with and trust your telepathic communication.

We all tend to communicate in the styles in which we feel most comfortable, especially when we are first beginning to flex our intuitive muscles.

If you are a person who is primarily *verbal*, you might receive a few words or sentences from the animal. The animal's thoughts and concepts might flash into your mind very quickly, leaving you scrambling to fit them to words.

If you are a person who is quite comfortable with your emotions, chances are that you will pick up many feelings from animals. You will sense their emotions.

If you are a person who is *visual*, perhaps an artist or a creative person, you probably experience the world as a series of snapshots or scenes. That will very likely be the way you'll perceive and transmit your early animal communications. You will receive mental pictures and images.

If you are a person who practices medicine or healing, then you may first sense an animal's *physical* imbalances, because this is the kind of information you are most attuned to. You might perceive disharmonies through simple knowingness, because you are drawn to a particular part of an animal's body, or even by sensations echoed in your own body for a second or two. A fleeting malaise—such as a backache that pops up for a few seconds when you encounter an animal—is often an intuitive glimpse of the animal's condition. You will sense what is off-kilter in its physical body.

If you are a person who has done a lot of *spiritual* exploration, you may receive insights at a level beyond conscious thinking. We humans struggle for spiritual knowledge, but for animals, who are more in touch with nature than we are and not as distracted by rational thought, spirituality comes naturally. You will receive information on a spiritual level.

Ultimately it doesn't matter how you achieve your communications with animals, for no one mode is better or more accurate than any other. Follow your instincts. Develop your own style by recognizing and trusting your strongest intuitive skills. In time and with practice, most people find that they're opening new avenues of intuition. They begin to receive and transmit communications on several levels or even through all four channels at once—mental, emotional, physical, and spiritual.

Now you are ready to attempt actual communication and receive feedback about how your telepathic abilities are working. In the next step, you will practice exchanging messages with a human partner and receive feedback and validation to show you how well you are doing. Remember, your job is to:

- *Think the thought clearly.* Be focused; don't let your mind wander.
- *Feel the emotions.* Before you can convey an emotion, you need to bring it up into your own mind, heart, and body.
- *Visualize the images and pictures.* Picture the message you want to send in your mind, like a series of shots in a slide show.
- *Feel the physical sensation.* Just as you can convey an emotion, you can transmit a bodily sensation by summoning it up in your own body.

Step 7: **Exercise Your Telepathic Muscle**

When people are first learning to communicate intuitively with other humans, there may be issues of safety; no one wants their mind "read" by anyone else, nor do they necessarily want to know what others are thinking. This next exercise will enable you to practice sending feelings, thoughts, and images to another person using color. I developed it as a safe way to begin sending to and receiving information from another person, paring down the communication to a simple concept. Because we experience color in so many ways—through seeing, sensing, feeling—it is an easy and effective way to get our intuitive powers moving, and a real confidence-builder. Animal communicator Penelope Smith liked it so much she asked to use it in her own workshops.

PARTNERED EXERCISE WITH COLOR

To do this exercise, find a partner—perhaps someone else who is reading this book or someone you know who loves animals. Then read through the exercise first before attempting it.

Each of you will get to experience both sending and receiving a color. You will both know what the color is before you begin, because the point of this exercise is not to guess what color your partner is sending. Instead, this is a complete telepathic exercise in which you will send and receive feelings, images, and thoughts about that color to develop the various aspects of your intuitive communication skills.

Your job as the sender will be to feel the color in your heart center as best you can. Does it feel soft, peaceful, cool, or vibrant? Then visualize the tone and shade of the chosen color—is it light or dark? Then be aware of any images or thoughts you associate with the color—such as a baby blanket, a holiday, a particular plant. The more energy you bring to envisioning each color, the more powerful the communication will be. Use all your senses in invoking the color in your heart. This exercise works so well because you experience telepathy on so many levels: feelings, images, thoughts, and even some physical sensations. You will now have a chance to apply what you just learned in the previous exercise of sending and receiving (focusing) by sending information to another person.

Your job as a receiver will be to allow yourself to receive the color from a state of relaxation. You might even get impressions of what your partner is feeling, picturing, and thinking about before the color is intentionally sent. Those perceptions may be your own about the color rather than your partner's. You will find that out when you have discussed your impressions with the sender at the end of the exercise.

If you're doing this exercise in a group, you may even pick up thoughts from someone other than your partner. At a workshop many years ago, one woman kept seeing scenes and images that her partner was not sending. She felt she'd failed. During the lunch break, however, she struck up a conversation with a man who was videotaping the class and found out it had been his thoughts she'd been receiving! It's not uncommon to pick up feelings and thoughts from other people. Consider our verbal language; we eavesdrop on others all the time. You're sitting with a friend in a restaurant, talking about her latest adventures, and all of a sudden you've simultaneously tuned in to a heated discussion between a couple behind you. Once you've honed your intuitive skills, you may find the same thing happening telepathically, but just as with spoken language, you'll be able to tune it out at will.

Let yourself be encouraged by this experience so you can let your mind quiet down and have some fun. To start, get situated with your partner in comfortable chairs sitting across from each other, with about a foot of space between you. Decide which one of you will be the receiver and which one will be the sender, center yourselves, and begin.

♥ Close your eyes and put your feet flat on the floor. Imagine roots growing from a very old and wise tree that extend deeply into the ground. These roots will help keep you connected to the earth and well grounded throughout the entire exercise. (Pause approximately 30 seconds.)

♥ Take a few deep breaths, knowing that with each breath you take you allow yourself to find that place within your heart where all of your love lies. Take a moment or two and allow a most wondrous, loving, white light to emerge from your heart. Surround your partner with this light for support and encouragement. Remember that this exercise is done with a great deal of safety and joy. (Pause approximately 30 seconds.)

♥ Quietly reassure yourself that you already have this telepathic ability and are willing to let your logical mind step aside in order for you to have this experience with your partner. Remind yourself that this is not a test but simply an exercise you choose to experience. Allow yourself to be focused in your heart's center. As the sender, allow yourself to feel the color pink in your heart center. Be aware of how it feels to you, be aware of the tone and shade, and be aware of any images and thoughts that are there. As the receiver, allow yourself to enjoy the relaxation. *(Pause approximately 5 minutes.)*

❤ As the receiver, allow the doors of your heart to open. As the sender, allow this color pink to flow from your heart center to the heart center of your partner. And as the receiver, allow yourself to feel this color pink. Be aware of the tone and shade and of any images or thoughts that are there as well. *(Pause approximately 5 minutes.)*

❤ When you feel complete, open your eyes, taking as much time as you need. There is no rush. *(Pause approximately 20 seconds.)*

❤ Now it's time to compare notes with each other. As the receiver, tell your partner what you experienced in detail. And as the sender, validate your partner wherever you can. Look for the similarities and try not to get too critical with yourself. You grow from these building blocks. If you got one image or one feeling, or the shade of the color was correct but you were off on the other aspects, don't worry. Focus on what you did get and not what you didn't get. This is where you will need to be disciplined, patient, and very loving with yourself to improve your skills. *(Exchange information for 5 to 7 minutes.)*

Once this stage of the exercise is complete and you've seen how successful you can be, exchange roles and begin again. The sender will be the receiver, and the receiver will be the sender.

❤ Close your eyes again, taking some deep breaths to allow yourself to find that place within your heart where all of your love lies. Take a moment or two and allow a most wondrous, loving, white light to emerge from your heart. Surround your partner with this light for encouragement and support, with the understanding that you already know how to do this.

❤ As the sender, allow yourself to feel the color green in your heart center. Be aware of the tone and shade, and be aware of any images and thoughts that are there. As the receiver, allow yourself to enjoy the relaxation. *(Pause approximately 5 minutes.)*

♥ As the receiver, allow the doors of your heart to be open, and as the sender, allow this color green to flow from your heart center to the heart center of your partner. As the receiver, allow yourself to feel this color green. Be aware of the tone and shade, and be aware of any images and thoughts that arise. *(Pause approximately 5 minutes.)*

♥ As you feel complete, open your eyes, taking as much time as you need. There is no rush. *(Pause approximately 20 seconds.)*

♥ Now it's time to compare notes again. As the receiver, share what you experienced in detail with your partner. And as the sender, validate your partner wherever you can.

Make sure that you share everything you received with your partner so he or she has a chance to validate your experience. No matter how mundane, silly, or insignificant the information may seem, it may be totally accurate and make perfect sense to your partner. If you feel you've failed at the exercise, ask yourself if you're trying too hard to control your thoughts. Typically, we give so much power to our conscious minds that when we start to use other aspects of ourselves, our fears and insecurities convince us we're losing control. We shut down our intuitive processes in order to feel safe. I encourage you to relax and try again. Let your imaginative, playful self take over, just for a little while, knowing you can opt to move back into your logical mode when the exercise is over.

Look for opportunities to practice these exercises. They're fun and stimulating. Instead of playing charades at a party, suggest doing this "color game." Practice with your spouse, child, neighbor, or friend, and experiment with other colors such as blue and violet. You will notice that your experience and degree of success will be different with each person. It is natural to have a stronger connection with one person than another. We have a great time in the workshop with this exercise. Everyone is astounded to have actually communicated with each other without the use of words and almost always pleased with their success.

These exercises are designed to help you experience telepathic communication for yourself. All these steps have been necessary to prepare you for your communication with your animal. And they show you how well you can do this with humans as well as with animals.

The next chapter is where it all comes together, what all this practice has been building to—the chance to connect intimately, heart to heart, with an animal.

3

Talking to the Animals

In my Introductory Animal Communication Workshops, we start by reaching out to animals as a group, using my dog, Jessie, as our test case. Everyone in the group asks Jessie to share how she feels about certain things, such as "Share with us what your favorite activities are." Then each of us shares the responses he or she has been able to intuit.

But how do we actually ask the animal a question? It's easier than you might imagine. We simply think the thought—"Share with us what your favorite activities are"—clearly in our minds without distraction. We allow the inquiry or question to be sent to her from our hearts, just as you sent the color to your partner's heart center in the Partnered Exercise with Color. Then we simply wait for information to come back from Jessie.

We might receive the message in a myriad of ways—a picture of her running or swimming, a thought about how much she loves the beach, or a feeling of pride in teaching people at the workshop. One person might receive a list of five activities from Jessie, another two or three, and some people pick up only one thing.

Jessie answers us by sharing everything she likes to do, and we receive what we allow in.

The whole point of this exercise is to show that such a range of responses is entirely natural—just as in our human relationships. We are selective in what we attract from others, what we tell them, and what we want to hear. You might decide to confide in Mary that you're having a fight with your husband, but when your friend Susie calls, you say, "Everything is just fine." You will be just as selective with animals. What matters at this point is the act of connection, not the quantity of information or the fact that someone else got a few different details. We each connect with a given animal in our own way because we are unique individuals.

Animals have the same variabilities in personality that we do. For instance, some are private and guarded, or perhaps shy and withdrawn, while others are real talkers. I remember talking with one rabbit who had so much to say that I had to ask him if we could continue the next day. I was exhausted!

Remember that when we meet someone who does not speak our language, we don't assume he doesn't have anything to say or can't communicate. We recognize that we just can't understand him. If we want to communicate with him, we know we must learn his language—or use a translator. It's the same with animals. To understand them, we have to know their language. Luckily, we don't have to learn a new language to accomplish this; we merely need to recover our native tongue—intuition.

As we begin to open up to animals, we have the ability to recognize them as emotional, physical, mental, and spiritual beings. Although their mental processes are different from ours, they experience the full range of emotions we do. They experience grief, sorrow, joy, confusion, frustration, anger, disappointment, fear, and love. They may differ in thought and perception because their brains and bodies are different, but that does not mean that they don't think or feel. It is well known that elephants grieve and bury their dead and that dogs experience joy and happiness when we return home for the day, with their wagging tails as evidence. I believe that animals' emotions are more powerful than ours because they are in the moment and don't allow the mental distractions we do in our lives. So, as you practice and grow more adept at these techniques, you just might find "talking to the animals" easier than talking to humans.

PREPARING TO COMMUNICATE

All your work so far has prepared you for this moment, so feel confident! Don't let fear, high expectations, self-judgment, or over-analysis undermine you. The goal is not to achieve but to *experience* connection, which will not occur very readily if you feel timid and self-conscious rather than open and receptive. Now is the time to lock your critical mind in the closet and expand your sense of the possible. You are about to embark on a wonderful adventure!

It may be helpful, in the beginning, to initiate communication with an animal you don't know very well. With your own animals, who are so familiar, it might be hard to distinguish what you know and think about them from what they're telling you. With an animal whose habits you do not know, you can ask simple questions and check the responses you get with the animal's guardian. This can be a great confidence builder. It confirms for you that you are on the right track.

To gain this kind of validation when communicating with your own animal, go into a room with your animal and close your eyes. Connect with him, ask him what he is looking at. Get a description from him, open your eyes, and see if what he is looking at matches what you saw through his eyes. This is a good beginning test when working with your own animals. It will afford you the confidence to trust other responses you receive.

Be confident, but also be realistic about your first efforts at communication. When you begin to connect with animals, you might feel that you're watching an old television set without cable. The picture may be fuzzy, and static may drown out the sound. This is to be expected in the beginning. You'll need to fiddle with the antennas—your intuitive powers—until you get a couple of channels to come in. Then, as you keep trying and refining your skills, you'll keep adding more channels until you get them all, as clear and sharp as if a cable line had been installed.

I remember asking a cat, on behalf of my client, what he enjoyed doing. At first I felt a rocking sensation, and as I stayed tuned to him, an image of a rocking chair started to emerge ever so slowly, becoming clearer only as I remained focused. Finally, I saw him on the chair, rocking. He loved the sensation he felt with the motion. But I had to be ever so patient, watching the image emerge in slow motion.

Remember that telepathic communication occurs in any number of ways—through emotions, bodily sensations, thoughts, and images. There are no limitations. Some people say they hear words or hear sounds; some smell odors; some experience hunger or nausea; some sense an animal's fear or excitement through the pounding of their own hearts. Some feel an animal's sadness in the form of their own tears. And some people say they "just know" what an animal is communicating; it is a natural knowingness. Sometimes communication happens so quickly that we need to stop and think about how we received it. I often find that there is no way I can communicate verbally at the same rate of speed that telepathic communication occurs. It happens in a flash.

TRUST THE PROCESS

People often talk of having a "gut" feeling about something. This sixth sense is very real; people in primitive times survived on it. You've probably experienced your own gut feelings, whether you've trusted them or not. It's so natural, it's almost like breathing.

When a telepathic communication arrives, we can think we've imagined it and say, "I feel like I'm talking to myself!" The messages can be that subtle—or they can come so fast that we almost miss them. That's why it's critical to trust the *first* response we sense, feel or see from the animal, without interpretation.

When we are beginning to recognize intuition and distinguish it from our own emotions, it is important to be receptive and to validate whatever we receive, especially if it is subtle. It is very important not to explain it away as "just my imagination" or "just a feeling."

To understand how this works think about what happens when you go to a restaurant and decide right away what to order. It just seems to pop off the menu. However, if you keep looking at all the choices, you get confused about what you want to eat, and you decide on something different. Then the person you are with orders your initial choice, and when the waiter brings the food, you look at his and say, "Oh, I wish I had gotten that! It looks so much better." Because you struggled to decide, you didn't end up getting what you really wanted, what your intuition told you to order.

Many of us have the old mind-set that we have to struggle for whatever we want. But in the restaurant example—and in making connections with animals—the right response is not necessarily the one we've worked for but the first response. Trust it!

Trust is eminently important in animal communication. You will trust yourself more when you realize how natural and effortless the process really is.

Try this: Visualize someone holding up his hand, with fingers tightly closed. This closed hand represents a person who is neither sensitive to nor open to the possibility of telepathy with animals. When an animal tries to communicate with this person by sending thoughts to him, there is nowhere for the thoughts to enter, since the fingers are not open and receptive.

Now imagine yourself, an individual who is very sensitive and open to animals, allowing the fingers of your left hand to spread apart and open. Imagine the fingers of your right hand spread apart to represent an animal's thoughts. When the animal sends her thoughts to you from the fingers of the right hand, they enter the open spaces between the fingers of the left hand. The fingers on the right hand interlock with the fingers of the left hand. The two hands become one. In other words, the animal's consciousness becomes your consciousness for that moment; for that instant, her thoughts become your thoughts. This is why you may feel that you're either making it up or talking to yourself rather than recognizing the thoughts as belonging to the animal.

Be willing to accept what you get from an animal, even if it doesn't make sense to you. When my dear friend Sheri Davidson was a novice animal communicator, she was lucky enough to receive a very simple but inspiring affirmation of this principle. As she was talking to a dog one day, she could only see the color red. She didn't believe she had connected with the animal. However, when she told the dog's person about seeing the color red, the woman knew exactly what it meant. Her dog's favorite place in the house was a room with red carpet. How about that for validation!

The good news is, you already listen to your animals telepathically. You just may not be aware of it on a conscious level. To believe that it is truly happening may take a while, but be patient. You simply may need more validation.

I was at a ranch in Santa Rosa Valley, California one day, standing by the entrance to the riding arena. The ranch owner, Claudia, was having her trainer ride her horse for her, as she often did. She felt the trainer could work more effectively with her horse than she could. As the horse passed by, I heard him telepathically say to me, "Why is this person riding me? I want my person to ride me." I communicated back to him, "Let me talk to your person for you."

After the trainer had finished riding, Claudia and I talked. She said, "You know, Carol, I don't know why I keep having my trainer ride my horse. I think I'm going to start riding him myself."

I smiled at her and said, "Claudia, I bet you think that's your own thought." She looked at me a little strangely and said, "Well, who else's could it be?"

"Your horse sent you that thought," I told her. "He wants you to ride him again. That's what he told me just now."

She had to catch her breath. "But I didn't know it was him; I thought it was my own thought. Things like that happen to me all the time. I can be going down the barn aisle and I'll know if a horse is not feeling well. I just know." I reassured her that she had been listening to her animals telepathically without knowing it because she is so sensitive and open to their needs, but she had been unable to distinguish her thoughts from theirs.

To believe what is happening is "real" (even though it's not tangible) takes a deep desire to communicate, a lot of practice time, and even more validation. Eventually, you will distinguish your thoughts from the animal's thoughts, his feelings and sensory experiences from your own. Until then, try to relax. Remember that we are the passengers, not the drivers, on this journey. We will go where the animal wants to take us.

INITIATING CONTACT

Before trying to communicate with an animal, it is polite and respectful to ask if he is interested and ready. I always open a session by asking an animal, "Are you willing to communicate with me?" For all I know, he might be busy with his own thoughts or might not be in the mood to communicate. I don't assume that animals will automatically want to engage at the time I want to.

A client of mine, Ginny Townsend of Garland, Texas, breeds German shepherds. She told me she had practiced long-distance animal communication with her male German shepherd one day on her lunch break. She knew she had reached him because she could physically feel the connection in her heart, but she kept hearing him say, "Later, later. I'm busy." She checked in with him again after a few minutes had passed, thinking that she might not have received the message clearly, and she heard him say the same thing. Ginny questioned her abilities because she couldn't understand why he wouldn't want to communicate with her. When she arrived home and found her bitch in heat, his message of "Later, later. I'm busy" was clearly understood!

Once you have received a welcoming response from an animal, you may well wonder what to say, how to begin. I always recommend that beginners start by asking questions that can be validated, so they can learn to trust the information they receive. And keep it simple. When you are just learning to process an animal's responses, you might be overwhelmed by what he or she has to say on the meaning of life!

Be respectful in your communications. Rather than pepper an animal with demanding, interview-style general questions ("What are your favorite activities?" "What do you like to eat?"), it is more gracious to formulate them in a caring, personal way ("Tell me your favorite activities." "Share with me what you like to eat.").

Some people think that when they ask questions, there has to be a "right" answer. This keeps them in their logical, conscious mind. At that point, they stop listening with their hearts and begin to analyze the situation. They freeze up and become worried about getting the "correct" answer, which blocks them from receiving information. When we approach with caring inquiries, it implies a freer, more openhearted state, inviting broader communications.

Before you attempt your first communication with an animal, jot down a list of questions that can be answered simply, such as these:

- Are you willing to communicate with me?
- Share with me what your favorite meal is.
- Tell me what your favorite activities are.
- Share with me your dislikes.
- Tell me who your best friend is.
- I'd like to know where your favorite place in the house is.
- Share with me what your relationship is like with each of the animals in the household, one at a time.
- Tell me what your home looks like.
- I'd like to know how you feel physically.
- Share with me what you like about being a dog (or cat, horse, bird).
- Tell me if there is anything you would like to change about your environment.

- I'd like to know what your purpose in life is with your person.
- Share with me if there is anything you want to tell me.
- I'd like to know if there is anything you want me to tell your person.
- Tell me if there is anything additional that your person can do for you.
- Share with me your age.
- Share with me anything about your past you would like me to know.

Some people wonder whether they can ask the questions aloud. Of course you can, if that's what feels comfortable for you. However, I prefer to silently think the thought in my mind and then send the thought from my heart to the animal's heart. It is the inner message that is sent and received, whether you say it out loud or not.

REACHING OUT

Congratulations! You are now ready to attempt your first communication, applying the following seven steps with your animal. Know that what you are about to experience will not be new or unusual, because it happens to you every day of your life. Now, however, you will be consciously experiencing it with better awareness. Approach this as an adventure, as a wonderful experience where there is no right or wrong, no judgment or criticism. This is where we leave our egos in the closet and expand our sense of what is possible for us.

Be realistic with your expectations regarding your first efforts at communication. It takes time to change your ways and habits. Be patient and loving with yourself, most of all. Sometimes we have a hard enough time understanding other humans with the same spoken language. Remember that this is like practicing a foreign language that we have forgotten. It will take time to become comfortable and fluent again. The more time you put into practicing your meditation and getting to know and love yourself, the easier communication will be with all beings—four-legged, two-legged, winged, or finned. So let's begin the process, step-by-step, with your animal.

7-STEP HEARTTALK PROGRAM℠—MAKING THE CONNECTION

Step 1: Be with the animal in a peaceful place
Step 2: Invite the animal to get quiet with you
Step 3: Find your still point
Step 4: Ask the animal if the time is right
Step 5: Go heart to heart with your animal
Step 6: Ask your questions from the heart
Step 7: Listen, trust, and enjoy

Step 1: **Be with the Animal in a Peaceful Place**
The best time to start is when you're just waking up, while you are still in your "being" mode and not in your "doing" mode. If you're at home, bring the animal with you into the room you have created for meditation, where you will feel peaceful and relaxed.

Step 2: **Invite the Animal to Get Quiet with You**
Make sure that there are no distractions in the room, such as toys or other animals, and turn off the TV or radio. Soothe the animal by speaking softly, or with a gentle touch. It isn't necessary to have eye contact with your animal, but you do need to make sure that he is aware of you and comfortable.

Step 3: **Find Your Still Point**
Close your eyes and do your breathing exercises from Chapter 2 until your mind and body have reached the still point. It may also be helpful to play the tapes of the relaxation and meditation exercises from Chapter 2 to bring your mind into a receptive, listening state.

Step 4: **Ask the Animal If the Time Is Right**
When you are quiet and centered in yourself, extend yourself to the animal by asking, "Are you willing to communicate with me?" Usually you will get a welcoming response. You might imag-

ine seeing the animal's head shake up and down, or you may find yourself filled with a sense of enthusiasm. If you sense that the animal has answered in any positive way, trust it.

Step 5: **Go Heart to Heart with Your Animal**

Open the doors of your heart to the animal. Just as you felt the properties of the color in the partnered exercise in Chapter 2—its softness, its tone and shade, any images it aroused, and how peaceful it made you feel—allow yourself to experience the essence of the animal. Imagine that a laser beam of light is between you, connecting you with his heart and soul. How does the animal feel? Descriptions, emotions, and other thoughts might pop up, such as "curious," "compassionate," "explorer," "teacher," "healer." All the impressions you receive will be aspects of this particular animal. You will be tuning in to his core essence.

Step 6: **Ask Your Questions from the Heart**

Once you have connected heart to heart, invite the animal to share his feelings. You can allow the animal to talk openly, or if you have prepared a list of questions, begin asking them one at a time. Simply think the thought clearly, and imagine the thought going out from your heart to the animal's, just as you sent the color to your human partner's heart. You can imagine, if you like, that the thought is carried to the animal by a soft and loving ray of light or as an electrical cord that connects the two of you. Or simply allow the thought to go to the animal, knowing it will reach him on the current of energy that connects your heart to his.

Step 7: **Listen, Trust, and Enjoy**

After you send the thought to the animal, wait patiently in a receptive, relaxed mode to receive his response. Remember that his message will reach you as an image if you are more visual, as a physical sensation if you are more physical, and as a feeling if you are more emotional. Or you may receive a simple knowingness or thought. Acknowledge the response, however it happens to come in. When you've received a communication, it is respectful to acknowledge the animal's participation; for example, say, "Thank you for sharing with me."

Don't feel that you have to stick to your prepared list of topics. Be adventurous and ad-lib to find out more about just who the animal is. He will appreciate your efforts to bridge the species gap with him. Trust yourself and enjoy!

That's it! You have just experienced a telepathic communication with your animal friend. What a great and fulfilling accomplishment! Now keep practicing. Know that with any language, we need to practice to become fluent. For some people it takes hours, for some months or even years.

MAKING A LONG-DISTANCE CONNECTION

Once you feel comfortable communicating with animals that are in the same room with you, you can expand your skills by practicing with animals in another location or state. For many, long-distance communication comes faster and sometimes more accurately, because no physical distractions, such as body language, contribute to misinterpretation. When connecting with someone else's animal, choose a time the person isn't aware of to communicate with him. This helps avoid being distracted by the person's thoughts and influences, which can overpower the animal's message.

It's hard at first to believe long-distance communication is possible. The only way to prove this to yourself is to experience it. We all know everyday stories of intuition. A woman on a business trip feels a flash of urgency that she needs to go home. When she calls, the baby-sitter says she was just about to page her because the baby came down with a sudden, high fever. Or you might have experienced it yourself in other ways. Have you ever suddenly thought of someone from your past, seemingly out of the blue, only to have her call you the next day? Such things occur all the time, and we generally accept them as normal.

Knowing this, know also that we can communicate with animals anywhere in the world. Think of radio waves. Although we know they exist, we cannot see or touch them. However, a ham wave operator can fine-tune his equipment to pick up on those waves, even very specific ones.

Just as the radio operator can distinguish between signals, we can distinguish between different beings by tuning in to their energies. Like fingerprints, no two beings' energies are alike. We all vibrate at certain "frequencies." So I may be 92.4 on the dial, and my dog, Jessie, may be 107.5. All we need to do is tune in to the particular frequency of the animal. We are able to do this by first collecting some important facts up front:

- Name and address of the animal and his person
- Complete physical description of the animal:
   -Gender
   -Breed
   -Age
   -Size and approximate weight
   -Body color, fur length and type (short, medium, long, curly, or straight)
   -Eye color
   -Distinguishing marks

Some people find it easier to use a photograph of the animal, but that is up to you. Experiment and find which way works best for you. With all this information, you then put out the intention that you want to connect with the animal fitting this description, living at this location. Your intention needs to be absolutely clear.

Use the same exact steps as when you communicate with an animal in the room with you: relax yourself, find your still point, and open your heart center to the animal. Then imagine a laser beam of light reaching out to the animal, and wait for a connection to be made. When I first started practicing long-distance animal communication, I would state the intention of wanting to connect with the animal in my mind three times. "I want to communicate with Susie," for example. Try this if you're having trouble focusing your intent.

Long-distance communication will feel very similar to other telepathic connections. There is no difference. You will feel a slight sensation within your heart that the connection has been made. You can ask the animal: "Are you there?" When he responds, introduce yourself and explain why you want to communicate with him, and ask him if he is willing to communicate with you. If you get that "yes" feeling in your gut, it's a go.

Now you are ready to talk. If anything, your connection will feel clearer and stronger, with less static.

Enjoy getting to know animals on a much deeper level and know that they will be forever grateful to you for taking a sincere interest in them. When I first discovered that one could actually communicate with animals, my heart and soul longed to have this connection. It was one thing to know that someone could understand an animal's inner thoughts, but the idea that I could *feel* that connection was the biggest dream come true for me. Now it's your dream to realize.

4

Overcoming Communication Breakdowns

When it comes to communicating with animals, there is no difference between your innate abilities and mine. I have become skillful only through many years of practice. And because I wanted to share this incredible experience with others, I used my own trials and tribulations in learning to develop the HeartTalk Program^{SM}. Since then, thousands of students have attended my workshops—and every single one has established a connection with an animal before they left. So, if you're feeling discouraged or as if you'll never get the hang of telepathy, keep trying and have patience with yourself. The rewards will be well worth it.

Most people struggle with their early attempts at animal communication. I certainly did. Learning to communicate with animals requires recovering the ancient language of intuition. To become fluent takes dedicated practice. You wouldn't expect a single course in Spanish to teach you to communicate fluently in that language—nor can you expect a few (or even what feels like many) attempts at communicating intuitively with animals to result in automatic success.

If you wanted to communicate with a Spanish-speaking person, for instance, you might start with some basic gestures, rudimentary sign language, to get your point across—a wave for "hello," upheld hands and a shrug for "I don't know." After taking a Spanish course, you might progress to a simple word—*gracias* for thank you, perhaps—then a phrase, a sentence, all leading to a complete thought. Through continuing education and lots of practice, your communication would continue to expand and you would eventually become more fluent.

And so it is with animal communication. For some reason, however, people seem to place more pressure on themselves when learning this intuitive language than they do when learning a foreign language.

It is natural to experience mental or emotional blocks when learning to communicate with animals. You may feel nervous and anxious, or try to distract yourself through "busy-ness" to avoid the exercises (otherwise known as procrastinating). You may have performance anxiety, fearing that you will simply draw a blank. Fret not; these anxieties are normal and happen to just about everyone when they first start to learn.

My students often share two chief complaints: They are unable to quiet their internal chatter, and they doubt that what they receive is real and not their imagination. This chapter addresses these and other communication breakdowns and offers exercises to help you overcome them.

INTERNAL CHATTER

The most common problem in learning telepathy is approaching it from a state of mental clutter rather than from one of mental ease and clarity. It's no wonder. We all feel, from time to time, that we are caught on a treadmill and don't know where the OFF button is. In our culture, we are programmed to be productive, compelled to fill each and every moment of our day with activity. We think so much that it inhibits us from hearing the subtle voice of our intuition. Because we are more comfortable being busy than being still, the slowed-down feeling of meditation and receptivity may make us nervous and resistant to the silence.

If you find meditation too difficult at first, consider a meditation class or group offered by a local metaphysics bookstore or continuing-education program. You may find it frustrating to meditate alone; many do, so don't pressure yourself. Again, find what works for you. Start in a group where you have the support of others. Begin to develop your own style, build your confidence, and soon you will integrate meditation into your quiet time at home.

Be realistic about your goals and your expectations of meditation. You may never be able to entirely quiet your thoughts, but you will be able to limit them. Accept the fact that your thoughts will come and go sporadically during meditation. When this happens, acknowledge the thought and let it go. Be aware without judgment. You will find your own unique still points, even if they feel different for you each time.

Approach your communication with similar acceptance. Say to yourself, "Let's see what happens when I connect with this animal," rather than, "My mind is so busy and full of thoughts that I wonder if I will be able to get anything from this animal." You probably won't get through with such negative thoughts. Ease up. We all have a tendency to do this to ourselves, but we need to stop the negative internal chatter and be more gentle. Here are five exercises to calm and quiet your thoughts.

PARTING OF THE SEAS

If you know the story of Moses and the parting of the seas, then you know the basics of this exercise. You will do the same thing with your thoughts. Start from a relaxed and centered state, using the relaxation exercises from Chapter 2. (In fact, before beginning any of the exercises in this chapter, it's always best to use this or another relaxation technique that works for you.)

Visualize your mind as a large pool of water. See your thoughts swimming in that water. There may be just a few calm thoughts floating or doing the backstroke, or the water may be crowded, churning with activity. Now visualize a dry pathway in the middle of the pool; separate the sea of thoughts to each side of the pathway. You have just created a clear space through which you can connect with an animal and receive his thoughts with clarity and confidence.

THOUGHTS IN A BOX

In this exercise you will relax, notice your thoughts, and acknowledge them. Then you will store them away, just for a while. In order to do this, you need to imagine a container that pleases you. For this exercise, visualize a box. It doesn't matter what it is made of or what it looks like, as long as it is something that will contain and still your thoughts. Some people visualize a gift box tied with a lovely bow; some need a metal box with a padlock. Once you have imagined the best box for you and placed your thoughts into it, allow that box to be tucked away somewhere safe. You now have some distance from your thoughts and emotions, allowing you to mentally relax in order to receive an animal's thoughts or feelings. Know that you will easily retrieve your thoughts from the box when the time is appropriate.

THOUGHTS ON A TRAIN

This exercise is similar to Thoughts in a Box, but in this one you allow your thoughts to be placed in a compartment on a train to go for a ride. All you need to do is acknowledge the thought and allow it to get on the train. When all are aboard, send the train on a peaceful journey. When you're ready, simply call the train back and retrieve your thoughts.

THOUGHTS IN A BALL

Visualize your thoughts wrapped in a soft ball of yarn and roll the ball to the side. Again, retrieve the ball at a later time that is more appropriate for you.

THOUGHTS IN A BUBBLE

In this light and magical way of unburdening yourself of thoughts, visualize them floating away in a bubble. Imagine a beautiful bubble, like the ones you might have blown as a child. Place your thoughts in the bubble, then watch it float away. When you're ready, the bubble will float back to you.

Hopefully, one of the above visualization exercises or one of your own creation will be helpful to you in quieting your mind and putting your thoughts on hold. Then you can focus on listening to the animals.

TRYING TOO HARD AND WANTING INSTANT RESULTS

These common problems are almost always connected and reflect a desperate state of mind—the exact opposite of what you are striving for. Your goal is to achieve the state of open receptivity that makes communication possible. When you first learn to communicate telepathically with animals, you may want this connection so much that you push. This drives your energy outward, not allowing you to be receptive. It's like hearing a tune and trying to remember the name of the song—the harder you try, the harder it is to remember. Your mission is to let go and let the thought come to you.

Have you ever noticed that when you don't have a care in the world about something, it comes to you easily? And, conversely, when you really want something, it is difficult to attain? Or have you ever met someone who wanted your friendship so badly, she tried too hard and pushed you away? Think about relationships in general—when we least expect them, they come to us without effort. Your relationships and communications with animals will come to you the same way—with ease and when you're not pushing or trying too hard.

Many people expect the floodgates to open or to feel a bolt of lightning when telepathic information finally comes. Most often, the gems of information come in subtle ways. Be patient, keep trying, and, most important, be willing to make mistakes. I call them "missed takes." We get to "take" them over—sometimes, over and over!

You may feel that if you don't get a lot of information, you're not succeeding. Be assured that when you're starting out, even one thought, one word, or one feeling is something to celebrate. You have a good start on which you can build. It's like constructing a house: If you want the house built before you lay the foundation, you won't have a very sturdy or secure house. Ultimately, as in most things, it's not the quantity but the quality of the information that will be important.

Animals communicate simply. For instance, they would not ask us what we did during our day at work. Conversations are most often initiated when they have a need; they don't talk to fill up space. If you get one picture, it can equal many words. Be grateful for the simplicity of their language.

Like anything that is worth doing in life, animal communication takes time and practice and a willingness to open your heart. You have the capacity to do it—heart talk is our first language!

EXERCISE: QUICK WORD ASSOCIATION

When you are trying too hard, all of your energy is focused in your conscious mind and it is almost impossible to relax. This word-association exercise will help you let go. You've most likely seen this exercise performed before, in the movies or on television.

Ask for help from a partner. After getting yourself into a relaxed state, have your partner say a word out loud. Then you respond with the first word that occurs to you. For example, when I do this exercise with a student, I sit across from him and say a particular word out loud. I might say "blue." His job is to say the first word that pops into his mind. He might say "sky." That's as simple as it is. I say "water" and he says "ocean." I continue to exchange words with him until I have a sense that he is relaxed and comfortable, and that his mind is willing to go with the flow.

The Quick Word Association exercise gives you the ability to respond freely, without overthinking or self-judgment. There can be no right or wrong answer, since endless associations are possible for each word. It gets you talking, which helps you feel more relaxed and less vulnerable. It is like dealing with stage fright or performance anxiety. Once you start talking, you automatically get into the flow of things.

When you are comfortable with this exercise, try it with the animal you want to communicate with in the same room with you. Do a series of words back and forth with your partner until you feel mentally relaxed. Then sit quietly with the animal, opening your heart to his. Feel the connection. Invite him to talk with you freely, or ask him a question or two. Allow yourself to receive the information back easily and effortlessly, just as you did with the exercise.

If this is still difficult, have your partner ask you questions: "What is the dog's favorite activity?" Reply by saying the first thing that comes to your mind.

If you don't feel ready to ask the animal questions, then simply sit with him, allowing your two hearts to blend. Allow the core essence of that animal to be revealed to you in whatever way it comes: through feelings, images, thoughts, or knowingness.

PROJECTING YOUR FEELINGS ONTO ANIMALS

When we are just learning to communicate with animals, it is common to want to interpret their responses, to jump to conclusions based on our human experience or by reading their body language. Such was the case of a seventeen-year-old Lhasa apso named Ozzie, whose story you will read in Chapter 10. The guardian was struggling with the very difficult decision about whether to put Ozzie down. If the decision had been based on the dog's physical appearance, all indications would have been to put him out of his misery. But once asked, Ozzie told us he was not yet ready to go and gave many good reasons. So, while I'm not asking you to ignore an animal's body language, I *am* asking you to go beyond it and not base decisions only on what you see.

As humans, we may have the tendency to read too much into what we receive from animals. We need to stay with the feelings, the words, the thoughts, or images we receive from them. Especially when working with someone else's animals, we may not understand what we receive, but we will once we express it to their guardians. They will almost always validate our findings.

Raymond from Chapel Hill, North Carolina called me one day because he was having difficulty with his new show dog, Tandy. She was not responding to his commands in the ring, although she performed perfectly when practicing at home. Raymond was frustrated, feeling that she wouldn't amount to much in the show world. He was considering giving her away.

After the phone call with Raymond, I contacted Tandy long distance. I asked her what the difficulty was. All I got from her was a picture of another dog. She told me an image of this dog flashed in front of her every time Raymond gave her a command at the show. She tried to focus on him but became so disoriented that even her walk was unbalanced.

I had no idea what any of this meant, so I simply relayed the information to Raymond. As is so often the case, he knew what it meant. "Tandy looks exactly like my prize show dog who just died," he said. "That's who I see every time I look at her. Whenever we're in the show ring, all the memories of the successes I shared with my other dog come flooding back." He realized these feelings surfaced only when showing and not when training at home. At competitions, even though Raymond would give the proper command, Tandy could only understand his feelings and the imagery he projected. For animals, emotion and images nearly always over-ride words.

I cannot stress this point often enough: When you are receiving a communication from an animal and you find yourself saying "Let me just figure this out," stop. You are no longer listening. It is your job to receive and trust the information, not to interpret it.

For example, if you want to know why a cat is urinating outside the litter box, you need to stay open-minded when asking the question. If you think you already know why (perhaps you think she's angry and trying to punish you), you bring that thought to the forefront and don't hear the animal's actual response. You allow your preconceived notion to interfere with your communication. You are not listening to the animal.

Animals are not complex in their communication. One thought can hold much information; one word can say it all. If they trust us, they will share their feelings. They will say if they are lonely, scared, tired, angry, or frustrated. Unlike many humans, they are not afraid of their feelings. Obviously, their communication style differs greatly from ours.

We may also project our own feelings onto animals. For example, a person who works may feel that her animal is lonely and sad when left alone all day. This might actually be how the person would feel in a similar situation and not how the animal feels. In fact, the animal may feel absolutely content being by himself.

We may do this if we have not dealt with our own feelings and anxieties about loneliness or if we experience guilt from leaving animals alone. Again, your job is to be *receptive*—to listen to the animal and detach your own feelings from what he tells you. To communicate accurately, we need to recognize boundaries and learn to be accountable and responsible for our own feelings.

EXERCISE: BECOME THE ANIMAL

If you are struggling with having preconceived notions, jumping to conclusions, or projecting your own feelings onto animals, then you need to get out of your own way. A good way to do this is to practice "becoming the animal." This exercise gives you the opportunity to experience an animal's perceptions rather than staying stuck in yours. You see things through his eyes, feel things through his body, and think thoughts through his mind.

Begin from a relaxed place and sit with the animal. Think about what you want to know or discover about the animal. Then simply imagine yourself becoming that animal, as you did in the gestalt exercise in Chapter 2. This takes more work for some than others. If you're having difficulty, ask yourself questions: What does it feel like to be in his body? How do things look through his eyes? How does it feel to be so low or high to the ground? Once you understand what it feels like to be him, then imagine how he would answer your inquiry. What would he say? Let him answer you, and trust that answer.

This exercise is a terrific way to hear animals' viewpoints and understand them better. It allows you to listen without interpretation or projection. Give it a try!

DOUBTING YOURSELF

I understand this subject very well because of my own self-doubt when I started in animal communication. In fact, almost everyone feels this way at first. It can be a positive factor in the learning process, because it helps keep us honest. In time, with the help of the exercises in this section, you will learn to deal with your doubts, controlling them so you can accept validation and feel good about your progress.

Be patient with yourself and the animals. Animal communication need not be intimidating. It is extremely simple, so much so that we often don't trust it.

Pay attention to what you receive, not to what you don't receive. Remember, you're building from the foundation up.

In the beginning, you may mix some of your own thoughts with the animal's thoughts. That's okay. Through practice and continuing your own inner work and meditation, you will eventually filter out your own thoughts. Your communication will grow more clear and accurate.

Try not to compare yourself with others. At my workshops, I often hear people say things like "I'm only getting feelings. I want to get pictures, like she is." You can be assured the person who is getting pictures is thinking "I'm only getting pictures; I wish I could get feelings." If you find yourself thinking "I wish I were getting . . ." you need to stop. Instead of looking at what you're not getting in the communication, look at what you are getting. Acknowledge that you are indeed communicating with the animal and feel elated about that!

Instead of trying to communicate as someone else does, embrace your own unique style and develop it. Find what works best for you. Is it better for you to communicate long distance, or do you prefer to have the animal with you? Do you like using a photo of the animal? Do you want to be alone with the animal or is it okay to have others around you?

The grass isn't necessarily greener on the other side of the fence; it's just a different kind of grass. If you see it as greener, it's only because you allow it to be.

EXERCISE: DESCRIBE THE ANIMAL

To overcome self-doubt, it helps to have a method of starting your communication sessions that you know will be successful. This can be something as easy as describing the animal's physical attributes. By starting here, you begin to connect with the animal whether you realize it or not. Once you physically describe him, you will most likely be able to move on to describe the animal on different levels.

Begin by sitting quietly with the animal. Do any relaxation or meditation exercises that help you, such as those in Chapter 2. Then, from this relaxed, open state, simply describe the animal physically. For example, if you do this exercise with my dog, Jessie, you might say, "I see a black-and-white dog with short hair and freckles, a black nose, and brown eyes. She has a shiny coat and crosses her front legs in the cutest way." As you describe her and hear yourself talk, you become more relaxed with the process and ever so gently begin to describe her personality, perhaps saying "She seems sweet and happy. She loves people and feels very confident." You begin to build on what you see.

It's like asking a child to build something from blocks scattered around the room. At first, the task might feel overwhelming to him. But as the child gets a feel for the blocks in his hands, moving them around, he eventually builds something. It doesn't matter what it looks like. This exercise is similar. You need to start some- where, building from what you do know. Then you can progress from there. You may be surprised how successful this simple exer- cise is.

NOT ASKING FOR CLARIFICATION

When asking animals questions, people often get nervous that there has to be one right answer. They often become fearful and retreat into their conscious, logical minds. Instead of asking a question, try an inquiry. Approach the animal by asking him to share how he feels about a certain situation. For sample inquiries, refer to the list in Chapter 3. Remember, however, that the answer you receive may not always make sense. Accept it and realize you now have options. You can tell the animal you don't understand the message and ask him for more detail. If you're working with someone else's animal and you don't receive any additional infor- mation, tell the guardian what you receive. She will most likely un- derstand the animal's message.

Often, when people don't understand what they're hearing from an animal, they feel too shy or scared to ask for clarification. They don't realize it's an option. But wouldn't you ask a human be- ing for further explanation if you didn't grasp what he'd said? It's perfectly logical and acceptable to ask an animal to repeat some- thing you don't understand. He won't judge you. For example, if you sense that an animal is disappointed, don't stop there. First, find out whether you indeed heard him correctly. Then ask why he feels disappointed and how you might be able to help him feel better. Your only way of resolving conflicts with animals is to know what's wrong and what they need to resolve the problem. Say to the animal, "I sense that you feel disappointed. Are you? Tell me why you feel that way. Tell me what you need in order to feel better." Have a real conversation with him, going back and forth between your inquiries and his answers.

Sometimes we need to be like detectives with animals, so we need to feel comfortable asking them exploratory questions. Never be afraid to ask. You can even tell the animals you are a beginner. The animal will be patient with you.

The barriers listed in this chapter are just some of the common problems that block communication or lead to incorrect interpretations. With the strategies in this book—and with a little faith in the process—every one of them can be overcome. Try not to overanalyze. Relax. Allow yourself time to fit heart talk into your life until it becomes as natural as breathing. After you have reviewed and experienced some of the previous exercises in this chapter and feel ready to move on, experiment with the exercises that follow. They will enhance and reinforce your telepathic and intuitive skills. Some of them require a partner, and some you can do alone. I've included suggestions and ways to help support yourself while developing your telepathic abilities.

EXERCISES TO ENHANCE AND REINFORCE YOUR TELEPATHIC SKILLS

EXERCISE: FEELING ENERGY

This is a simple yet profound exercise that gives you the opportunity to trust that what you feel is true. You will find it easy because it is so tangible and concrete that your mind can't negate what you feel, and you'll learn to use words to describe feelings and things that you cannot actually see. It is a great experiment to help you feel your life energy and know that it is, indeed, alive.

Sit in a comfortable chair and relax. Vigorously rub the palms of your hands together until you begin to feel heat between them. At that point, hold your hands about six inches apart; then slowly move them farther apart and back together, without touching. Keep moving them back and forth, as if you were playing an accordion.

You will feel something happening between your hands. Some people describe it as a tingling sensation, a sense of warmth, a magnetic pull, or like electricity. What you feel is energy, your own energy that you have trapped between your hands. To feel your energy more intensely, cup your hands slightly and move them in circular motions, as if you are moving your hands around a soccer ball. Your energy is alive—you're feeling it right now—and you can name it, describe it, even though you cannot see it. This exercise helps you to trust your feelings and ultimately your intuition.

EXERCISE: COTTON BALLS

Everyone laughs when I bring out the cotton balls in a workshop. They wonder what I'm up to. But I don't know one person who hasn't enjoyed this exercise or found it extremely helpful in developing intuitive and telepathic abilities.

It is beneficial to start with the Feeling Energy exercise, warming up before moving on to this advanced version of it. The Cotton Balls exercise is best done with other people—as few as two or as many as you'd like. Assemble so that you all sit facing one another. Each person needs a handful of cotton balls, about six inches in diameter. Have the group close their eyes and place their feet flat on the floor. At this point you can play your tape of the relaxation and meditation exercise from Chapter 2 or ask another participant to read the following to the group:

♥ Take some deep breaths while scanning your body for any tension. Breathe into those areas where the tension lies and then allow all the tension to be released on the exhale.

♥ Imagine you have roots from a very wise tree growing from the bottoms of your feet and extending far into the ground. These roots will help keep you connected and grounded throughout the entire exercise.

❣ Allow a brilliant white light to enter through the top of your head, relaxing every muscle in your body. As the light flows gently and easily throughout your body, down your legs, into your feet, and back up into your hands, allow the light to flow into the cotton balls.

❣ As this happens, be aware of how the cotton balls feel to you. You can hold the cotton balls lightly. You can fluff them up or squeeze them if you'd like. What's most important is to be aware of how they feel. *(Pause approximately 5 minutes.)*

❣ Now open your eyes and pass your cotton balls to another person in the room. Close your eyes again and allow yourself to feel these cotton balls. What do they feel like? How do they feel compared to yours? Do they feel the same, similar, or very different? *(Pause for 5 to 10 minutes, or until everyone feels complete.)*

At this point everyone opens their eyes and, one by one, explains how the cotton balls of the person they exchanged with felt and how they were different from their own.

You will be astounded at what you are able to feel in the cotton balls and at how you can articulate it. Let's review what happens in this exercise. First you allow your energy to flow easily into the cotton, which I have found to be a great absorber of energy. When you switch cotton balls with a partner, you are able to distinguish and note how their energy feels different. You are no longer feeling mere cotton balls, you are experiencing energy, and you can articulate your experience in words. You are becoming aware of the subtleties of energy. Give yourself a giant pat on the back.

People have amazing reactions to this exercise. One workshop attendee said that the cotton balls she received felt very organized, as though each one was separate and had its own place or purpose, as though each one had a job. She then said they also felt very warm, loving, and caring. What she was describing was the energy of the person who'd originally held the cotton balls. He was very organized and had everything in order in his household, he reported. We could all sense that he was also a very caring and loving person. All of his attributes, as different as they were, could be felt as energy within the cotton.

Another person described the cotton balls as feeling confined, compacted, like they needed space and air. She said they felt as if they needed some lightness and fun. Once she had shared this information, the person who started with those cotton balls agreed that she had been feeling very isolated and confined, with a great deal of pressure from her workload. She told us she was in desperate need of space and time out for fun.

When you share your experiences, validate one another where and whenever you can. This helps build confidence. This exercise is always a big hit and helps almost everyone experience the intangible.

EXERCISE: PHOTOGRAPHS

We use this exercise in my workshops when people begin to learn to communicate long distance with animals. It requires that each participant have a photograph of his or her animal. It will help you build your confidence since you know nothing about the animal you will work with other than what he looks like in the picture.

You can do this exercise with as few as two people. If you are in a group, have each person place his or her photo facedown into a basket. Then each person chooses a photo. You may tell the person who drew your animal what his name is, but that's all. If you are working with just one other person, exchange photos, telling each other only the animal's name. Have everyone sit back and relax, get comfortable. You may want to do a meditative exercise as a group, or let people quiet themselves in whatever way they choose.

Take the next five to ten minutes to sit with your photograph. Look at it. See the animal and just be with him. From time to time, close your eyes and open your heart to the animal. Go back and forth with eyes open and shut, looking at the animal, then relaxing and opening your heart center.

Then allow yourself to experience the images, feelings,

thoughts, and impressions you receive. It is best to have a pad and pen or pencil with you. Jot down some of the things you receive so that you don't have to hold on to all the information in your head. If you get it down in writing, it leaves space for more information to come through.

It doesn't matter if you see a flying banana in your mind. Write it down. Believe it or not, that animal might like eating bananas. Remember, don't judge the information. Simply accept it. It might make absolutely no sense to you, but it will likely make sense to the animal's guardian.

When everyone has finished, take turns sharing the information received. These discussions are usually very revealing and help validate everyone's experience.

For example, you might see a chain-link fence and have a sense that the animal loves water. You might see an image of a gray cat and get a good feeling about him, or see a bunch of carrots and horses on a hillside. While these items may seem disjointed, you've probably just perfectly described the animal. It might just be that the photo you chose is of a dog who lives in a yard fenced with chain link. The dog loves to swim, has a gray cat as a buddy, loves to eat carrots, and spends a lot of time with the neighbor's horses on an adjoining hillside.

You will be surprised at how much information you receive through the photograph. By simply relaxing and sitting with the photo, you will receive many particulars about the animal. And you don't even have to work at it—it just happens.

This exercise works so well because it puts you in an open frame of mind. Because there are no questions to be asked, you don't feel the fear of not knowing the answers, nor do you put demands on yourself. You are free to simply see what happens.

This exercise can also be done with a photograph of a person. Some people prefer this to working with a photo of an animal, because it takes even more pressure off. Since they are not trying to learn telepathic communication with humans, they don't care as deeply about their sense of success. They aren't hobbled by fear and doubt, and they're thrilled with the results of the exercise.

They usually tell me they're surprised at how easily the information came to them. This is often the result when you let go of expectations.

EXERCISE: FOCUS ON A FEELING OR AN IMAGE

This exercise is best done with a partner. One of you starts as the sender and the other is the receiver; then you can switch roles. Similar to the Partnered Exercise with Color in Chapter 2, this time you will send a feeling instead of a color. After doing the relaxation and meditation exercise together, sit across from your partner. As the sender, choose a feeling to send. It might be peacefulness, joy, fear, or sadness. Allow yourself to be totally absorbed in that feeling. When you feel the sensation of it strongly in your gut, focus on sending the feeling to your partner. As the receiver, allow yourself to be open, like a sponge—soaking in the sensations and, most important, trusting what you feel.

You can also try this exercise with simple images. In a group setting, for instance, draw simple images on individual pieces of paper, such as a circle, a square, a triangle, and a diamond. Then put the pieces of paper facedown into a basket and have the first sender select one. The sender then focuses on that image as strongly and clearly as possible and sends it to the receiver.

EXERCISE: VISIT EACH OTHER'S HOME

This is a great exercise that will help you trust your intuition and develop your long-distance communication skills with animals. Pam Oslie, a well-known psychic and author from Santa Barbara, California, teaches this exercise in her workshop, which I attended. My first response was that I would never be able to do it; happily, I was wrong.

Do this exercise with a partner. Each of you will have a turn experiencing it—don't try to do it simultaneously. The object of the exercise is to psychically visit your partner's home, through your mind, to see what it looks like inside and out. You will notice details, such as colors, materials, and furnishings, and relate them to your partner for validation.

Begin by sitting across from your partner. Decide which of you will go first. Together, surround each other in a lovely golden light, feeling safe, comfortable, and supportive of each other. As the first to try it, extend that light (as a symbol of your consciousness) outward, a few feet beyond your body. Then extend it into the entire room. Allow the light to continue to move outward into the environment outside the building, knowing that your consciousness is not limited by walls. Extend the light ever outward into the environment, until you reach the front door of your partner's home. Visualize what the front of her apartment, house, or condo looks like. What is it made of? What color is it? What surrounds it? Then walk inside and see what the interior looks like in detail—the color of the walls, the rugs on the floor. What does the furniture look like? What else do you see?

Be a detective. Go exploring, and go for the details. Give yourself about ten minutes with this exercise. When you feel complete, take a few deep breaths. With each breath you take, your body will become more aware of the current environment and your physical body. Allow yourself to easily and gently bring your consciousness back into the room. When you are ready, share your findings with your partner. Describe what her home looks like in detail.

Then switch roles and have your partner take her turn exploring your home. As the occupant of the home, validate your partner wherever you can so she knows how well she did.

When I did this exercise, I saw that my partner's house had blond hardwood floors accented with red Oriental rugs, and white furniture with red accents. There were many windows, which made the house light and airy. I felt it was located near the beach. I saw a fireplace and stacks of magazines and books throughout the house. The artwork, which was primarily red, was displayed in Plexiglas shadow boxes. It was so incredibly exciting to discover that this visual journey was even remotely possible. To my amazement, my partner validated that the images and impressions I saw and felt fit his house exactly.

EXERCISE: AUTOMATIC WRITING

I encourage everyone to try this exercise as a way to begin writing down information when communicating with animals. When you write the information down, you get the thoughts out of your head and onto paper. You don't need to remember everything the animal told you, and you open space to allow more information to come through. You may choose to write in great detail, or just use key words and symbols, or you may want to sketch or draw what you receive, if that is more natural for you. You can also use this skill to help when you are feeling stuck or blocked in your communication.

Once you are relaxed and have the animal with you, focus on what it is you would like to know from the animal and send that message to him. Now, with your pen or pencil in hand, write spontaneously, noting anything you feel or sense from the animal. If you feel blank, as if nothing is happening, then write exactly those words on the paper—*I feel blank, like nothing is happening*—even if it feels silly to you. The important part of this exercise is to keep writing, no matter what. Just record your flow of thoughts, whatever they may be. You will eventually become relaxed enough to start receiving the actual communication from the animal.

Automatic writing helps open the doors for receiving more details. Again, these details may not initially make sense to you, or they may seem out of whack with one another. Eventually, all the puzzle pieces will come together to create a complete picture. This exercise is similar to the Quick Word Association exercise, but you can do it without a partner. Practice automatic writing every day; make it a part of your routine. Many people love this exercise and adopt it as their permanent method of communication.

SUPPORTIVE MEASURES

Throughout the process of learning to communicate with animals, you will most likely have ups and downs, with good days and bad days. Sometimes you will feel connected and accurate, and other times you will feel as though you've lost your abilities. This is perfectly natural and part of the learning curve. Along the way, it's important to support yourself so you don't lose patience and give up. Many of my students have tried the following self-support methods and found them to be helpful.

AFFIRMATIONS

Affirmations are a good way of clarifying your intentions and of silencing negative inner chatter. Before you begin a communication session, try saying a few affirmations to yourself. Here are a few examples, or come up with your own.

- I know I have this ability.
- I ask for divine guidance.
- I want to receive information that is accurate and that is for the highest and best good of this being.
- I ask that my mind sit on the sideline in observation.
- I choose to have this experience for myself.
- I give thanks for this experience.

SUCCESS BOOK

In my workshops, I often suggest that students find themselves a lovely covered book with blank or lined pages. The book is only to be used for success stories regarding your telepathic communication with animals. Record every accurate response you receive, whether it is an image, a word, a feeling, a thought, or a concept. Most important, number each validation you receive so that you can see them piling up. Then, when you doubt yourself and are in need of support, you can refer to your Success Book. Reviewing all your validations will prove to you that you are really communicating with animals. I also encourage you to put stars next to those words, sentences, paragraphs, or pages you feel particularly thrilled with. Try using self-adhesive, shiny stars, the kind teachers use to put on your homework assignments in grade school. They're available in most office supply or stationery stores.

SUPPORT GROUP

Surround yourself with people who will be supportive of you in your new adventure. You need encouragement, not discouragement. Perhaps you can find a meditation group to participate in. Many metaphysics bookstores offer classes, lectures, and groups; you may find one of them very supportive. Or start your own support group with others who have studied animal communication or who have read this book. Start by meeting once a month and practice your telepathic communication with one another's animals. You might want to have a potluck afterward. Many of my workshop students have formed support groups, and their skills have improved dramatically as a result.

ASK THE ANIMAL FOR SUPPORT

If you are struggling with animal communication and finding it too difficult, simply ask the animal for support. Intuition is a language that is natural for animals, so ask them for assistance. Sit back and relax; tell the animal that you are unsure if you are receiving anything from him and that you would like his help. Ask him if he is willing to help you. Watch for a response in your gut. What does it feel like? Does the feeling seem positive, with a sensation of excitement or enthusiasm? This is the "yes" you're hoping to receive. Or does the feeling seem uncomfortable, unsure, or unenthused? Perhaps the animal doesn't want to help at the moment. If so, that's how it might feel. It's unlikely that you will get such a response, though, since most animals are thrilled just to be invited to help.

The following confidence-building exercises can be extremely validating when you work with your own animals. Because you know them so well, it is more difficult to trust that what you receive is actually coming from your animal and not from your preconceived thoughts or feelings. These exercises make sure you are getting through to your animal companions.

❤️ Telepathically ask the animal to sit, lie down, or come to you. Do this by sending images of what you want him to do; clearly picture him doing the task in your mind. If you are clear with your "sit" message, your animal will sit down, and that will be your validation.

❤ Ask the animal to give you a sign when he has received your communication. Choose a specific action, or leave it up to him to decide how he will notify you. When you think you've received a sign, trust yourself.

❤ Ask your animal to give you a sign if he feels that you have received the message he sent. Again, watch for the sign, and when it comes, believe it.

By asking an animal for help, you allow yourself to flow into his world. Instead of trying to reach out to him, let him gently pull you into his world. Ask him to show you what it feels like to be approached by you. Do you push too hard, give up too easily? Perhaps he can help you see what you need to do to create a strong yet gentle connection. Remember to allow the animal to talk freely to you without judgment.

If you doubt an animal's response, tell him that you are just a beginner and coping with doubt, and ask for his patience and guidance. If, however, you continue to doubt, the animal might stop talking to you, because you do not believe him.

If you seem to have reached an impasse, realize it is usually only temporary. Allow yourself a time-out. When the time feels right, find your quiet space and gently ask yourself, "What would it take for me to understand this, to be able to do it?" Notice what issues come up for you. You might want to write them down or discuss them with a supportive friend to help you gain some perspective on things. Give yourself time and then try again with what you have learned. Sometimes a new approach can make all the difference in the world.

Scooter, at age 4, the
master of harmony
for 21 years.

Joy Boy looking on as
he teaches one of his
last classes with Carol.

MARTIN VAN WIJNGAARDEN

matters
of
the heart

5

The Animals in Your Life

Animals offer some of the most rewarding relationships in our lives. It is important to choose your animal companion carefully, just as you would a friend. But once you choose an animal, your job isn't over. Just as with humans, some effort is required to get the most out of the relationship and keep things running smoothly. And just as in all relationships, communication is the key. This chapter will help you find the right match in an animal companion, using the communication techniques we learned in Part I, and help you sustain happy relationships with the animals in your life.

MAKING A CHOICE TO HAVE AN ANIMAL

Choosing to have an animal is an important and life-changing decision. Before you bring an animal into your life, it is essential that you recognize the level of responsibility you are assuming. After all, you will be taking care of another living being for his or her lifetime. Do all you can to make the right choice for yourself and for the animal.

Before you fall in love with an animal, it is important to consider his or her needs along with the needs of current family members, both human and animal. Later in this chapter, you will go step-by-step through the process of communicating with a potential family member and your current animals. Just as in making the decision to have children, the choice to bring an animal into your home needs to be taken seriously.

Answer these questions to determine if you are ready for this commitment.

- Why do you want an animal in your life?
- What are you looking for from the relationship? Companionship? Protection? An animal to train and show in competition?
- What amount of effort are you willing to give to the relationship?
- Do you have the time that is necessary to care for the animal physically and emotionally? For example, after a long day's work, are you willing to allow time for a walk and to play? Animals require regular exercise, and you need to decide if you can schedule such a routine into your life.
- Can you provide an environment that is appropriate for the particular animal you are thinking about getting?
- Are you aware of the costs of having an animal? Expenses include a good nutritional diet, possible grooming, veterinary care (preventive care as well as unexpected illnesses), training, possible boarding and pet-sitting, toys, comfort items, and general supplies pertaining to each species' needs.
- What is your lifestyle? Are you willing to make the necessary adjustments to include an animal in a considerate and compassionate manner? Are you willing to share your home with an animal by allowing him to have total access to the house, or is he expected to lead a separate life by living in the garage, yard, or basement until you return home? If you're considering a cat, are you willing to adjust your decor by having climbing/scratching poles available to address her basic instincts to claw and climb?

- Is your work schedule conducive to having an animal? If you travel often or work long hours, you might decide it's not appropriate to have an animal at this time.

These are just a few of the things to think about and consider before plunging into this major decision. Remember, it will have a lifelong effect.

KNOW WHAT YOU'RE GETTING INTO

Because animals are cute, people often fall in love with them without realistically assessing their needs. Some animals are much higher maintenance than others, such as birds, horses, and even some dogs.

People buy bunny rabbits for children because they're cute. They don't do the research to find out that rabbits can be high-strung and hard to handle. Rabbits may chew through electrical wires and not use a litter box. Parents find themselves exasperated at having to take care of these high-maintenance animals themselves. A more appropriate choice for children might be a calmer, lower-maintenance animal, perhaps an older dog who is already trained and housebroken and anxiously awaiting adoption by a family.

No matter what animal you choose, ask yourself if you have time to both train and supervise your children in the proper handling of an animal. Are your children old enough to assume responsibility for the care of an animal? Be sure to assess these issues honestly so that our animal friends will face no undue harm.

Also, consider whether you are ready for the responsibility a particular breed or animal may require. You would not bring a rottweiler into your house unless you were ready and able to provide proper guidance and direction, and an abused animal may have greater emotional needs than you are prepared to fill. Be honest with yourself about what you can manage.

Physically speaking, an animal may be too big or strong for you to live with comfortably, as one of my clients, Judy Daggs from Simi Valley, California, came to learn.

Judy had recently purchased a palomino horse named Oatie and was becoming increasingly fearful of him. Oatie would pin back his ears and charge, not only at her but at just about everyone who came near him. He would make every attempt to throw her— or any beginning rider who would dare mount him—off his back. Judy felt intimidated by his size, power, and temperament.

When I arrived at the ranch, I talked to Oatie and found out that he felt sad and angry for having been gelded without his per- mission. He felt he was a "leader" and had been robbed of his role in life.

I asked him how we could help him feel better about the situa- tion. He wanted to belong to the trainer of a ranch rather than to a beginning rider. In this way, he would be a leader by being with a human leader. Pam O'Neill, the trainer of Majestic Equestrians of Moorpark, California, gladly took him in, but told Oatie that in order to be her horse, he would have to give lessons to beginning riders.

Oatie shocked and amazed everyone. As soon as Pam took him on, his ears perked up; he stopped charging people and happily started giving lessons to beginners. Oatie found his match, his home, and the ability to express his leadership role through his hu- man partnership with Pam, the trainer.

CHOOSE THE RIGHT ANIMAL FOR YOUR LIFESTYLE

Just as we choose our family of human friends with great sensitiv- ity and care, we need to use care in choosing animals with whom we intend to share our lives. For example, if you have young chil- dren, you should determine whether the animal you are consider- ing has the temperament and willingness to be loving and patient.

Charlotte Podrat, the owner of Purple Hills Ranch in Malibu, California, called me one day about a horse that she wanted to purchase for her daughter. She was attracted to the horse because of his spunkiness, but when her daughter first rode him, the horse bolted. Charlotte was worried that he would do it again.

When I got in touch with the horse telepathically, he conveyed

that he did not want to belong to a child—that he was not inter-
ested in "baby-sitting." This was an important discovery for Char-
lotte, who had to recognize that the horse she had admired was not
temperamentally suited to this particular job. Now her daughter is
happily matched with a horse who accepts and responds appropri-
ately to the child.

Consider the environment you can offer the animal. Are you
thinking of adopting a working breed such as a Border collie and
planning to coop him up in a small apartment? This kind of dog
needs space and something to do all day long. If you choose a
working dog and live in a small setting, then you need to make
sure he gets plenty of exercise. Put yourself in his paws: Imagine
living in your bathroom (that's about how big an apartment feels to
an outdoor animal) and getting out to eat and play only when your
parents allow it. It would be a horrible, boring existence, yet people can't understand why their dogs bark all day long when confined. Find a dog who will fit comfortably into your environment.
If you do not plan to give him much exercise, do not get a working
dog; choose a dog content to live in a small space.

Many good books are available on this subject, including
Adopt the Perfect Dog: A Practical Guide to Choosing and Train-
ing an Adult Dog by Gwen Bailey, and *Simon and Schuster's*
Guide to Dogs by Elizabeth Meriwether Schuler. Visit the library,
or ask your veterinarian for advice.

When choosing an animal, think about what you are asking
him to deal with in order to be a part of your life, and keep that
thought at the forefront of your decision making and in your heart.

USING TELEPATHY TO HELP YOU
CHOOSE AN ANIMAL

This section will explain how to use the communication skills
you've learned so far in choosing an animal. Let's review what
you've learned in the previous chapters to prepare for your telepathic tasks when bringing an animal into your home.

In Chapter 2 you experienced telepathically sending a concept to your partner through the Partnered Exercise with Color. You had to blend or "be" with a color to sense it completely before sending it to your partner. This happened for you because you sat quietly with a color with the intention of wanting to feel, sense, visualize, and think about it.

You experienced it again in Chapter 3 when you learned to go heart to heart with an animal. You allowed yourself to experience the essence of the animal by reaching out with a laser beam of light from your heart. And you felt the essence of that animal through impressions, words, feelings, or a general knowingness. You were able to identify with his energy.

In Chapter 4, you experienced feeling another person's energy in the Cotton Balls exercise, then you practiced communicating telepathically through many of the other exercises in that chapter. Now you're ready to put your skills to practical use. Remember to start from a relaxed place when working with an animal. If you need to, use the exercises from Chapter 2 to center yourself and open your heart center to any animal you want to talk to.

EVALUATE THE PERSONALITY

Before bringing any animal into your life, it is beneficial to assess his or her personality to make sure the relationship will be a good fit for both of you. We are going to apply the same steps you've already learned to evaluate an animal's personality through reading his or her energy.

Let's use an example to go through this process step-by-step. Suppose you see a puppy at the shelter and you want to know if this is the right animal for you. In order to determine that telepathically, you need to tap into her core essence, or personality. Begin by getting quiet. Close your eyes, take some deep breaths, and find your still point. Then allow yourself to connect heart to heart with the animal, as though a laser beam of light were reaching from you and touching that animal. Once your connection is made, ask yourself what it feels like to be with this puppy. Imagine, just as when you had those cotton balls in your hands, that you are holding the animal. What does her energy feel like? Write down what you're sensing so you can free your mind to receive more information. You might sense that the animal is strong and domineering, or perhaps shy and timid. You might feel a sense of sweetness and compatibility, or of mistrust and fear. Just allow the feelings or words to emerge.

As you continue to be with her, you might pick up feelings about her situation. You might feel a sense of sadness from the puppy; perhaps she thinks no one will adopt her. She may be missing someone, especially if she was separated from her litter mates or mother too soon. Does she feel anxious being around people? She might not understand why she was dropped off at the shelter. You might even sense that the animal feels sickly, which would signal you to get her a complete checkup before making your final decision.

When you've taken this kind of time to be with an animal, you will have a sense of whether she or he is the right choice for you or not. For instance, if you have a timid cat at home and you feel that the puppy is feisty and domineering, you know that the combination will not work very well.

Usually, all this information comes from the animal without you having to make any inquiries. Just allow yourself to be and connect with the animal, and all else happens naturally.

Most puppies and kittens will not have reams of information to give you, because they are just entering this world and getting used to their own bodies; they haven't experienced a whole lot yet. However, you can certainly get a sense of their energy and if they will fit nicely into your family.

When adopting an adult animal, you may receive more information on which to base your decision. Inquire about his or her past to make sure the animal will feel comfortable fitting into a family with children or with other animals. Refer to the "Questions to Ask a New Animal" section in this chapter to help you explore how to feel secure in your choice.

It is also critically important to know what the animal wants to do with his life and how he wants to express himself. What really matters in life to this animal? It's now time to ask for more information from the animal.

CONSIDER THE ANIMAL'S GIFTS AND EXPECTATIONS

We need to be sensitive to an animal's abilities and to allow him to express his talents naturally. If you were a ballerina and your parents took your ballet slippers away, how would you feel? What if they told you that you could never dance again? How would you deal with all that emotion and repressed energy? Animals have desires and need to be fulfilled just as we do.

Ask the animal about his natural abilities and desires—does he have the gifts to be a show dog, or a dressage horse instead of a trail horse? You may be surprised at how definite animals can be about their needs and expectations. Before I adopted my horse Dudley, I asked him what was important to him. He answered, "My well-being." I then asked him what he needed to achieve that, and he replied, "I want to be treated with respect," then stated firmly, "I am *not* a machine; I am *not* a machine."

It was so important to Dudley to have productive work that when my life became busy and I could no longer ride, jump, or show him as often, he begged me to let him go. He asked me to help him find a home where he could continue to participate in the competitive events he loved, where he could have constant excitement and activity, and where he could be surrounded by other horses. He even selected the new person to adopt him. Because I loved him, I had to honor his wishes. He wasn't ready to retire, and he was determined to live a full, action-oriented life.

The key words here are *he begged me*. We should never assume that we know what an animal needs unless we ask, as my client Jody Hilker of Nipomo, California learned.

Jody came to me for help with a horse her neighbor had recently purchased, a nine-year-old Arabian named Starlight. She had been sold to Jody's friend by a man who'd had the horse for seven years. Having just become a father, the man feared that his new responsibilities would prevent him from riding Starlight very often. He believed it would be kinder to find the horse a more attentive home.

Starlight was obviously unhappy, frequently pawing at the ground and shaking her head. Jody noticed that every time she was near her, she felt extremely emotional and occasionally even broke down in tears. Knowing that Starlight was unhappy, with her friend's blessing she brought the horse onto her property so she could have the company of other horses. To Jody's surprise, rather than enjoy the respite, Starlight grew even more agitated and began to kick the corral fences. That's when Jody called me to see if I could get through to her.

When I spoke with Starlight, I learned that Jody was right— she had been reaching out to her for help. She desperately missed and wanted to return to her family of seven years. She didn't care about being ridden. All she wanted was to live out her life with them, loving and watching over them. No one had considered whether she thought it was kinder to have a new guardian.

Jody called Starlight's original guardian and told him how unhappy and lonely his horse was without him. Reassured by Jody that riding meant little to Starlight, the man gladly took his horse back. As soon as Jody took Starlight home she could feel her relax. The pawing, the head shaking, the kicking all stopped. Starlight was back where she belonged.

It is important always to ask the animal what his or her wishes are.

QUESTIONS TO ASK A NEW ANIMAL

- How do you feel about living with others? Do you want to be the only animal in the house?
- How do you feel about children?
- What are you afraid of? What bothers you?
- How social are you? Do you like being with a lot of people, or do you prefer to live with a couple or a single person?

- What kind of relationship do you want with your human companions? Your animal companions?
- How do you feel physically? What is your current condition?
- Have you been abused in the past? Have you experienced any trauma?
- What is your greatest interest in life? Do you want to be a house cat or a show cat?
- What kind of physical environment do you want—indoor, outdoor, or both?
- What will make you most happy in life?

When asking an animal the above questions, think the thought or question in your mind clearly and succinctly. You can formulate a mental image to go along with the thought, if it's appropriate, and then imagine the thought being sent to the animal, heart to heart. You can visualize the question being transmitted through a laser beam of light, if you wish. Then just wait for a response.

For example, if you ask an animal, "Have you been abused in the past?" you might receive an image of a person yelling at the animal or of the dog being struck by someone. But remember not to impose your assumptions from reading his demeanor or body language. Wait for his reply. He could be cowering because he hurt his leg playing and no one has yet noticed.

If you ask the animal, "What will make you most happy in life?" you might see an image of the animal sitting on your lap or following you wherever you go. This dog simply wants to be your best friend and companion.

CONSIDER THE ANIMAL'S IMPACT ON THE OTHERS IN YOUR HOUSEHOLD

Your existing family of both humans and animals needs to be consulted before adding another animal to the household. Regardless of how friendly and loving your current animals are with other animals in the park or at the neighbors', there will definitely be ramifications when introducing a new animal. Some animals may not want the new addition as a companion, but will agree to the adoption because they know it will make you happy. Other animals may not want another addition at all.

Know that even if your animals are willing, they will need your help with the transition—just as children need help in dealing with a new baby sister or brother.

Maggie Gilday-Herbert of Quartz Hill, California called me one day with a very common problem—sibling rivalry between her animals. She had recently adopted a new yellow Labrador retriever puppy named Fauna. Her situation was complicated by the fact that another female golden retriever, Leah, had passed away some months before. Luke, Leah's brother, who was usually a gentle, nonaggressive dog, now threatened to hurt Fauna. She was responding by going to the bathroom all over the house. Maggie wondered if she should find the puppy a new home.

When I talked to Luke, he confirmed that he was angry at Fauna because he missed Leah and felt she was irreplaceable. It was much too soon, in his view, for Maggie to have brought another dog into the house. I relayed his thoughts to Maggie, who completely empathized. She, too, was still grieving for Leah. She said she'd never considered Fauna to be Leah's replacement. I suggested that Maggie take Luke alone into a quiet room to reassure him by telling him exactly what she'd told me.

She did and tried to comfort Luke further by explaining that no one could ever take away her love for Leah or assume Leah's special place in her heart. When she was finished talking with him, Luke went over to her and nipped her on the nose, ever so gently. She said it was as if he was saying "It's about time that you said something." Within a few days, she found Fauna and Luke lying together as if they were best friends.

As Maggie learned, explaining her reasons for bringing Fauna into the house could have eased Luke's anxiety and made the transition much easier on everyone. Inevitably, animals will feel betrayed and abandoned when a new animal comes into the household, fearing that they're losing both their human's affection and their place and role in the family. Sometimes an explanation is all that's needed to help your animals welcome a new companion. You may need only to provide simple reassurances to an animal that he hasn't lost his place in your heart. All you have to do is ask them what they need.

When I was teaching several workshops in Chicago, Illinois, I stayed with Barbara Rycki, one of the most jubilant, generous, and positive people I know. Barbara had added a third cat, Buzz, to her household. She had two other cats, PeeWee and Tasha. Tasha was taking the addition of Buzz quite hard, acting depressed and withdrawn. Barbara was beside herself, not knowing what to do. How could she get Tasha back to her former happy self? She asked me for my help.

After sitting with Tasha for a while, I was surprised that all I received from her was "I want to be greeted first." When I told Barbara what I got from her, she said Buzz was always at the front door when she arrived home because he was so anxious to go outside. So naturally, because she saw him first, she would greet him first, not knowing that this was hurting Tasha's feelings.

The next day Barbara did what Tasha asked and greeted her first, even when Buzz greeted Barbara first. That's all it took. From then on, everyone was happy as could be. Buzz and Tasha even began to play with each other. One very simple change—straight from the cat's mouth—turned the entire situation around.

Animals have strong feelings about with whom and how they wish to live—and even about their names. Some animals definitely do not want to share their homes with others. Very often, people who work full-time assume that their animals are lonely and, feeling guilty for leaving them at home all day, adopt new animals to keep them company. Only when it is too late—when the animals run away or get depressed to the point of illness or even death—do the people learn how much their animals cherished their privacy and territory.

If you ask an animal whether he wants a new companion, you should be prepared to honor his wishes. You can ask what would help the animal accept the change, and you may get some solutions. But if you don't, know that your animal is adamant. Don't assume that he or she will get over it in time.

QUESTIONS FOR THE ANIMALS CURRENTLY IN YOUR HOME

- How do you feel about having a new family member? If you don't want one, are you willing to compromise?
- Would you welcome another cat (dog), or would a different kind of animal be more acceptable?
- Do you care how big the animal is? If it's male or female? Young or older?
- What would help you welcome a new animal? Do you have any special requirements?
- Would you like to help choose the new animal?

BRINGING A NEW ANIMAL INTO YOUR HOME

Now that you've used your telepathic abilities to make a wise decision about a new animal, you can continue the communication to make sure he settles in happily with you and your family. After all, you have already established a heart connection together.

MAINTAIN YOUR HOUSEHOLD ROUTINES

When you bring in a newcomer, it is important to uphold your other animals' daily routines to keep sibling rivalry in check. Greet the original family members first and the newcomer next so you can avoid hurt feelings. Usually, the newcomer receives a whole lot of attention and playtime with you. This can be where jealousy sets in. The older members find their time with you halved and are not happy about it. They may see having this new animal as a loss to them. Make sure that the original family members' playtime is just as it was before, and prevent the new animal from going after their toys. Buy new toys for the new family member and, if you need to, separate the animals at playtime. Even an animal who is happy to accept a newcomer will feel threatened if his role in the family seems to be usurped, as the following story shows.

Rebecca Adler, a client from Mundelein, Illinois, called me about a problem with her family's cat, Justine. The problem had developed when they brought home a new cat, named Burgess, one year before. Until then, Justine had been the "only child." They assumed she wanted a companion. With the addition of Burgess, Justine had begun hiding under the bed, and her whole personality had changed. She was resentful of Burgess and became a very antisocial, angry little girl. Her family's hearts broke as they watched her change. To make things worse, Burgess chased her, picked on her, and there was obvious jealousy between the two of them.

Justine's misery was evident through her hiding when they had company, striking people who tried to pet her, opening her mouth without a sound, recurring bladder infections, and an unwillingness to play. Her people forgot the music of her purr, as she never purred audibly anymore. Rebecca felt they had ruined her life.

It was extremely difficult for me to communicate with Justine, because she was so depressed and withdrawn. I suggested the use of Bach Flower Remedies (flower essences available in most natural-food or vitamin stores) to calm the cat. I also suggested Rebecca tell Justine just how sorry they were for bringing Burgess home, that they hadn't realized her feelings at the time, and, of course, that they loved her very much.

I also suggested that Rebecca begin to do the things they used to do with Justine before Burgess arrived. She needed to play with Justine—without Burgess in the room—so that all the attention was hers without worrying if Burgess would jump her.

Justine started becoming herself again. She was more sociable with company and made herself more visible. She began to talk more, purred quite audibly, slept in their bed again, and her bladder infections were markedly reduced.

TENSION TAMERS

Here are some tips that you might find helpful for adding new members to the family, whether the current members were asked how they felt about the addition or not.

- Make sure that each animal has his or her own sleeping area to feel secure.
- Since animals are instinctively territorial, be sure to give them each an undisturbed area for mealtime so they don't have to compete for their food.
- Cats can be fastidious about their litter boxes. It's important to keep boxes extra clean and to provide a sufficient number of boxes to satisfy the number of cats in your home.
- Give each animal a job. (This will be discussed in detail later in the chapter.) Make sure they know how they fit into the household and how important their individual roles are. Remind them by congratulating them on their new job so they know they are not taken for granted.
- Keep things as they were before the new members of the family arrived. Maintain your relationship with each animal.
- Make sure that the original family members get their usual playtime. Try not to let the new animal go after their toys. You might need to separate them at playtime.
- Greet the original family members before the newcomer to avoid hurt feelings.

In general, it is easier to bring a new dog into a family than a cat. For more information about how to physically introduce a new cat to the other animals in your household, read Anitra Frazier's book, *The New Natural Cat*.

ENHANCING LIFE WITH YOUR ANIMALS

As in human relationships, we need to be mindful in our relationships with animals. Don't take them or the relationship for granted. Be aware of their feelings, what they are communicating to you, and the messages that you give them. This will maximize the pleasure you take in each other's company.

LEARN TO LISTEN

Of the many rich ways we can enhance our relationships with animals, one of the most important is a fundamental of this book—learning to listen to them telepathically. If the majority of people can communicate with a computer, it's a sure bet they can communicate with animals.

We need to become better listeners in general. Observe how well you listen to people. When someone talks to you, where is your mind? Are you drifting with your own thoughts, thinking about what you will be doing the next day? Or are you thinking about what you'll say to that person? Perhaps interrupting him to say it?

Every story I share in this book should drive home the importance of listening to animals. The following story shows how sophisticated, detailed, and accurate animals' messages to us can be.

One of the most disturbing cases I've ever worked on involved finding out who was shooting cats in a Van Nuys, California neighborhood. Within three weeks, seven cats had been shot. One had died, and another, named Samantha, had to have her leg amputated. I tried to talk to Samantha about what she might have seen during the shooting, but she didn't have much to say. She only showed me a picture of something blue on a balcony nearby.

The neighbors suggested I talk with Wilma, the busybody cat of the neighborhood. Wilma told me the whole story. She described seeing a young man who wore a baseball hat backward over clean-cut hair, had a scar on his face, and was dressed in baggy pants. He wore a white T-shirt and carried an oversize bag.

The neighborhood committee put out the description that Wilma gave, and everyone went on watch. They found the balcony where the shooting took place. It was trimmed in blue, and the owner, who turned out to be the young man's father, drove a blue truck. *The young man who lived there indeed had a large bag, and inside it was a BB gun. Here's a case where the cat solved the crime. Because of Wilma's description, the criminal was caught and the shootings came to a halt. Everyone within the community was thankful for Wilma's role.*

As you can see, animals can be quite observant and aware of their surroundings. Often, they can provide us with detailed information.

BE MINDFUL OF YOUR THOUGHTS

We also need to be mindful of our thoughts around our animals. If you think a thought long enough and give it a lot of energy, the animal will probably pick it up even though you didn't consciously sit down and direct it to him. This happens because your thought is strong and because animals are telepathic. Some people might say, "Well, then, why don't animals pick up everything from me without my having to direct the communication to them consciously?" Animals do not sit around all day listening to us and to our internal chatter. They have better things to do than monitor us. And if they did, they would be totally exhausted by us. But they can and will reflect what we are thinking, as the following story shows.

A client from Kuna, Idaho called me because her colt was sickly and, after numerous vet visits with no results, she didn't know how to help him. His hair had fallen out, he was itchy all over, and no medication or remedy was helping. When I asked the horse to share with me how he felt, I kept getting the thought that he was disappointed with the fact that he was a colt and not a filly. His diagnosis was that he was allergic to himself. When I told this to the family, they were shocked. When the mare was pregnant, all they had thought about was how much they wanted a filly and how disappointed they would be if they got a colt. How could this horse like himself when he felt nobody else was going to?

Our thoughts can be picked up even by those in the womb. Thoughts that aren't mindful can affect an animal's self-esteem, and can possibly result in physical illness.

ASK THEIR VIEWPOINT

It's important that we discipline ourselves not to make assumptions about animals and about the way they feel or think. They are individuals with their own thoughts, feelings, and perceptions. We need to hold ourselves back from jumping to preconceived notions regarding our animals' behavior. We can learn from our animals. Let them help make a difference in your life. Let them be who they are.

At a workshop I was conducting in a home in Tampa, Florida, twenty of us sat in a circle in a large living room. Our host's cat, Precious, was hiding in the closet. Everyone assumed the cat was frightened and didn't want to talk. No one thought to ask him. When I asked the cat why he was in the closet, he said he wanted to talk with us but needed some reassurance to feel safe around so many people. I asked everyone to focus on their heart centers and muster up all the love they had for this cat and imagine a lovely, light-pink energy being emitted from their heart centers to the cat. Lo and behold, guess who came out of the closet? Precious came to the edge of the circle and looked at me, asking for reassurance that it would be okay, which I gave him.

Next, he surprised us all by jumping into a woman's lap. She told us she'd been silently asking the cat to come to her. He rubbed his furry face lovingly against hers, kneading her with his paws. The guardian of the cat was in tears watching. She told us that Precious never let anyone other than her near him, and that this was the way the cat showed his love for her. He had never done it before with anyone else. She was touched to witness her cat displaying such affection for another human being.

What a gentle and tender moment for all of us to witness and experience. We were able to watch one being offer love to another being. These tender moments with animals happen more than we realize and often go unrecognized, because we are too busy to notice or to be involved in the moment. This cat was teaching us how to be present in every moment.

You can see it was important to ask him about his behavior and to consider his concerns. As a result, the group consciously made an effort to settle into their hearts, changing the energy they were expressing. Then he felt comfortable in letting his love flow in a spontaneous manner.

ACKNOWLEDGE THEIR FEELINGS

Animals are thinking and feeling individuals. It is unkind and thoughtless to expect your animal to do your bidding without realizing his needs in the situation. If your animal does not want to engage in a particular activity with you on a certain day, rather than simply forging ahead, acknowledge his feelings about it, ask for his cooperation, or consider adjusting your plans. You will need to compromise. This is an important element in making any relationship work.

I learned this with my cat Joy Boy, a spirited and independent hunting cat who helps me run my workshops. One beautiful day, he was visibly itchy to go outdoors, but my whole class was assembled, ready to begin. "Joy Boy," I said, in front of everyone, "I know you want to go outside right now, but I really need your help." He thought about it for a moment and then he stopped sniffing around the door and trotted over to the ottoman in the center of the classroom, lay down, and spent the next several hours at full attention, helping everyone in the class understand what relationships are all about. It's a better way of communicating when we respect our partner and acknowledge his feelings and ways of doing things—and it gets results.

GIVE THEM INFORMATION

For most people, it is disorienting and uncomfortable not to know what is going on—not to know what our day will hold, where our meals will come from, where we'll be taken, or who will be entering and leaving our lives. Yet many of us subject our animals to this anxiety every day. We assume that they know what is going to happen. How could they if we haven't told them?

Information gives us the ability to make decisions for ourselves. Given the information, we feel empowered, more in control of our lives. When someone else is making decisions for us and we are unable to participate, we feel powerless. Feeling powerless can cause depression in animals and in humans.

Animals need information, just as we do. If you are going out of town on vacation or business, tell your animal how long you will be gone. Tell him if you will be gone for two days, five days, or ten days, whatever the case may be. Then show him a mental image of you coming through the door, excited to see him again. This way he will focus on your return rather than on your leaving.

Though we've always been told that animals don't understand time, we're now understanding that they actually do. Several books have been written on the subject, including *Dogs That Know When Their Owners Are Coming Home and Other Unexplained Powers of Animals: An Investigation*, by Rupert Sheldrake (see Bibliography for more). From my experience, I know that animals understand time. They know what age they are. They know that the sun sets and rises and that it constitutes a day. Some people use a technique where they count the number of sunrises and sunsets and visualize this to the animals. I simply tell them the number of days I will be gone. Don't worry about explaining the concept of time. When you communicate with an animal, much of it happens automatically, behind the scenes, as we've learned. They will receive the information in a way that makes sense to them.

Visualization can be a powerful tool when letting animals know what to expect. It certainly helped with my client Judy's dog, Bosco.

Bosco, a black cocker spaniel, used to become very depressed when his person, Judy from Fairfax, Virginia, went on vacation. When I asked the dog what he wanted or how he could feel better, he said that he wanted to join Judy on vacation. Here's where information from the person benefits the animal. He really needed to know what traveling with Judy would mean for him. I sent Bosco mental images of the long car ride to the airport. I showed him being put into a carrier in a holding area. I told him he would probably spend several hours there, alone, until being put on the plane. Then he would travel for more hours before arriving at their final destination and being reunited with Judy. Once Bosco heard the scenario of what "vacation" really meant for him, he was quite content to stay at home until Judy returned. Judy also carefully chose the right pet-sitter for Bosco's needs and reassured him that he would be lovingly cared for.

It is important to be this thorough in your communication with your animal. Instead of simply accepting his answer or request, make sure he understands fully how it impacts his life. He hears in your mind how excited you are about your trip, so of course he wants to join you. But what he hasn't heard about is the journey he would need to make in order to vacation with you. Your responsibility is to make sure he understands the whole picture.

If your animal needs to stay overnight at the vet's office, tell him. This is where your visualization techniques come in handy. After communicating that he will be staying there, show him a mental image of you coming through the door to pick him up the next day. Show him an image of you hooking the leash onto his collar or placing him in his travel carrier, both of you riding in the car, and then arriving back home. This way the animal can feel less stress and know what is happening. Can you imagine what it would be like to stay overnight in a hospital, not knowing if anyone was ever coming back for you? How can animals know what our plans are unless we tell them, in detail? Focus your thoughts and communicate, communicate, communicate.

GIVE YOUR ANIMAL A JOB IN THE HOUSEHOLD

Giving an animal a job—or recognizing the role he has chosen for himself—may be the most fundamental interaction you will ever have with him. You will, in a sense, be acknowledging his identity. Just as humans want to know their roles or positions in life, animals love to have a purpose, and most of them know what their purpose is.

Think of a retiree, depressed because his life seems to have little purpose since he has nothing to do—no job. He becomes cranky and extremely lonely. When he worked, he felt needed, important, and social, with a real sense of belonging. This applies to animals as well.

When the family consists of multiple animals, there is an even greater need for each family member to feel a sense of purpose. A lot of sibling rivalry can be avoided if boundaries between your animals' jobs are clear from the get-go.

Occasionally, I have seen animals who did not want jobs, but they have been very rare. These animals are usually here this lifetime just to relax, enjoy life, and rest. Animals have differing personalities and needs, just as we do, and, like their human counterparts, some animals may just be lazy!

My dog, Jessie, assigned herself jobs within our family. She never asked for any; she just set out to do her thing from the very beginning. She knew what she wanted to do and what was going to make her happy. She is the official welcoming committee, she alerts us when anyone arrives, she guards the property, she watches over the cats, and she helps me keep my playtime in balance. She also assists me at all my local animal communication workshops. One student, while attending an introductory workshop with Jessie and me, got an image of Jessie as my office manager. She said the more Jessie took on and organized things, the more time she freed up for me to have fun, with or without her. It's not unusual for animals to act this selflessly.

Allowing animals to have jobs is vitally important in our relationships with them. Having a job is so crucial that it gave one dog a new lease on life.

Toni Tucker of Sharon, Connecticut called me one day about Winni, her bichon frise, described by Toni as an enchanting little powder puff with black eyes and a coal-black nose. It was Toni's intention to show her, but there was only one problem: She was too petite for the show ring. Toni started having thoughts of selling her. Over time, Winni's demeanor changed. She became shy and tentative and lost all of her joy and puppy enthusiasm. She remained on the outside of the pack of the other bichons in the household.

When I talked with Winni, she felt less important than the other dogs and insecure about her place in the family. She thought Toni didn't like her anymore and wanted to get rid of her. Toni remembered all her indecisive thoughts and her confusion over whether to keep Winni or not. I advised Toni to decide one way or the other. It was too hurtful for Winni to live in this limbo of indecision.

Without hesitation, Toni picked her up, held her lovingly, and reassured Winni how special she was, how loved she was, and that they would be together forever. I recommended that Toni give her a very special job because she felt so unimportant.

After meeting an animal agent, Toni found the perfect job for her. Winni began a modeling career. The change in her behavior was immediate. Winni loved the attention, the lights, the grooming and primping. She loved being center stage. She had clearly found her niche and purpose and developed quite a portfolio: books, television, magazines, and catalogs. To everyone's surprise, she also went on to become a champion in the show ring.

We need to give our animals jobs that fit their personalities and ambitions in life and that they want to do. Base your animal's job on her best qualities and special gifts. Congratulate her (and each of your animals) daily and individually for doing such a great job. Notice her attitude and sense of pride! For instance, if you have a dog who loves kids, ask her to take care of the children when they are in the backyard. You wouldn't want to give this job to a dog who didn't like baby-sitting. Or you wouldn't want to ask your cat to be the official welcoming committee if he was shy around people. These would be assignments that neither animal would enjoy or feel successful in fulfilling for you.

Here are some possible jobs that your animals might embrace:

- Being the official greeter
- Being the guard dog
- Hunting for all the bugs in the household
- Taking care of the children when they are in the backyard
- Looking after other animals in the household with special needs, especially if one is dealing with chronic illness
- Alerting you when visitors approach
- Being the peacemaker. Resolving conflicts with family members through peaceful and forgiving means
- Showering love on everyone who visits the family
- Keeping the household full of laughter and lightness
- Providing special company to a senior in the family

The more animals you have in your household, the more important it is for each of them to have his or her own role. If you have a family of eight cats and you bring in a ninth one, that cat may look around and say, "What am I supposed to do here? It looks like all the jobs are filled." That might be true—and you will have to create a role for that animal.

My friend Jackie has multiple cats, and one of them appeared to be very depressed. Since this cat seemed to like heights, she decided that a low, flat rooftop, which he could safely jump to and from, would be the perfect place for him to perform his new job: protecting the house. Now the cat is so happy with his job that she has a hard time getting him in for meals!

One of the unspoken jobs that animals are very willing to accept is the job of sheltering us from pain, emotional or physical. Animals have been known to take on our pain, especially when we are not dealing with a given situation. This is where we need to relieve them of their duty. We must tell them that we appreciate their help in assisting us, but they should take care of themselves and let us take responsibility for ourselves. Treatment with Bach Flower Remedies (natural flower essences) can be of tremendous help to animals in letting go of their caretaking for us. Read more about Bach Flowers in Chapter 6, or refer to the Resources section at the end of the book for information.

It is important that we be accountable for ourselves. We need to consistently nurture those aspects of ourselves we criticize, judge, or feel uncomfortable with. If you sweep matters under the carpet, that's not where they will remain. Your animal will pick them up telepathically and try to resolve the situation. If an animal holds on to those feelings long enough, illness can set in, as it does with humans. So help your animal out by keeping yourself emotionally balanced.

No matter what size, shape, color, breed, or species, animals are all creatures of love, comfort, and joy. They can make us laugh, protect us physically and emotionally, and help us to understand ourselves a little better.

Finding Solutions to Behavioral Problems

Our goal is to live with our animals in a loving and harmonious fashion. This is accomplished by our willingness to listen, communicate, learn, and adapt. By doing this, most problems can be avoided. However, when they do occur, there are some simple and practical measures that can help resolve conflicts.

One of the chief reasons people consult me is their desperate need to understand—and hopefully change—unusual, peculiar, or even destructive behaviors in their animals. While many books and training programs deal with some of the problems addressed here, such as aggression and house-training, simple communication can be a very effective means to a solution. Using the telepathic skills you've learned in this book, you can work with your animals to understand and deal with their problems.

Animals will do anything they can to gain our understanding, and strange behavior is often a sign that something is awry in their lives. We often make assumptions and misinterpret what they are trying to reveal to us. Until we can correctly ascertain what is wrong, we will only spin our wheels. To find a solution, we need to determine whether the problem is mental, emotional, or physical—or some combination—and address it on that level. If we try to apply a physical solution to an emotional problem or one that is derived from misunderstanding or confusion, we'll never fully resolve it.

We may not only misdiagnose problems but we may also ascribe inaccurate motives to our animals' behaviors. They often have reasons we'd never suspect for the way they act. Furthermore, animals can often tell us exactly what it will take to curtail their troubling behavior. All we need to do is ask!

WHY ANIMALS ACT OUT

Let's review some of the reasons why animals may exhibit unusual behavior. First, it is important to seek the advice of a veterinarian to rule out a physical cause. Animals who are in pain or distress may exhibit unusual, aggressive, or destructive behaviors.

If the problem isn't physical, it is most likely emotional. Because animals are emotional beings, much like us, they respond in various ways to their experiences and environment. An animal may act out because of fear, insecurity, abuse, or simply because you have not communicated your expectations. Animals also respond to the stresses of competition and territorial conflicts in a multi-animal home. Unhappiness and depression may result from lack of attention and neglect. And it is not unusual for animals to respond to tensions and imbalances within the human family. Just as humans do, they will react to changes occurring within their home and environment.

FIND OUT WHAT IS GOING ON

When emotionally upset or troubled, animals act out in many different ways. No matter what the behavior—whether digging holes in the yard or growling at the mail carrier—the process to finding the problem and the solution is always the same.

Begin by approaching your animal in a gentle, patient, and

nonassuming manner so he will feel free to communicate with you. If you approach an animal with an attitude of anger and blame, he will most likely shut down, be unwilling to communicate with you, and be unreceptive to exploring solutions.

It is never more important to feel relaxed and centered with an animal. You may want to revisit the basics in earlier chapters to feel confident in your ability to communicate effectively. When you are ready, sit with your animal and make these basic inquiries:

- Tell me why you are behaving this way (visualizing a clear and specific picture of the behavior).
- Tell me if something is bothering you, physically, mentally, or emotionally.
- What do you need in order to change your behavior?
- Is there anything I can do to improve the situation?

It may surprise you to find how easily some problems—even serious and long-standing ones—can be resolved.

FINDING SOLUTIONS

The simplest solution is almost always the best solution. Some behavioral problems can be solved just by having a heart to heart session with your animal and expressing how you are feeling about his misbehavior or possible misunderstanding. Humans often underestimate how much our animals want to please us and how effective it can be simply to make our distress known. If they know that we are frustrated or angry at what they are doing, they will usually change their behavior—or at least try.

When working with your animal, realize that it may take several attempts to talk him out of a long-term habit. Don't think you've failed to make your point if you don't get instant results. It takes time for an animal to break a bad habit, just as it does for humans—think about how hard it is for smokers and nail-biters to give up those habits. Repetition is the key; you may have to repeat the process several times with an animal before he finally incorporates the information. We need to grant animals the same patience we would hope to receive ourselves.

Marty Meyer of Ventura, California, a student of mine and now a successful animal communicator, often took her dog, Jessy, along on trail rides with her horse. But when Jessy started chasing bicyclists on the trail, Marty was upset and told the dog of her discomfort. The dog explained that she got bored on the trail unless Marty's attention was focused on her. Marty started paying more attention to the dog and, for a while, it worked.

Soon, however, the dog resumed chasing bicyclists. Marty was extremely frustrated and upset. It was becoming too stressful to bring Jessy along anymore. Marty told her so and got results, but she had to repeat the information a few more times before the behavior finally stopped for good. With such an ingrained habit, it took several repetitions to drive the point home.

Each problem you encounter with an animal will have a unique solution, which you will usually learn from the animal himself. Using the basic inquiries on the previous page, you can get to the heart of your animal's distress and learn how to solve the problem. Here are stories of how many animals and their people found solutions to classic behavioral problems, including aggression, house-training difficulties, and destructive habits.

AGGRESSION

Aggressive behavior—snapping at, biting, or attacking other animals or people—is one of the primary reasons that humans banish animals from their homes. But aggression does not always mean that an animal is ill-tempered or unmanageable. It is often a sign that he or she is suffering great emotional stress or physical pain. One of the saddest misinterpretations of an animal's behavior that I have ever seen came from the loving owner of a Border collie, who feared her dog was turning vicious.

My client Judith, of Laguna Beach, California, called me about her previously friendly Border collie named Nicole. Nicole had started snapping when anyone came near her. She would wolf down any paper products left around the house—not just shredding but totally devouring them. Whenever Judith would use her barbecue grill outside, Nicole developed the bizarre habit of lying on the first step of the swimming pool. This might have been typical behavior for a water dog, but Nicole clearly disliked water and would never even touch it with her paw.

Because it didn't seem like a physical problem, Judith did not think she needed to consult a veterinarian and instead consulted animal behaviorists. (As you will learn from this story, it's always best to first see a veterinarian when your animal has problems of any kind.) None of the animal behaviorists Judith called upon could explain the dog's strange behavior and suggested that the only solution might be to put her down.

I was her last resort. When I approached the dog to introduce myself, she immediately shot me the message: "Don't touch me!" I assured her that I would respect her wishes and keep my distance, attaching emotion to the thought. I then asked her to describe what happened to her when Judith barbecued. For the first time in my experience with animals, I got a sensory impression so strong that I could actually smell meat cooking. I heard Nicole say, "When I smell that, I feel so sick. My stomach gets hot," and I instantly experienced the same feelings in my own body. She then sent me an image of herself racing to the pool and lying down in the water. She said, "It helps the pain go away." I understood—her stomach was on fire, and the water was cool. Clearly the poor animal was very sick and in desperate need of medical attention.

Judith took her to the veterinarian right away, who found that her liver was dysfunctional. There was so much bile in her system that it was actually eating her stomach. That explained why Nicole had been eating all the paper she could find—it helped absorb the bile. She was so uncomfortable in her body that she could not stand to be touched and, as animals often will, snapped to warn people to stay away because she felt so ill. Take a moment to consider the intelligence of this dog, who was using such great ingenuity to try to help herself.

What a lesson for Judith, and for me. This animal was crying out for help, only to have her behavior misinterpreted as viciousness. If Judith had asked what was wrong, she would have known of Nicole's physical problem, the burning in her belly. If Nicole had been asked why she was gobbling down paper and lying in the pool, Judith would have learned that she was trying to relieve her own pain. Yet this dog almost lost her life! I can't even contemplate the number of animals who have been euthanized because their behavior was misunderstood. And all they need us to do is ask and listen.

HOUSE-TRAINING

House-training can be a major source of frustration for humans, who quickly lose patience with puppies or kittens who don't comply, and who lose their tempers when older animals soil the house. Punitive training methods, such as rubbing an animal's nose in the carpet or hitting him with a newspaper, don't get to the root of the problem. What's more, these methods are inappropriate and degrading. Don't assume that a young animal doesn't know he shouldn't be soiling. He simply may not know what else to do. He may need to be shown the entire sequence of steps he needs to take to go to the bathroom, including how to go through the doggie door or scratch or bark to alert you to let him out. Sometimes, this single missing step causes all the confusion.

Patti, a two-year-old Chihuahua, had been house-trained but was still having accidents inside the house.

When I arrived at my client Colleen's home in Burbank, California, Patti announced that she was confused about her soiling situation and was not sure how to tell her person when she needed to go out. Apparently, there had been no precise signal established between Patti and Colleen, who would occasionally open the door when she felt the time was right for Patti to go outside. Colleen suggested that Patti use the same signal Chad, her male boxer, used

*to let her know. Patti refused. She wanted her own signal. We mu-
tually decided that she would run her paw on the carpet or on
Colleen's leg when she needed to go outside.*

*Within five to ten minutes, I heard Patti scratching the carpet
from another room and I asked Colleen to let her out. Patti was already putting her signal into action. Sure enough, Colleen opened
the door and out went Patti. We congratulated her for learning so
quickly. However, there was still one missing link. She needed to
give the signal in front of Colleen. If Colleen had been upstairs and
Patti gave the signal from the first floor, all of our efforts would
have been in vain, leaving Patti even more confused than ever.*

Adult animals may soil for a wide variety of reasons—to mark
territory, especially in a new house; because of physical problems,
such as bladder infections; or because of stressful environmental
factors, such as the arrival of a new animal or the upheaval of re-
decorating. With cats, they may simply want their own litter box.

When dealing with soiling problems in an adult animal, always
take the animal to the vet to rule out physical problems. If no
health problem exists, then ask the animal what's causing the behavior. Again, the biggest mistake you can make is to assume you
know the cause.

*Paul Asselin of Culver City, California called me in frustration,
because for ten years his cat, Raspberry, had been soiling the living
room rug whenever the family went away. The family had consulted vets and tried various solutions, to no avail. Paul assumed
that the cat soiled to punish them for leaving, and he asked if I
could finally put a stop to the behavior.*

*When I connected with Raspberry, she said she wasn't angry
with the family. On the contrary, she was terrified whenever they
left, scared they might never return. Soiling, to an animal, is mark-
ing territory. To Raspberry, it meant that this was her home. She
was soiling to make herself feel secure.*

*I asked her what she needed to relieve the fear of abandonment
that was underlying her behavior. She replied, "I want to know*

that this is my home forever. I want to know when they are going and when they are coming back."

I asked Paul and his family to sit down with Raspberry before leaving town the next time, to explain how long they would be away. I assured them that animals understand time very well. I also recommended that they send her a mental image of them arriving at the front door at the end of their trip, excited to see her. With a strong image of a happy homecoming in her mind, Raspberry could stay focused on their return rather than their departure, and feel secure that they truly intended to come back.

Many people, when asked to fulfill their animals' wishes so directly, say, "You've got to be kidding!" But this family was at their wits' end. They gave the cat the reassurance she asked for, and she in turn kept her part of the bargain. She has not soiled the living room rug since.

CONFLICTS BETWEEN ANIMALS IN A HOUSEHOLD

Animals who live together inevitably have conflicts, just as people do. They may compete for territory or for the affection of their humans. They may act out when they feel unsure of their role in the family—the job that gives them a sense of purpose, as we discussed in Chapter 5. They may squabble and get their feelings hurt and respond by attacking others or by withdrawing. Usually animals clear up such disagreements between themselves, but we can improve a problematic situation with a little mediation. The following story illustrates several of the most common conflicts that arise between animals in a household.

Laurel Graham of Hoffman Estates, Illinois has several fine cocker spaniels and shows some of them. She called me because her cocker spaniel house dog, Goldie, was acting depressed. When I asked Goldie why, she told me that one of the show dogs, Mindy, constantly picked on her, antagonizing her both physically and mentally. But what made her feel worse was the fact that all the other dogs, including Mindy, always brought home prize ribbons and received special attention. Goldie said she didn't want to be a show dog, but she did want to feel special.

In a flash, I got an image of Laurel parading Goldie around the house wearing a special ribbon. I told Laurel of my vision, suggesting that she do this, announcing to the other dogs how special Goldie was and what a great job she was doing taking care of the household. Laurel tried it. Not only did Goldie's spirits pick up but she was never tormented by Mindy again. In fact, all the dogs in the household treated Goldie with newfound respect, thanks to what Laurel calls "the ribbon ceremony."

Mindy, however, did not abandon her bullying ways but started picking on another cocker spaniel, BB, who was gravely ill with a tumor. Mindy started biting her. When I asked her about it, Mindy confessed that she resented the attention BB was getting and didn't understand why BB was being so pampered. I suggested to Laurel that she explain BB's illness to Mindy and ask her to be patient with the situation. Once Laurel communicated this information to Mindy, the behavior stopped and the household became harmonious again.

Sometimes animals fight not because of jealousy, competition, or misunderstandings between them, but because they are taking out their individual problems on each other. Again, realize the importance of keeping an open mind rather than judging situations according to preconceived notions. In the following case, for example, it would have been easy to assume that the cats were angry at each other, but that would have been a complete misinterpretation of what was actually going on.

Charlene from Kihei, Hawaii called me because one of her cats, a gray tabby named Silver, was regularly beating up the other cat, Whiskers. Subsequently, Whiskers had developed a spraying problem. My client was at the end of her rope. When I asked Silver why he was fighting, he said he was miserable cooped up indoors and wanted to go outside. The house they lived in had a walled-in pa-

tio, but my client explained that she was afraid to let the cats out unsupervised. She worried that they'd climb over the wall and not be able to get back or that they'd be attacked by the tomcats prowling on the other side. Silver told me that he could hear the tomcats yowling, and it tormented him not to be able to see them. It made him feel out of control and that he wasn't doing his job as the protector of the household. He unleashed his frustrations on Whiskers.

Whiskers told me that his spraying was not a reaction to being beaten up, but that it brought him a great sense of physical relief. He was in pain, but the veterinarian had not been able to diagnose his problem. I gave my client the name of a holistic veterinarian, who diagnosed and treated a hard-to-detect infection, gave Whiskers supplemental treatment with acupuncture, and adjusted his diet.

That solved one problem. Next, Charlene cleared off a bureau in an upstairs bedroom overlooking the patio. This perch provided the aggressive cat a panoramic view over the top of the patio wall. Loving his new sense of guardianship, Silver stood lookout in his new "crow's nest" every day for three weeks. One day, to Charlene's great angst, he sneaked out onto the patio when she wasn't looking. Just when she began to panic, he popped right back over the wall and came back inside. It was as if he just needed to see what freedom was all about and then, satisfied, he decided that the bureau was the best spot for him.

The spraying and aggressive behavior stopped. The cats began to play with each other, and the household returned to normal.

WHEN AN ANIMAL DOESN'T KNOW WHAT'S WRONG

At some point you may ask an animal what's wrong and get no answer, no matter what you do. Don't assume it's your fault if this happens to you. When I get no response from an animal, I first suspect that he can't explain what's wrong because it's not his problem. He's likely to be acting out some strong emotion experienced by his human. We will talk more about this common problem in Chapter 11, "Learning to Love."

However, there are other reasons why an animal won't answer. An animal might not respond because his mind is temporarily occupied with other things. Other times, an animal simply does not know what is wrong. In some cases, he may know what's wrong but not want to talk about it. This is especially true of animals that have been abused.

There may be no simple solution for long-standing or complex problems, and if an animal has been verbally, physically, or emotionally abused, he or she may not know what is needed to resolve the behavior. In such cases, finding the solution can be like peeling the layers of an onion, allowing them to fall off easily and gently, one at a time.

ALTERNATIVE THERAPIES

When working with an animal with long-standing problems, it's often helpful to try alternative healing methods. I often incorporate therapies such as Bach Flower Remedies, Tellington TTouch, and energy work into my work with animals. (You can learn more about them in Chapter 9, "Comforting Sick and Injured Animals," and from reading the books I suggest in the Resources section.)

Bach Flower Remedies are simple flower essences that were developed by British physician and scientist Edward Bach in 1930. His thirty-eight remedies provide animals and humans with a gentle and safe way of relieving emotional stress. I often recommend one in particular called Rescue Remedy for animals who are distressed or agitated. Most health-food or vitamin stores carry these products, which come in small brown dropper bottles. Each flower essence addresses a certain problem, and they can be mixed and matched to address compound problems. Send for the company's literature to learn more about the essences.

They can be given to animals in a variety of ways, including in their food or water. In the company's pamphlet, Barbara Meyers, a certified Bach Flower counselor, offers these guidelines for administering the remedies:

- Add ten drops to the animal's water dish, even if it's a communal dish. The remedies are safe for all animals to consume, whether being treated or not.

- Dilute two drops to one tablespoon of water to give to the animal by mouth or to add to his food (use four drops if Rescue Remedy).
- Rub two drops of remedy onto the animal's nose or ears.
- Administer four times per day. In cases of extreme stress, you may use the remedies as often as every half hour. Rescue Remedy can be used every five to eight minutes in times of crisis.

I find Bach Flowers and other alternative therapies extremely beneficial when working with very troubled animals, such as Tamra King's dog, Shayna.

Tamra King of Los Angeles, California, took in a six-year-old husky mix named Shayna after the dog's original guardian passed away. Shayna, who was smart and well trained, had been inseparable from her person. The man had been sickly for a while, and every time he was hospitalized, Shayna went to the kennel. The last time, she stayed at the kennel for two months and the man never came to get her. Shayna was now frantic, missing her human and pacing around Tamra's house all day. The only time she seemed happy was when Tamra and her family took her for a hike. Then, as soon as she got home, she would start to pace again, and Tamra wondered what they could do to ease her suffering.

When I arrived at Tamra's home, the dog was apprehensive. Previously, her entire life had revolved around her guardian and included very little socialization. As Tamra and I sat in the living room, Shayna paced around the house, stopping only for water. All Shayna knew was that she wanted to go back home. Before I could communicate with her, I needed to get her attention.

She needed to be physically close to someone so she wouldn't be absorbed by her worries and panic. I put Shayna on her leash, which comforts some dogs because it offers them a connection and closeness with a human. Next, I did a "grounding" technique with Shayna, an exercise to redirect her energy away from her anxieties.

I walked her around the room and asked her to look at certain things. I said, "Shayna, look at that coffee table," as I gently tapped the table with my fingers. When she looked, I told her what a great job she did. I then asked her to look at another object in the room, tapping it gently. I always congratulated her after she focused on the object. This grounding technique allows the animal to have a point of focus and to calm down rather than stay caught up in her own distractions.

Once I had her attention, I asked Shayna if she knew why she was in this new home. She said she was confused. All she knew was that she wanted to go back home. She knew the man was dependent on her and she wanted to lick his face to wake him up, as was her daily routine. She was frantic that she couldn't do her job.

I had to tell her the truth. He was not coming back to get her— he was now in the spirit world. Shayna was tormented by the fact that she couldn't say good-bye. She felt, in some way, that she had let him down because she couldn't get back to him. I told her there was nothing she could have done to help him and that no one had been aware how important it was for her to see him and say good-bye. This was a critical part of our communication. Shayna was stuck on a misperception and it was essential that she understood the truth of the matter.

Little by little, Shayna began to relax. From touching her, I determined that another important part of her healing process would be to help her body, which was tight and stressed from her constant worrying and pacing. With her permission, I began to do some "bodywork" on her, using a combination of a movement therapy called TTouch and something called energy work. Energy work is simply allowing energy to come through your hands with the intent of soothing, loving, and healing the animal. I also recommended Tamra use Bach Flower Remedies to aid in Shayna's healing process. To ease her anxiety, I suggested Rescue Remedy, which also helps alleviate grief, and other Bach Flowers to help her cope with loss, change, and homesickness. After her bodywork session, Shayna fell into a deep sleep for the first time in weeks. Tamra said she never had seen the dog so peaceful.

HELPING AN AGITATED ANIMAL

When an animal is agitated, there are some easy calming techniques. They include the grounding technique I shared in Tamra and Shayna's story and simple breathing exercises. Just as we use breathing to calm ourselves, we can use it to help our animals relax. In fact, I suggest that you use these exercises with all your animals as a preventive measure and not wait until they become agitated or are in crisis. Then, should an animal become traumatized or ill, you and the animal will already be familiar with this breathing technique.

Sit calmly with your animal in a quiet place. Talking aloud, ask her to work with you as a team. Begin to take some slow deep breaths, making sure that the animal can hear your inhale and exhale. Continue for five minutes or so, until you can see the physical relaxation in the animal's body. That's it! This simple exercise works wonders in my sessions with stressed and upset animals.

I used breathing exercises with my cat Scooter when I took him to the vet for surgery. The vet tech needed to shave some of his fur to apply a pain patch. When she approached Scooter with clippers, he leaped from my arms. The tech tried again, but with no success. I asked her to wait for a moment while I talked to him. I told him why they needed to shave him and that the clippers would make a funny noise. I put my fingers on the side of his body and jiggled them, showing him that he would experience a vibrating feeling on his body. Once he understood what was going to happen, I asked him to breathe with me. We regularly did our breathing exercises at home, and I knew this would calm him. We began to breathe together—in and out—and he followed right along with me. When I signaled for the vet tech, Scooter sat relaxed and calm as she shaved away. She was astounded and said she wouldn't have believed it if she hadn't seen it for herself.

TIPS FOR CALMING ANIMALS

1. Consult your veterinarian or a qualified alternative-health practitioner if an animal is chronically distressed or acting

strangely. Rule out physical causes before you explore other solutions or try any of the healing methods listed here. Unusual behavior can be a sign of serious and even life-threatening illness.

2. Make sure you are calm in the presence of an agitated animal. Set a good example. Be aware of your body language and your voice. Avoid staring at the animal, which can be very threatening.

3. Allow a lovely light-pink energy to flow from your heart center to surround the animal. This can feel very relaxing and soothing to him and help him feel safe in your presence.

4. Do the simple breathing exercises described on the previous page, with the animal. Breathing exercises can help both humans and animals relax, clear their minds, and change their physiological responses to stress.

5. Talk to the animal in a soft, gentle, and slow voice. Allow your movements to be slow and fluid.

6. It may help to create physical closeness with the animal, either by going into a quiet room together or, if the animal responds well to a leash, by putting a leash on him and walking around the house or yard together.

7. When you have the animal's attention, try a grounding technique to help him focus, such as the one mentioned in Tamra's story.

9. If the animal is willing to be touched, stroke him gently. Once the animal responds well to touch, he will also respond well to bodywork, such as massage, or to energy work. If the body is tense, the animal will react automatically from fear rather than from a calm, focused place. Calming the animal's physical body can help release his emotional tension, increase his self-confidence, and restore his self-respect. In Chapter 9, "Comforting Sick and Injured Animals," you will learn an energy-balancing technique. The Resources section at the end of this book lists excellent sources for learning about many useful techniques. For a hands-on experience, I offer a two-day Body Balancing Workshop. Call 818-597-1154, or refer to my website, www.animalcommunicator.net, for information.

9. Consider other alternative therapies for animals. I often refer clients to Tellington TTouch practitioners for their unique movement therapy as well as labyrinth work, a powerful grounding and confidence-building technique in which you walk your animal through a series of obstacles. In addition, acupuncture, acupressure, massage, and herbal and homeopathic treatments all work well with animals.

Communicate with the animal to assess what is causing the problem behavior. Whatever it is—aggressiveness or housetraining problems—make sure you find out the cause directly from the animal. Once you understand the root of the problem, you will know how to respond. Then continue to communicate to assess his progress and any additional needs he might have. Remember that solving complicated problems may take time, repetition, and patience.

THE PSYCHOLOGY OF COLOR

If you have an anxious animal, be aware of the colors he wears in such items as collars, blankets, and sweaters. The color red may amplify his anxiety, while blue and green will soothe.

Although we've always heard that animals don't see color, only black and white, recent research is starting to indicate otherwise. As stated in the *Journal of American Veterinary Medicine Association Scientific Reports: Leading Edge of Medicine—A Review:*

> *The ability of dogs to distinguish color has been the subject of several studies with often conflicting results. Many early behavioral studies indicated either that dogs lacked color vision, or that if they could discriminate hue, it was without importance to dogs, and form and brightness were more important. Many of these early studies, however, were poorly controlled, and more recent, well controlled studies have clearly documented that dogs possess and use color vision.*

This is hardly a concrete statement of evidence, but it's a start. Scientific research being what it is—that is, conflicting, confusing, and often inconclusive—we have to go with what we know in our hearts to be true. From my work, I feel absolutely positive that animals see colors, because they often describe their situations using color, telling me the color of a building or car or other things they see around them.

Color has an amazing psychological effect on both animals and humans. Many alternative-health practitioners believe that different colors align to the seven energy centers of our bodies, or "chakras." The color pink is closely aligned to the heart chakra. This is why I use it to send calming energy to animals. You'll learn more about using color in telepathic communications with animals in the chapters to come.

As Chris Griscom says in her book, *The Healing of Emotion:*

> *Color is a much more significant energy on earth than we have realized. Color contains certain frequencies that act according to physical laws and directly affect us. We know that the cooler colors such as the blues and greens create a relaxing atmosphere, that the reds and oranges are the fiery colors that stimulate body and psyche.*

She says that violet dissolves negative energy; blue is the color of relationship and spirit; green is the color of balance and healing; yellow is the color of consciousness and the mind; orange *lends courage and creative expansion*; red is the color of action, energy, and anger; and turquoise is the color of protection. Consider these properties of color when choosing bedding, collars, even food dishes for your animal.

WHEN PEOPLE ARE THE PROBLEM

As we've discussed, animals are sensitive to our emotions. Often without knowing it, we may be the cause of their problem behaviors. As hard as that may be to admit, it is our responsibility to change our behavior to help them.

The easiest thing to do is to be aware of your behavior and the example you set for your animal. Your calm and loving energy can be reassuring when she is at the vet's, the groomer's, competitions or shows, or any place where she would normally experience anxiety. It is important to have realistic expectations of your animal and reassure her of your unconditional love—win or lose—whether in the show ring or at home.

COMMUNICATING WITH SHOW ANIMALS

Because animals want to please us, they can feel pressured by what we expect of them, especially in such competitive situations as animal shows. Several dogs have told me that at shows, their humans get so nervous that their anxiety travels down the leash! When worries clutter our minds, we can't communicate clearly with our animals. No wonder some animals don't do as well in shows as they do at home.

Don't give your show animal the extra burden of your anxiety. Learn to relax so you can keep the lines of communication open with your animal. Use these tips:

- At a show, wear the same clothes you wear at home when practicing. You will have butterflies and anxiety in the show ring, and wearing unfamiliar clothing will make you even more uncomfortable. Wear the same clothes for both practice and showing, even if you wear a suit in the ring. Believe it or not, it can help tremendously.
- Try Bach Flower Remedies, such as Rescue Remedy, or breathing exercises to ease your nerves.
- Don't try anything new or make any changes to your routine at the show—keep everything the same as when you practice.
- Try visualization: See yourself with the animal, feeling relaxed, going through all of the movements beautifully. Picture you and your animal exactly as you want to appear in the show.

- When we are fearful, our energy rises through our bodies and out through our heads, allowing our energy to scatter. Try these grounding techniques:

    Visualize roots growing from the bottoms of your feet and extending deeply into the ground. These roots will help keep you connected.

    When you do breathing exercises, exhale your energy downward and through your feet to stay grounded.

    Many years ago, it was common to see dolls in the rear windows of cars. You could knock them over and they would always spring back to center. This was because their base was very heavy; no matter what happened, they would always return to center. Apply this image to yourself so that you always return to center. Think of your energy as moving downward to create a solid base.

    This next suggestion may seem odd, but bear with me. Certain elements in nature are grounding forces; why not use them to help ground yourself? Copper is one such element. Tape pennies to the bottoms of your feet to help keep your energy closer to the ground. The semiprecious stone tiger's eye is also good for grounding. Purchase two small stones (easily found at fossil and mineral stores or metaphysics bookstores) and wear them in the sides of your socks.

- Keep your routine with your animal fixed in your mind. Don't crowd it out with worry. Remember that the animal will feel your anxiety and be confused by it. When your dog is off-leash, visualize an invisible leash attached to the animal so you have more connection. Continue to communicate with him telepathically, showing him what to do.

If you show or train horses, you may want to ask for input regarding your riding abilities or training methods. Ask the horse how he enjoys being ridden and trained. Does he like his saddle? How does it fit? How does his bit and bridle feel to him? How does the person feel in the saddle? How can the rider improve his or her skills? Does he like the method of training? Does he like his trainer? What does he need to feel more comfortable with his schooling? How does he feel about competing in shows? What could be done to make it less stressful? Does he like his stall and accommodations?

There are endless questions you can ask to improve your skills and performance together—don't be shy. It gives the horse a chance to have his "say" about how he wants to be ridden or trained. I've done this many times with my own horses and with clients' horses, and the information provides great results for both rider and horse. One horse told me he felt his rider was like a student driver, but he didn't mind giving her "driving" lessons. He told me he wanted her to sit back more in the saddle and to stop leaning to one side. The trainer was both amazed and delighted, since she had been trying to convince the rider of this for a year. Another horse was able to achieve wonderful things once his trainer heard what he had to say.

Duane Knipe, a sports-medicine race trainer at Florida's Tampa Bay Downs Racetrack, asked me to help a horse named Twisted Stitch, who had a habit that kept costing him races. During every race, Twisted Stitch balked rather than go into "the hole," the space between two horses running side by side. When I asked why, the horse explained that he was afraid of the hole because he felt certain the horses he cut between would knock him down. Going into the hole felt claustrophobic to him.

I asked what would help him overcome his fear. He said that he couldn't go through the hole alone. He was so overwhelmed by his fears of falling and being trapped that he needed someone to talk him through it. He wanted the jockey to encourage him so he could feel connected and supported every step of the way. You can imagine what the jockey said—"You want me to do what?!"—but Duane convinced him to try it. After all, they had tried everything else to help Twisted Stitch fulfill his great potential as a racehorse. What did they have to lose?

During the next race, the jockey began talking to the horse as they approached the hole, and sure enough, Twisted Stitch plunged straight through it, coming in second and losing first place by a nose. It was the best race he had ever run in his life.

Animals want to perform their best, and their input is often required to help them achieve that goal. Ask your show animal how she feels about showing. Does she like the competition? How does she like the method of training? Does she like her handler? Is she being handled roughly in any way? What would she need to feel better about training? What can you do to make things go more smoothly at the show? Again, be curious and you'll discover ways you can work together better as a team.

CODEPENDENCY AND DESTRUCTIVE BEHAVIORS

You often hear of animals who wreak havoc on their homes when their people are away or who chew personal items or dig holes under fences. Animals' problems with such destructive behaviors are usually linked to codependency. We need to establish healthy and balanced relationships with our animal companions. It may not be healthy to be with our animals twenty-four hours a day. What they learn is that their lives revolve around us and only us, for better or worse. We need to be mindful of any tendencies we have to emotionally smother and control them. It is important that they have experiences that build their confidence and sense of individuality so that they develop a healthy sense of security when they're not with us.

Bobby, a client from Philadelphia, Pennsylvania, has a dalmatian named Brandy and lives in an apartment complex. The two go everywhere together. They travel together, eat together, go to work together, and sleep together. The dog had never been off-leash or able to run free with other dogs, except for a few brief encounters.

Brandy is now showing signs of aggressive behavior. When she is able to escape from the condominium, she lunges at people. On walks, she aggressively charges other animals, pulling Bobby to the ground. Bobby is now so fearful of Brandy's actions that she has become even more protective of her.

I've recently started working with them, and much work lies ahead in order to bring a sense of relaxation and freedom to their lives. I will continue counseling sessions with both of them and suggest Bobby use Bach Flower Remedies and bodywork on Brandy. Linda Tellington-Jones's labyrinth work will be implemented along with new and gentle training methods. Brandy will be given an opportunity to run in a safe, contained area and a chance to develop some socialization skills so she can live a normal life.

The flip side of the coin is the animal who has become so dependent on a human—and perhaps vice versa—that he or she has tunnel vision. The world has narrowed to nothing but the person–animal relationship.

Molly from Kansas City, Missouri called me when there was nowhere else to turn. Molly had not worked for several years and, during that time, had adopted a large mixed breed named Gypsy from a shelter.

When Molly returned to work, Gypsy's behavior became alarming. She jumped a six-foot fence in the yard, so Molly built an eight-foot fence to keep her contained. But eight feet didn't seem to matter to Gypsy. She became the Great Houdini of the dog world and escaped regularly. Molly's after-work routine became looking around the neighborhood for Gypsy. She finally decided she would just have to keep Gypsy inside the house and hire a dog walker.

Again, she thought she had solved the problem. However, Gypsy was overwhelmed by being alone inside and was determined to find a way out. I found out later that she felt the need to be with someone; she didn't know how to be by herself. Her life had revolved around Molly twenty-four hours a day and she did not understand why she was now being left alone.

Gypsy was so tormented by her feelings of loneliness that she crashed through the living room window to find companionship. Luckily, she wasn't injured, but the results could have been devastating.

While both of these examples involve dogs, no animal companion—or human—is immune to the unhealthy attractions of codependency. It can cause intense separation anxiety for the animal when you need to leave him alone. Animals will do almost anything to relieve their emotional pain.

If, for instance, you get a new job that requires you to travel, your animal may not know how to take care of himself when you leave. He may resort to odd behaviors such as chewing up things in your home. If he has a doggie door, he may resort to jumping over the backyard fence so that he can be with someone. He can't stand the feeling of being alone. The animal may never have had to cope with these feelings before, and now his emotions are too great for him to manage. Animals have even been known to go through plate-glass windows, as Gypsy did, and eat or scratch their way through garage walls, because they can't stand being alone and need to get out that badly.

Our first impulse in such situations is to adopt a new animal to keep the first one company. This is often the wrong thing to do, for it may distress the animal even further and increase his feelings of anxiety and abandonment. As we discussed in Chapter 5, before bringing home any new animal, check in first with your current animal companions.

If your animal has abandonment issues—fears of being left alone—you can help him manage those fears. Every time you leave the house, tell your animal that you will be returning. Make sure you tell him how long you will be gone—two, four, or eight hours. Then visualize a mental image of yourself coming back home and excited to see him. He will be assured that he is not being abandoned and will be able to focus on your return rather than on your leaving. In the beginning, start with short trial runs, leaving for fifteen minutes or so. Keep increasing your time away in intervals of ten minutes or whatever increment seems appropriate to help him adjust and feel reassured that you will indeed come back.

There are other easy ways to decrease an animal's fear of abandonment. While you're gone, play music that your animal is accustomed to hearing when you are home. Give the animal a job to perform while you're away. Tell him to help keep the house clean by hunting for bugs, or choose whatever job suits his personality. And, of course, every time you return home, tell him what a wonderful job he did. This makes the animal feel good about staying home and helping you while you are away. If possible, create variations in your daily routine so your animal doesn't become overly sensitive to change.

Expand the animal's world in as many healthy ways as you can think of. Have him or her spend time with other animal friends, with other people, out walking around the neighborhood or the local park, and home alone. Introduce him to a variety of situations early in life so he can feel good about new things rather than apprehensive and insecure. Help him to feel secure about all his surroundings and about meeting new people.

Codependency is a two-party syndrome. If your animal is exhibiting symptoms, it's important for you to look at your own life. Codependency is no healthier for you than it is for your animal. A healthy animal plays, eats, and sleeps when he or she wants to. Make sure you're doing the same thing to take care of yourself. Create a balance of exercise, playtime, balanced meals, social time, and plenty of rest. If you do these things for yourself, it will lead to healthy relationships all the way around—with yourself, with others, and with your animal companions.

When trying to find solutions to our animals' behavior problems, it is critical for us to fine-tune our communication skills, knowing that it is always a two-way conversation. Be creative when developing inquiries to get to the root of the problem. Ask, listen, and ask some more, then listen again. Realize that solutions may involve negotiating, repetition, compromise, and redefining expectations. It is not just a matter of demanding that your animal change. You need to adjust your behavior as well to understand and be sympathetic to your animal's point of view and particular needs. With love and respect, almost any problem can be overcome.

Relocating with Animals

Moving to a new home is stressful enough for humans who know exactly what's going on. Imagine what it's like for the animals in our lives. Moving causes upheaval, disorder, and feelings of loss. Like humans, animals have many adjustments to make—new smells, new noises, new territories inside and out, and new friends to make. And, also like humans, they often mourn the loss of their friends from the old neighborhood.

In the anxiety and turmoil of planning and packing, people often neglect to consider their animals in the impending move and fail to prepare them for their new lives. I was guilty of this with my family of three cats when I sold my consultancy business and relocated to the country. The house was in upheaval, jammed with boxes, and I was distracted and busy. One day in the middle of all this, I received one of the most powerful animal communications I have ever had. Distressed about what was going on in the house, the three cats sat and faced me—one in each chair, like a mini-powwow. Then I heard words as plainly as if a person were saying them aloud: "You need to sit down and talk with us!"

Of course, I should have realized that I owed them an explanation—not only because their lives were disrupted and would change as radically as mine, but also for the sake of their health and safety. Moving is the time when many animals get lost in the shuffle and run away to escape the disruption of their environment. For those who do safely reach their new destination, they still may face many unfamiliar perils. Communication with your animals is essential during relocation. Now is the time to put all your telepathic skills to use as you include your animals in the process.

Rather than burden your animals with your anxieties and worries about the move, share your excitement with them. Send positive images of your new lives together and of everything working out smoothly. If you worry about how they are going to handle the situation, they may pick up on your worries and become resistant. They may withdraw or hide, run away, or develop unfavorable behaviors.

If you are planning a move, talk with your animal about it. Take quiet time to tell him what to expect and to instill a sense of calmness about the move. Fill him in on specifics, including every detail that may affect him.

- Tell him when the move is taking place. Will you be moving in two weeks or two months? Remember, animals understand the concept of time.
- Explain to him that all the boxes he has seen around the house will be picked up by movers and moved to the new location.
- Tell him that during the move he will be kept in a safe place. If you plan to kennel him, explain that to him, and include when you will pick him up.
- Tell him how the new location will enhance his life. How will it be different from your current home? Explain the advantages of the move. Will you have a bigger yard? Use visualization to show him this.
- Visualize what the new home looks like from the inside out. Send him mental images of each room and what the outdoors look like—trees, grass, and fencing. Cats, in particu-

lar, feel more comfortable if they know what their new
place looks like ahead of time.

- Explain how he will travel. Is he going by car or plane? Will he
  need to be in a travel carrier?
- Tell him how long the trip will take. Will it take two hours by
  car, or will you be flying for five hours? If you are going by
  plane and he is too big to fit under your seat, explain what it
  will be like to be in the cargo hold and that you will be there
  to greet him once you have arrived. Again, using your visualization skills, show him the process step-by-step.
- Ask how he feels about the move and if he has any concerns or
  needs. Let him have a say, and help him in whatever way
  you can.

In this chapter you'll learn many practical tips for moving
safely and happily with your animals, based on my years of working
and communicating with animals. But, in addition to these practicalities, I encourage you to keep the telepathic lines of communication open during this stressful time. Before, during, and after
the move, communicate with your animals daily, if not more often.
Speak in a soothing voice and be an example of calmness. Take
time to sit and listen to each one about their concerns. As their
trusted guardian, do your best to provide comfort, reassurance,
and safety.

In most cases, your animals will come to share your excitement
about the move, as mine did. In a few rare cases, an animal will flat
out rebel against a move, and a sensitive person will have little
choice but to figure out a way to honor the animal's wishes. The
following story is just such a case.

*A California client, Louise Jones, owned a second home in New
York. She was concerned about how her large tabby cat, Mr. X,
would react to going there for a month or two. Indeed, on the day
she was planning the move, Mr. X disappeared. Soon I was able to
contact him, but he was very reluctant to communicate or reveal to
me where he was. He had ascertained, by listening to Louise's*

thoughts, that she was about to cart him off to the East Coast. He did not want to be found.

Although Mr. X loved his family, his allegiance was to the land, the trees, and the garden at his Malibu home. He considered it his job to protect them. Securing his domain gave him a sense of purpose in life. He had run away to find a new home nearby, and the new people had started to feed him outside. Eventually, he showed me where his hideout was, but only so I could let Louise know he was safe.

Louise missed Mr. X so much that she scouted out the house he had described to me and found him. Lonely without him, she brought him back home, where he stayed for only a day. He had chosen a new home and made up his mind that that was where he belonged. He did not want to move to New York, even for a month or two. He knew Louise wanted to take him regardless of his feelings, so he decided to make his new home permanent.

Louise recognized his strong connection to the land and faced the fact that Mr. X had made a decision to remain there. Wisely, she understood that tragedy could result if she went against his wishes. She went to his new home and introduced herself to Mr. X's new people, who were thrilled to have him. Although it pained her enormously, she loved him enough to let him go.

MOVING SAFELY WITH YOUR ANIMALS

You've inked the deal, hired the movers, and started packing boxes. You're really moving. As you make plans and arrangements, don't forget to include a plan for your animals. Preparation is the key to making the move a safe and happy one for them as well as you. Begin the process early, at least a month before moving day, keeping your animals' health, safety, and emotional well-being in mind.

1. Moving causes stress, no matter what. I have found that Bach Flower Remedies can make transitions more manageable for animals. When animals are faced with the anxieties of a move, transition, or travel, I recommend two Bach Flowers: Rescue

Remedy and Walnut. Start using them two to four weeks before the move and continue until two to four weeks afterward.

2. If your animal is on any medication, be sure to have extra on hand before traveling. Prior to your move, find out the name and location of the nearest vet and emergency-care facility in your new neighborhood, and keep it with you.

3. Some animals are fearful of travel carriers because of unpleasant associations with trips to the vet's office. If you wait to get it out until moving day, your animal may retreat to a hiding place and then be impossible to locate. To help avoid this problem, bring it out weeks before the move. Cover it with a towel and place a soft bed and toys inside. Before too long, your animal will most likely become relaxed around the carrier and begin to take short naps inside.

4. Order identification tags for the new location ahead of time, and when you move, put them on your animal immediately. If you do not have new tags, use a permanent marker to write your new phone number on the collar. Be sure your animal's collar is secure and that he cannot slip out should he be startled or frightened.

5. Keep a piece of your unwashed clothing, used towels, or your animal's special blanket with him during the move. Scent is an important part of an animal's world, and having familiar smells around can be very reassuring.

6. On moving day, some people board their animals overnight at their vet clinics or kennels. If your animal is not in good health, veterinary boarding may be the best choice.

7. If you choose to keep your animals at home during the moving process, here are some tips that can keep them safe:

- On the day of the move, make sure each of your animals is in a safe environment. For dogs, this can be as simple as a dog run, fenced backyard, or dog crate. Cats should be isolated in a room where they will not be disturbed, such as the bathroom. Close the bathroom door tightly and tape a large sign to it that says: CATS INSIDE—DO

NOT ENTER. Alert each mover that under no circumstances is anyone allowed in that room. Make arrangements for the movers to use another bathroom. If an
animal is not contained in a safe area, he or she may run
out of the house, may get lost, and may never be seen
again.

- Make sure the bathroom windows are closed, even if
  they are screened. Many people have lost animals because screens can be easily clawed through if an animal
  is in distress and wants out.

- Keep food, water bowls, litter, and toys in the bathroom,
  as well as a box or travel carrier (with bedding). This will
  provide a safe place for a nap, or a sense of protection.

- Check on the animal periodically, reassuring him that
  you will be on your way soon. Speak in a soothing voice
  and be an example of calmness.

8. When the movers have gone, put your animal into a carrier,
making sure that all hinges or zippers are fastened or locked so
he can't escape. Place a thick pad or piece of foam on the bottom of the carrier, and place another piece inside the metal
door to mute travel vibrations, easing the animal's nerves and
adding to his comfort. Be sure to bring a change of bedding or
newspapers, paper towels or baby wipes, and plastic bags for
cleanups. Travel fears may lead to unexpected elimination.

9. Using your telepathic skills, remind him again how long the
trip will take. If you're traveling by car, enjoy the ride and talk
with him along the way about how much fun it's going to be.
Tell him that he will remain in his carrier, or in the new bathroom just as he did in the old house, until the movers have finished unloading the boxes.

10. Everyone, including animals, needs rest breaks on long car
trips. Be sure to take plenty of water and your animal's usual
food. Sudden dietary changes can lead to stomach or intestinal
upsets at the worst possible times. In hot weather, carry a spray
bottle of water to cool down an overheated animal. If your animal is uncomfortable traveling by car, you may want to prac-

tice short trips before the move to help prepare for a longer
journey.

11. Upon your arrival at the new location, repeat the same procedures outlined in number 7. It is even more important to be
diligent at the new location. This is when many disoriented animals run away and have no way to find "home."

12. Once the movers have departed, and with doors and windows
tightly secured, let your animal explore the inside of his new
home. With cats, some people prefer to let them into one
room at a time. Choose a method based on what you think
your cat is most comfortable with.

ORIENTING YOUR ANIMALS TO A NEW HOME

An animal moving to a new environment will need your help to
cope with unfamiliar experiences. In general, dogs typically take in
their new surroundings and adjust quickly. Cats need more time to
fully explore and accept their environment. They need to sniff
every nook and cranny of the household to feel comfortable and
safe.

Keep cats indoors for up to four weeks before letting them
outside for the first time. If let out any sooner, cats often disappear
permanently. They haven't had time to fully adjust. They need to
feel totally comfortable with the inside of their home before going
outside.

When I let my cats outside for the first time after I move, I
walk them on a harness and leash, showing them the boundaries of
safety on the property. I show them where it is not safe, where
there may be busy streets or unfriendly dogs. If your animal is unfamiliar with a leash and harness, start by putting a harness on him
in the house. Let him get used to this feeling on his body. Once he
is comfortable with the harness, attach a leash and walk him
around so he can get used to the slight feeling of pressure on his
body. Once he is comfortable with both, then try it outdoors, starting with short periods of time and increasing to longer periods.

Remember, however, that you need to do what works best for

your particular animal. If your cat would feel ridiculous wearing a harness and leash, don't do it. Do what is comfortable for both of you, but keep the animal safe. Once your cat feels safe with his environment (which you can ascertain by asking him telepathically), let him out without the harness and leash but under your supervision. Again, start with a short period, perhaps one hour each day, and work up to more. If you have multiple cats, let them out one at a time to begin with.

If you live in the country, you may have chosen to keep your cats indoors. If your cats are miserable indoors because they are hunters and yearn to be outside, my own solution might work for you. I have always lived in the country and I have never lost a cat to coyotes, even though I live in the middle of coyote country. This is because I have house rules; they aren't allowed to stay out overnight. If they were, I probably would not still have cats. Because coyotes hunt nocturnally, I let my cats out every day from 10:00 A.M. to 2:30 P.M. At 2:30 sharp, I call them in. This gives them plenty of time to hunt, climb trees, roll around, and explore. They are very content with this schedule and happy to have an assigned time to go out to patrol or hunt—it makes them feel like they've done a good day's work. Then they're ready to come in and help clean the house by searching for bugs.

Another way to feel safe about letting your cat out in the yard is to use a product called Cat Fence-In, which you can install above your current fencing. It is engineered to keep cats contained within their own yard and to keep other cats out. For information about Cat Fence-In, refer to the Resources section in the back of the book.

Dogs need different attention in making their adjustments to a new home. First, make sure you have secure fencing. Check for loose boards and holes underneath the fence, and make sure the gates are secured. Some people tether their dogs during a move. Unless your dog is already comfortable being tethered, I don't recommend it. Particularly at the new location, your dog might become extremely stressed and do anything to break free. Once you are settled, walk your dog around the neighborhood. Let him become familiar and comfortable with his surroundings beyond the backyard.

Having a job is important to an animal after a move, especially if its former lifestyle changes. Suppose your cat has been an indoor/outdoor cat most of his life and you have moved to a neighborhood with a busy street. You may have decided to keep your cat indoors in the new house. Your cat may become frustrated with your decision and display his frustration by howling at night, scratching at the door, or making mad dashes to get out whenever the door opens. Or perhaps your cat might even start spraying on the furniture or soiling outside the litter box. Know that this type of stress can even lead to illness in the animal. If this cat has been a hunter all his life, then ask him to help you keep the house clean by hunting for all the bugs in the house. You might also consider getting a "cat tree," or carpeted climbing structure, for climbing and scratching and a nice, high viewpoint. Or install a window seat so he can view the outdoors and get some fresh air.

In their explorations of a new, unfamiliar place, animals can find themselves in danger. Using your visualization techniques, communicate dangerous areas to your animals and show them the boundaries of your property. However, you need to focus on what you *want* them to do rather than on what you *don't* want them to do. For instance, visualize them staying on the inside of the fence. If you say, "Don't go over there," it means, "Go over there" to them because you are visualizing "going over there."

Creative visualization can be a powerful technique to help animals manage unanticipated dangers, as my friend Christine Ouang's experience with her cat, Miou Miou, shows.

During the last major California earthquake, Miou Miou vanished, and Christine and her roommate searched the house high and low for her. Finally they found her cowering behind the refrigerator—one of the most dangerous places for her to be! Grateful that she was alive, they used visualization to demonstrate that if another quake came, Miou Miou should seek shelter someplace safer and conveyed an image of her scooting under the bed. Then, to drive home what could have happened, they sent Miou Miou a mental image of herself crushed flat on the wall by a toppled refrigerator. Christine told me that when they transmitted that picture, Miou Miou instantly drew back her ears and put her paws on top of her head. Clearly, they had gotten through to her—and perhaps they showed her how to save her own life.

Just as Christine did, you can show your cat the safe havens on your property as well as the dangers. Before he goes out on his own, ask, "If you were startled and frightened outside, would you know where to go?" If he says, "yes," then he'll be fine. If he says, "no," show him the cat door again, then give him a little more time in the yard under supervision.

As a general rule, be conservative about judging when to let your animals outside after moving to a new home. Err on the side of caution. For most animals, adapting to a new place can take two to four weeks. Keeping them safe during that period may require a little more work, but it's well worth the effort.

8

Finding Lost Animals

Coping with the disappearance of your animal is a heart-wrenching and traumatic experience. However, with your new telepathic skills, *you* need not feel so lost. By becoming grounded and focused, you will find the courage and strength you need in order to take an active role in finding your animal.

One of the most challenging—and potentially rewarding—tasks I face in my professional life is finding animals who have gone astray. Some animal communicators prefer to avoid these assignments because it is so frustrating and painful when an animal cannot be found. I was reluctant to try it at first myself, thinking that it must be some very specialized ability, and referred clients to another animal communicator. My breakthrough came when I lost my own cat, Scooter, for two months. I'd almost given up hope when Scooter came home, as you'll read in his story later in the chapter. I realized the heartbreak people go through and I knew I could help.

Locating a lost animal is like tuning in to a distant radio frequency, and it can be very difficult to distinguish the animal's thoughts about where he'd *like* to be or what he's seen on his journey from his images of his actual physical surroundings. Imagine yourself sunning on the beach and dreaming about your winter ski vacation in Utah—what a confusing impression of your whereabouts your thoughts would give anyone who tuned in to you telepathically. That's just one of the difficulties long-distance communication poses.

Occasionally, a lost animal will want to be found so badly that his transmissions will overshadow other, weaker signals. In one comical case, I found a cat whose grateful person brought him in for a homecoming checkup with the vet—only to learn, since her own animal had been neutered, that the almost-identical returnee was not her cat! I had tuned in to a cat of the same description, and that animal, desperate for a home, had answered the call. This story had a happy ending (my client's cat mysteriously returned on her own, and we found her "twin" a good home). Mercifully, such mix-ups are very rare. More common, sadly, are the cases when I have to tell anxious humans that I have been unable to make a connection or, worse, when I have received information that an animal may no longer be in a physical body. Later in this chapter, I will describe the signs that indicate when an animal may not be in his body, and why it may be very difficult to determine that.

Locating missing animals has become one of my specialties. As arduous and emotionally wrenching as such cases can be, I continue to welcome them—from all over the world—because the reunions I've been lucky to achieve bring my clients such great joy. I must emphasize that you need not be psychic or have any extrasensory powers to locate a lost animal. Be forewarned, though, that the process can be hit-or-miss and difficult, even for professionals, so don't feel defeated if your efforts fail. But be assured that anyone who attempts it with a loving and open mind and heart has an excellent chance of locating any lost animal who is still in a physical body and willing to be found.

WHY ANIMALS STRAY

Just because an animal cannot be found at home does not always mean that he or she is truly lost. Quite often, an animal has left home for a reason that may or may not be negotiable. Sometimes the animal is simply seeking adventure, pitting himself against the big, wide world. Other deliberate reasons animals leave home are to return to a former home they never wanted to leave in the first place or to move on when they feel they've completed their job with the family. Some animals are truly lost because they've been stolen or chased by another animal, or have run away when frightened by something without paying attention to their surroundings. If your animal goes astray, knowing these scenarios can bring you some peace of mind and relieve you of some of the misplaced guilt you feel. In addition, knowing the reasons why and how your animal left might help you locate him once you understand the details.

BECAUSE THEY ARE UNHAPPY

Perhaps the most common reason that animals leave home is dissatisfaction with the present situation. The upheaval of moving, for example, can be upsetting enough to drive an animal away, as can the threat posed by a new animal who has joined the household. Sometimes animals become overstressed by the problems their humans are experiencing.

One of the most memorable animals I've ever worked with was Willy, Richard Segal's four-year-old white indoor cat, who unexpectedly disappeared from their Los Angeles home. Richard spent days searching surrounding neighborhoods, putting up flyers, and talking to everyone from kids to trash collectors. By the time he called me, he was understandably frantic and near despair, because Willy was deaf.

Willy's other senses—especially touch and sight—were very

acute, because when I contacted him he was able to send me an image of himself stuck under a house near a street corner within three blocks of Richard's house. The cat felt frozen in place and scared to death. When I asked Willy what he could see, he showed me the wheels of a car in a driveway, seen through a screen of latticework, and the color red. He had run away for an all-too-common reason—because he was upset with a new puppy whom an unsuspecting Richard had brought home. I explained all this to Richard, adding that when he went out to look for Willy, he would have to move extremely slowly and calmly. Willy would be easily panicked if approached abruptly.

Within three days of our conversation, Richard received a call one night from a woman who had seen a cat matching Willy's description beneath a house in the neighborhood. Richard took Willy's favorite cat toy and walked one-and-a-half blocks to the house she described. Unfortunately, it was during the riots following the Rodney King incident, and Richard was understandably nervous at being out when there was an imposed curfew. Not only that, but the residents of the house weren't home and Richard feared that neighbors would think he was a burglar.

As soon as he reached the house, however, he knew it was worth it. It was like seeing a neon sign, he said, pointing right at Willy. The house, on a corner, had latticework and not one but three red cars in the driveway. Sure enough, hiding beneath the house was a frantic Willy. In fact, when Richard approached, Willy flew out from under the house and jumped the backyard wall. Not about to lose him a second time, Richard hurtled the wall and caught up with Willy, using the cat's toy to lure him into his arms.

Richard was exuberant at having his beloved Willy back and could work out his conflict between the cat and the new puppy, now that he knew what had made Willy run.

BECAUSE THEIR JOB IS DONE

Animals often seek new homes when they sense that they have nothing more to teach and that their relationship with a particular family is complete. Sometimes they recognize that a certain situation or person will no longer prove challenging and satisfying and that they need to move on to grow, as was the case with my own Connemara horse, Dudley.

Dudley, a talented show horse, loved his work and was well known in his field of competition. We had lived together for six years when my life became so busy that I could no longer ride him in shows. Dudley loathed the prospect of early retirement, and he begged me to find him another home. Because I loved him I couldn't bear to let him go, but I knew it would be too selfish to make him stay if he would be unhappy.

All I could do was help him choose his new companion. As each new person came by for a test ride, I'd hear Dudley say, "Oh, no, it's not him." One day a twelve-year-old girl showed up with her mother. I asked if she wanted me to ride Dudley first, as all the others had, but she said no. She climbed right up and rode him as if they had been together their entire lives. When he did something that might scare another person, such as bucking, she just giggled. That's exactly what he wanted—and I heard Dudley say, loud and clear, "This is her." It was love at first sight for both of them. Some animals are truly meant to move on. Our job is to love them enough to let them go.

BECAUSE THEIR TIME HAS COME

Sometimes animals leave home out of love for us. An animal who is aged or ill may go away to die, partly out of instinct, but also from a wish to spare his family the pain of witnessing his passing.

I encountered an especially poignant case of such generosity when Allie from Dillon, Montana called me to find her missing dog. He'd been out in the unfenced yard with her brother, who was washing his car, and slipped away when no one was looking. When I made contact with the dog, he explained that he had left to die and showed me the calm and peaceful place where he had laid himself to rest. I had to break the news to my client, who was not surprised, for she had known it in her heart. Her previous dog had also recognized how unbearable she found death and decided not to put her through that agony. This loving dog, too, chose to leave on his own to prevent her from suffering.

I assumed that a similar situation had occurred when a Denver, Colorado client, Lori Callahan, called me to report that Magic, her seventeen-year-old cat, was missing. But when I actually sat down and tuned in to Magic, half-dreading the prospect of receiving sad news, I was astonished at the blast of energy she sent me. Elderly as she was in cat years, she was not only alive but also full of spunk. She had simply decided to go exploring and had jumped on a table to get over the wall into the neighbor's yard. However, once there, she wasn't able to make the high jump back over. All she needed was a little help.

When animals are lost, it is wise to set aside our fears, preconceived notions, and worst-case scenarios (which even I have been guilty of, as the above story shows) until we can get some inkling of the truth.

IF YOU LOSE OR FIND AN ANIMAL

Whether an animal has left home deliberately or involuntarily, it is wise to act quickly. Begin by following these practical steps:

1. Contact organizations whose goal is to help locate lost animals, are sources of information, and/or have listings of lost animals. These organizations include:
   - Pet Finders
   - Sherlock Bones
   - The Humane Animal Rescue Team

- Animal Recovery
- AKC (American Kennel Club) Recovery
- Local breed rescuers, whose numbers can be obtained from organizations such as the Humane Society, the SPCA, or your local municipal animal-control department. You can also find some local rescuers by looking in the classified section under *Pets*, *Pet Adoptions*, *Dogs*, or *Cats*.
- The Internet is a great source for listing animals who are missing and who have been found. Browse for subjects such as *animal rescue*, *pet rescue*, and *lost and found animals*.

2. If you've found an animal, you may choose to take him to a shelter. If you do, however, ask for the animal's impound number in addition to leaving your name. Then, if the animal is not picked up by his person, you can retrieve him before he is euthanized. If the animal is sick, which often happens to animals under such stress, or if the animal does not appear friendly or adoptable at the shelter, the animal may be put down. Ask about the shelter's policies. Another option is to board the animal at a rescue kennel or at your veterinary clinic.

3. Look for lost-animal posters throughout the neighborhood and outlying areas or create and post your own, marked ANIMAL FOUND with a photo of the dog or cat. Check in a breed book at the library to identify the animal correctly.

4. If you've lost an animal, make simple and clear flyers with a photo of the animal and your telephone number to post around your neighborhood. Place ads in your local papers. Most papers will run two lines free of charge for lost animals. If you've found an animal, check for ads. If you decide to run one describing the found animal, be careful how much information you put in the ad. When you get a response, ask the person to describe the animal in full detail: whether the animal is male or female, what his size and weight is, what color he is, what color his eyes are, what length fur he has, what his distinguishing marks or personality traits are, and what kind of collar or tags he's wearing, if any. Ask for a description of the tag: Is it plastic or metal, round, heart- or bone-shaped. You want to ensure you are returning the animal to the correct family.

5. Visit all shelters and veterinary clinics. Do not limit your visits to nearby shelters only. There are many cases in which animals have been taken or have traveled a great distance. Do not rely on phone calls. Regardless of good intentions, staff and volunteers may not receive or always convey accurate information. Many people avoid this step because it feels emotionally overwhelming to see so many displaced animals inside shelters. It is important to be strong and focused for your animal's sake; he may be anxiously waiting for you.

6. Speak to your neighbors, mail carriers, gardeners, and trash collectors. Ask if they have any clues for you.

7. Organize a search party. Ask children in the neighborhood to help. Remember not to use a strident, panicked voice when calling the animal, but rather a reassuring one.

8. Use your telepathic abilities, as outlined in this chapter, to find the animal. Sometimes, however, it is more difficult to work with your own animal because you have a strong emotional tie, which can interfere with intuitive clarity. If you are unable to connect with your animal telepathically, ask a friend who has telepathic abilities to assist you, or call a professional animal communicator.

Because the chances of finding a lost animal may diminish as his trail grows colder, you should take any unusual absences seriously. However, don't despair if an animal doesn't turn up right away. A few of my clients have found their animals after months have passed, and one cattle dog was missing for a year before his people finally located him.

Many an animal has left home voluntarily, only to find himself well and truly lost. That was the case with my cat Scooter, who jumped off my condominium balcony when I was out of town and disappeared for two months. Needless to say, I was devastated. I was not yet that experienced in animal communication, so I did what I could—I immediately put out hundreds of flyers and combed the neighborhood, with no luck. To make matters worse, I had plans in the works to move to another city. I despaired that I'd never see Scooter again.

One night, when all my bags were packed and waiting for the moving company, the phone rang and a voice on the other end said, "Are you the person who owns Scooter?" When I assured her I was, she told me she was my downstairs neighbor and said, "He just walked into my living room."

He was still wearing his collar, which is how my neighbor found me. Scooter and I had a joyful reunion. He was just fine, and he told me how much he had needed the experience of seeing the world. He had come up against some pretty rough cats and learned to defend himself. When I asked how he got back, he said, "I woke up one morning and just knew where to go." He just didn't know how to get to the right condo because there was no access to the second floor from the outside and all the doors were closed!

HELPING YOUR ANIMAL FIND HIS WAY HOME

I firmly believe that what brought Scooter home, just in time for the move, was the meditation I practiced daily for the two months he was away, as described below. I visualized sending him a beam of white light from my heart, telling him to look for the light that would lead him home. I now share this powerful meditation with my clients whose animals are missing, to help them establish a telepathic link. This white light is like the big searchlight you see in the sky when a store is having a grand opening—a good strong beacon that can help support and encourage the animal to find his way home.

MEDITATION FOR MISSING ANIMALS

Sit in a comfortable chair, feet placed flat on the ground, and close your eyes. Take deep breaths, scanning your body for any tension that you are holding. Allow yourself to breathe into those areas where the tension lies, and on the exhale let all of the tension release. Then focus your attention on your heart, feeling all the love you have for the lost animal. Feel all that love in your heart center. Then imagine that you see your animal in front of you. Once you have that image firmly in your mind, allow a beam of light to flow from your heart to your animal. As you send this big beam of light, say to your animal friend, "Look for this light. This light will bring you home. Keep looking for this light and it will bring you home."

USING TELEPATHY TO HELP AN ANIMAL FIND HIS WAY HOME

Once you've begun the practical search efforts detailed above in "If You Lose or Find an Animal," it's time to put your intuitive powers to work. Here is a step-by-step process to telepathically reach out to your animal and give him the assistance he needs to be found or find his own way home.

Step 1: **Shine the Beacon**

Start by using the powerful Meditation for Missing Animals. Some people like to do this exercise every day. It gives them a sense of involvement with their missing animals and helps them stay positive and calm. When you have a lost animal, it is essential to keep your thoughts on a positive track instead of entertaining negative thoughts, worries, and suspicions. See your animal safe and surrounded with a bubble of light, warm and comfortable, with plenty of food and adequate shelter. Put your energy into visualizing your animal finding his way home. See him walking down a path that leads back to you and your family. Positive thoughts are magnetic, while negative thoughts cloud and scatter your homing beacon. If you remain fearful, it will only muddy your animal's thinking, scatter his energy and his connection with you, and create static in your tracking signal. If it is in your belief system, ask for assistance from your spirit guides or angels. Ask them to help keep the animal safe.

Step 2: Make the Long-Distance Connection

Use the long-distance skills you learned in Chapter 3 to connect with the lost animal. It's helpful to know the date he disappeared, from where he left, and whether he was wearing a collar, identification tags, or other accessories.

The information you receive from the lost animal might include images, sounds, smells, and feelings, but it will be directed by the questions you ask, so be specific. Be aware that you will probably not receive addresses or street names or cities. This is not, in my experience, how animals see their world. If you can't immediately connect, don't assume that the animal is no longer in a physical body. Keep meditating and keep trying. The animal may be too frightened or too busy at that moment to pick up your signal.

When you first tune in to the animal, you might sense his fear—this is only natural, for he is probably disoriented and in unfamiliar surroundings. He may be hungry, thirsty, lonely, or even trapped or injured. Using the techniques you practiced in the partnered meditation exercise in Chapter 2, surround the animal with a gentle, warm bubble of pink light. Light-pink energy, as mentioned in Chapter 6, is soothing to an animal. Imagine the pale pink bubble of light gently easing the animal's anxiety so he can relax and regain his confidence.

Try some telepathic breathing exercises to calm the animal. Ask him to breathe with you, letting him perceive your inhales and exhales. Talk gently with him, reassuring him and telling him how you will assist him. Help him to regain his confidence and to know that he can find his way back home. If you lose the thread of communication because of the animal's fear, try again after a few hours, when he may be calmer and more coherent. When you can make a solid connection, you'll need to get concrete details from the animal. Try not to let more than twenty-four hours pass before you make a strong enough connection to communicate.

Step 3: Tell the Animal that Help Is on the Way

Once you have established a connection with the animal, try to determine if he is in immediate danger. Ask:

- Is he hurt?
- Is he trapped?
- Does he have access to food and water?

If the animal seems to be somewhere safe, urge him to stay put. Some animals, out of agitation and fear, run long after immediate danger has passed. Do as much as you can to give the animal support and encouragement to relax, for if he keeps moving, it will be all that much harder to find him. Reassure the animal that his family is looking for him and it will be best for him to stay in one place.

If the animal must keep moving, encourage him to:

- Travel when it is safe and quiet, perhaps at night.
- Watch out for traffic when coming to streets.
- Be brave enough to seek someone's help—someone whom he feels is safe and might be able to locate his home through the ads and flyers you've posted.

Record what the animal tells you on index cards, then group them according to the categories of questions listed below. Carry the clue cards with you when looking for the animal, as well as an open can of his food, his favorite blanket or toy, and a leash or carrier.

Step 4: Find Out How and Why He Left

Do your best to determine the circumstances of the animal's leaving. He may offer you good, solid clues about where he is.

- Ask why he left. Did another animal chase him? If so, what did he look like? How big was the animal? Did he run because he was frightened by a loud noise? Did he leave because the gate was open? Did someone take him? It's important also to remember to ask if he wants to be found. Most animals will be truthful about whether they want to return home or not.

- Ask him what he remembers about his journey. Does he remember in what direction he traveled from home? Did he go to the left or to the right from the front or backyard? Does he remember how long he traveled? Did it feel like miles or blocks? Was he running for an hour or just minutes? Did he travel in a vehicle? Ask him to describe what the vehicle looks like. Is he showing you a picture of a van, a sport utility vehicle, a sports car, a convertible? And what is the color of the vehicle? How far did the vehicle travel? Was it a short ride, perhaps minutes, or did it feel longer? How much longer? Was it day or night? In what direction did he travel? Which direction was the sun? Does he remember any landmarks?

- Ask if he's alone. Is he with another cat or dog? Ask for a description of his companions. Did a person pick him up? Ask him to describe the person and any others who may be around. What color skin and hair do they have? Do they wear glasses? Are they tall or short, light or heavy? Try to get an image rather than a specific answer to each question; you will get more detail. Ask if the animal is aware of any intentions the people have for him. Is the animal happy?

Step 5: **Ask About His Surroundings**

It may not be necessary to ask the animal every single question I have outlined below. What is required is that you get as much information as you can, ideally in the form of images. If the animal is not forthcoming—a common reaction when animals are afraid or distracted—you can probe by asking detailed questions.

- Ask if he is indoors or outdoors, and get details. Ask for an image of the area in addition to any thoughts, sensations, or feelings he is experiencing.
- Ask him to describe what he sees when he looks up. Maybe he's near an industrial area and will show you smoke from a

factory. Perhaps he sees airplanes, or a distinctive bridge, or treetops. Ask the animal to describe what he sees when he looks to the right and what he sees when he looks to the left. Have him describe the surface of the ground. Is it paved? Is it dirt, gravel, cement, or grass? Is there any fencing and, if so, ask him to show you what it looks like. Is it chain link, redwood, split rail, or perhaps stone or cinder-block walls?

- Ask him what he hears. There might be identifying noises in the area. Perhaps he hears the whistle of a train, or church bells, or traffic from a large highway.

- Ask if he is inside a structure. If so, what type of structure is it—a house, mobile home, apartment complex, industrial building? What color is the structure? What is the building made of? Is it brick, stucco, wood? What type of roof does the structure have, and what color? Is it red tile or black shingles?

- Ask about the terrain he sees or has seen while traveling. Get images if possible. Does he see open land and wilderness? Is it desertlike, forested, hilly? Are there buildings, houses, sidewalks, or brick walkways? Ask him to describe every little detail he sees. What kinds of trees, bushes, and plants are around him? How tall are they, what shape, what color?

- Is he near water? Is it a large or small body of water? Is it an ocean, pool, lake, pond, stream, or a puddle?

- Ask if he is around people or other animals. Are there children? Can he sense what ages they are? Are there cats, dogs, chickens, horses, or other animals around?

- Ask him how he is being treated. If he is with humans, is he being walked, and, if so, where? Do they go to a park or walk around the neighborhood? If so, what does that look like?

Step 6: Synthesize the Information

If the animal has given enough information for you to recognize the area where he is, bring food, familiar toys, and his carrier in the car with you when you go to look for him. If you find the area but not the animal, then get back in touch with him telepathically. Ask if he heard you calling his name. If he did, why did he stay hidden? Was he still too frightened? What can you do to help him come out? Where exactly is he hiding?

If you return to the area and still cannot find the animal, bring a chair with you, or sit on the ground, and do the Meditation for Missing Animals. Visualize a beam of light extending outward to your animal. Let the animal feel your energy while you are in that particular area, so he can become even more comfortable and confident. Call for the animal in an upbeat voice and have his food and toys with you to entice him.

If the animal does not come out of hiding, send him a visualization of how he could get back home on his own. Draw him a map in your mind. What houses or buildings would he have to pass, and on what side of his body would those structures, trees, or fences be? Be as clear as you possibly can. Your visualization techniques are essential. Visualize the animal walking back home, coming through the door, and lying down and relaxing in his favorite spot.

In addition, you can try going beyond the area you have been looking in. Sometimes you just need to go a little farther. The information you received may reflect things he saw along his journey that had some meaning to him, but may not necessarily be where he is now. Don't be afraid to ask friends to help you look. Put together a search party. Sometimes, going out very late at night is the best time; when it's quiet, the animal feels more secure than in the midst of the bustling daytime hours.

If you don't recognize the area he describes to you, keep trying for more details. Some people like to try to feel for the energy of the animal using a map of the general area. I have done this on occasion. Let your hand hover over areas on the map. If you feel a strong sensation beneath your hand, this may be representative of the energy of the animal in that particular spot on the map. If you are an experienced pendulum user, you can use it in conjunction with a map as well. Hold the pendulum over areas on the map to see if the pendulum picks up the animal's energy. If there is an energetic pull, the pendulum will usually move in a clockwise motion. For some, the pendulum moves differently.

Step 7: **Support the Missing Animal**

Your continuing communications can be a tremendous source of comfort to a lost animal, as Nancy Rowe of Woodstock, New York learned when her short-haired cat, Wasabi, was missing.

Wasabi was a two-year-old indoor cat who had never been outside until the day he escaped through a broken screen. Nancy lived on five acres in the country and was frantic because Wasabi had been gone a week. When I got in touch with Wasabi, he showed me that he was trapped in a tree and very scared—he had seen a coyote. He could see a house from where he was, but since he could see other animals at the house, he was afraid to venture there. He described the house he saw in great detail—white with green trim, a screened porch with lots of trees around the home, a gravel driveway, and a dirt road very close by. He was certain, however, that he did not know his way home.

After driving around, Nancy found the location but not Wasabi, so I asked him to give me more information. This time, he immediately showed me a huge bird flying past him. To me, it looked like a blue heron. He showed me a pond to his right. He said he had eaten a bird and was beginning to feel more secure because he had heard Nancy's voice calling him. He was beginning to get his confidence back. In the midst of all of this, he showed me a picture of how he enjoyed his belly being rubbed. (When I later told that detail to Nancy, she confirmed that it was his greatest pleasure.) He proceeded to give me more information regarding the house he saw, the plants, the dogs, and other details of his surroundings.

When Nancy went back out again, she saw a blue heron—a bird rarely seen in her area—which made us both feel much more

*hopeful. But there was still no Wasabi. The next day I gave my stu-
dents the assignment of locating Wasabi, and they received even
more information. One of the people in the group, Susan Clark
Ovitt, saw an image of Wasabi wet, with his ears slicked down. I
passed the new details on to Nancy, and we all wished her well and
put out our positive thoughts for Wasabi's safe journey back home.
Nancy took her chair and went back to the property to look for
Wasabi, following Step 6: Synthesize the Information.*

*The next day Nancy called with great news. Wasabi was home.
He came back on his own—with great directions, I might add,
from Nancy. And indeed, he was soaking wet, with his ears slicked
down!*

*What struck me most was how much we had helped Wasabi go
through some essential changes within himself. He went from pure
fright in the beginning—protecting himself in the tree, afraid to
approach the house—to feeling brave enough to come down once
he had talked with me and heard Nancy's voice (but still too scared
to come out), to finding the courage to make his way home alone.
Our communications with a lost animal can be tremendously en-
couraging and may even help keep him alive.*

TRUST THE ANIMAL'S INFORMATION

We've talked about trusting the impressions we receive from animals, but there have been a few cases where this point was especially vivid for me. One involved a female rottweiler named
Chewbacca, who had disappeared.

*Beverly Berger called me as a last resort when Chewbacca dis-
appeared, and fortunately, I was able to reach out to the dog. Unfortunately, Chewbacca revealed that a man who offered her food
had lured her into a pickup. Now she was in a small, yellow,
fenced-in house with a woman and the man, whom she visualized
for me as being tall, lean, well built, and dressed in a plaid shirt
and a cap. The detail that really stood out for her, and that she*

emphasized to me, was that he had a face full of wrinkles. Chew-
bacca told me that the couple hit her occasionally, almost as if they
wanted her to snap, and that she suspected they wanted to sell her.
She also told me that the man would sometimes take her to a park,
where he would jog with her.

Before any of us could figure what to make of these revelations,
the kidnapper showed up in the park, where he offered to sell
Chewbacca to another man. Suspecting that something was amiss,
the man bought her for fifty dollars and immediately checked to see
whether she had a tattoo or embedded identification microchip—
and indeed Chewbacca did. After this good Samaritan brought her
home, a neighbor volunteered that she had seen a suspicious man
around fitting the description Chewbacca gave—and what she re-
membered most vividly about him were the wrinkles on his face.

This is an important lesson, especially for those attempting the
tough detective work it can take to find a lost animal. Pay careful
attention to every single impression the animal conveys, no matter
how odd or unexpected it may seem, for even seemingly minor details may hold the key.

Such details were critical in helping Saul and Dina Smithson
of Sedona, Arizona find their thirteen-year-old Pomeranian, Rocky,
who was lost somewhere on their seventy-five acres of wilderness
land.

When some hikers passed the Smithsons' cabin, Rocky had fol-
lowed them. He'd been gone for two days by the time they called
me. Dina and Saul were especially worried since Rocky had a col-
lapsed trachea and often had a hard time breathing. Search parties
had gone out, but to no avail. Even his veterinarian was losing
hope of finding Rocky, suggesting that a coyote had probably made
a meal out of him. Nevertheless, Saul and Dina did not want to
give up.

When I tuned in to Rocky, I was quite surprised with his atti-
tude and conversation. He was quite sure of himself and showed
me good hiding places that were keeping him safe from predators.

When I asked him to show me in detail where he was, he was very forthcoming. He said that when he looked to his right he saw a tree that had fallen and looked like a bridge. He said that two trees nearby had grown together and looked like the letter V. He said he had plenty of water and could hear water trickling down rocks near him. He told me that all he could see was green; it looked like a forest to me. Although the Smithsons lived in Sedona, Rocky's description showed me no evidence of red rock. He said that he was headed downhill versus up and was facing south. He also said that if he kept going, he felt as though he would run into some cabins. This little fellow was certainly secure about his circumstances and was taking good care of himself. His feet felt prickly and sticky and hurt. He said that when Saul or Dina called for him, they should also whistle.

When I gave Saul this information over the phone, I could hear the disappointment in his voice. How was he going to find Rocky with these descriptions? He sent the search party back out anyway. They had gone about two miles when they saw droppings from Rocky and started following the trail. Within thirty feet, they saw the V-shaped trees and the downed tree that looked like a bridge, exactly as the little dog had described it. Saul checked his compass and found that they were south of the cabin. All of a sudden, they heard rustling in the bushes a few feet away and Rocky came bustling out to them, happy and healthy except for his bloody feet.

Later, a neighbor told the Smithsons he had seen Rocky's prints near those of a mountain lion and, of course, thought the worst. However, Rocky kept himself quiet and calm, knowing instinctively that any noise would alert predators to his whereabouts. What a smart little guy—he'd done a great job distinguishing details, and the information worked.

THE HARD QUESTION: IS THE ANIMAL STILL IN A PHYSICAL BODY?

There have been times when I tried to make a connection with a lost animal and received nothing—no feeling and no sensation. When I first started working with lost animals, I used to interpret that to mean that they were no longer in a physical body. But that proved inaccurate in many cases. Now I wait at least a few hours and try again. If, however, you have not been able to contact an animal after many tries, it may be time to face the question of whether the animal is still in his body.

It can be extremely difficult to ascertain whether the animal is still in a physical body or not. When an animal has met with sudden death, perhaps by the impact of a car or an attack by another animal, he may not be aware he is out of his physical body—it has happened too fast. Remember the movie *Ghost*, with Whoopi Goldberg, Demi Moore, and Patrick Swayze? Patrick Swayze meets with sudden death, but he is still walking around wondering why people don't notice him and why he can't make contact. This may happen with animals. So, when someone gets in touch with an animal, the animal may show where he is and what is around him, not recognizing that he is experiencing these things in spirit form rather than in physical form.

The reverse of this situation can also happen. When an animal is extremely frightened, it can feel as if he has left his body even though he is very much alive. And in a sense, he has—he has been literally scared out of his wits because the terror is so uncomfortable to deal with. The person contacting him can mistakenly interpret that state of fear. It might be impossible to determine, with complete accuracy, whether the animal is still in the body. But, through applying the skills you have learned in this book, you can try. You might practice the following visualizations even if your animal isn't lost, to give you some experience with it under less stressful conditions.

SENSING WHETHER AN ANIMAL IS IN PHYSICAL
OR SPIRIT FORM

Using your long-distance techniques from Chapter 3, connect with the lost animal and ask if he is still in a physical body. You might immediately get a strong yes or a strong no. If you get neither, then try these different approaches:

1. Feel for a heartbeat or a pulse. Can you sense that feeling and rhythm? Some people, when searching for a cat, also feel for a purring sensation. Oddly enough, cats sometimes purr under stress.
2. Check for a feeling of being grounded, of being connected to and part of the earth.
3. Imagine that you see two paths in your mind. Imagine that the path going to your left indicates that the animal is still in a physical body. Then imagine that the path going to your right indicates that he is no longer in a physical body. Now relax and see what path you are drawn to when you think of this animal. Are you drawn to the left or right? Where is most of the energy felt, on the right or left?
4. Visualize a candle that represents your animal. Is the flame lit or out?
5. Check for a feeling of entrapment. When an animal is out of his body but not aware of it, he may feel trapped, because he is neither here nor there but in between. Be aware, however, that the animal may still be in a physical body, but literally trapped or confined somewhere and terrified.
6. Check for a sensation of airiness. When the animal has moved into spirit form, you'll feel a very light, ethereal, expansive, almost floating sensation.
7. Watch for images. You may get a vision of how the animal met his death, which may be accompanied by a light sensation as he gently floated out of his body. If you do happen to see the event that caused his death, then see if the body was left there or carried away, or what else might have happened to it. If the

body is still there, pay careful attention to the surroundings so you will be able to locate and search the area for yourself. As painful and difficult as this may seem, I encourage you to seek a sense of completion with your animal companion. For many, not knowing is far more painful to live with.

While I hope most of you never need these guidelines, I hope they are useful for those of you who do.

Comforting Sick and Injured Animals

When an animal is sick or injured, loving communication can be of tremendous comfort. Using your telepathic skills, you can ask your animal what would help him feel better, such as a gentle massage, or offer him some of his favorite toys. If you listen, you can find out how the animal feels, where the discomfort is located, what degree of pain he is in, and what he needs to feel more comfortable. Communicating with your animal allows you to take an active and productive role in his overall care and well-being rather than feel like a helpless bystander. You can work hand-in-hand with your veterinarian to fine-tune the diagnosis by knowing exactly how the animal feels physically and emotionally. Telepathy can be a tool for revealing important clues that can solve a "tough case"—perhaps saving an animal's life.

FINDING OUT WHERE IT HURTS

When sitting quietly with your sick or injured animal, it's a natural opportunity to put your telepathic skills to good use. Chances are that you're already on a heart to heart level with the animal, empathizing with his situation, and trying to make him feel better. Now you can help him further by gathering important information about his condition.

You will ask for a complete description of how the animal feels, physically and emotionally. Be specific in your questions, to get as many details as you can. Your questions should include:

- How do you feel physically, emotionally? Are you in any pain?
- Where in your body are you uncomfortable? Ask for specifics. Is it his back, stomach, head, eyes, teeth, ears, intestines?
- What does the discomfort feel like? Is it a sickish feeling? A burning sensation, or a feeling of great pressure? Be as specific as you can with the animal.
- Is the pain constant?
- When does it occur and how often?
- How severe is the pain?

As you ask these questions you might actually experience, in your own body, the physical discomfort the animal is having. People often resonate to their animals' bodies, feeling the exact sensation for a split second. If, indeed, you are experiencing your animal's pain, the feeling will dissipate quickly. For example, if the animal has a headache, your head might hurt for a split second, long enough to know that the animal has a headache.

If the feeling lingers, however, it might be your own ailment. It's also possible that you have taken on the animal's pain because you are so empathetic. To avoid taking on an animal's sensations, clearly state at the beginning of the session that your intentions are to be a facilitator only.

Just as we've used color in other chapters, you can use it to protect yourself from taking on another's energy. Visualize surrounding your body with a clear, sky-blue light. This color allows good energy in and keeps negative energy out. Judith Pynn, an intuitive and an intuitive trainer from the Santa Cruz, California area, says, "When you visualize sky blue, you're affirming your boundary. You're less likely to take on negative energies around you." Judith also recommends using the color gold, saying "Gold is love, which allows us to feel safe enough to be vulnerable, connect with our deep selves, and let healing take place." She teaches her students to generate enough of their own energy to repel negative energy. The concept is similar to the age-old advice of eating well and getting plenty of rest to ensure good energy levels. You have to have enough of your own energy to do this type of work.

In addition to physical sensations, you might also receive information from your sick or injured animal in thoughts or mental images. You might see a particular part of his body that feels uncomfortable. You might sense a feeling of heat, inflammation, or throbbing in that area. The information can come in many different ways. You might also discern an animal's discomfort by touching his body, or determine his flow of energy by moving your hands above his body, which you'll learn more about later in this chapter in the Energy-Balancing Technique.

To ascertain an animal's level of discomfort, you can visualize a meter with a scale from zero to ten—no pain to intense pain. This method has been an invaluable tool for me on many occasions. As you ask the animal questions about the pain level in specific parts of his body, in your mind's eye watch where the needle moves to on the scale. If you are familiar with using a pendulum, you can use it to detect pain levels. Hold the pendulum over the animal's body, setting your intentions that the pendulum will move in a clockwise motion. Then begin to count. When the pendulum stops moving—for example, it might stop at "three"—that is the degree of pain the animal is in.

I found the pain meter to be an invaluable tool in helping Mikki, a Yorkshire terrier who'd had chronic diarrhea for one year. His human, Madeleine Carteron, called me in desperation because none of the treatments they'd tried had worked. When I tuned in to Mikki telepathically, I felt his discomfort not in my stomach, as you might expect, but in my back. The needle on my telepathic pain meter swung to six, moving toward seven. This number was very high, and I suspected a problem with his vertebrae. I strongly recommended that Madeleine have a chiropractor look at Mikki.

By this point Madeleine's husband, Bernard, was convinced that she was throwing her money out the window trying to treat the dog. All the vets had been bad enough—but now an animal communicator and a chiropractor? Nevertheless, Madeleine took my suggestion, and sure enough, the chiropractor confirmed that Mikki's back was out of alignment—and that his crippling diarrhea was the result of his constant back pain.

The chiropractor made the spinal adjustment, and soon Mikki, who had been almost an invalid for a year, was running around like a puppy. His diarrhea was gone. You can imagine the expression on Bernard's face. He was dumbfounded! After that, he even signed up for my weekend animal communication course and started talking with Mikki.

After you've assessed the animal's pain level, question him about any symptoms you have observed in him, such as not eating, drinking large amounts of water, unusual posture, frequent urination, or any changes in his routine, attitude, or mood. If the animal is taking medication or receiving some kind of treatment, such as acupuncture, find out how it makes him feel and whether he believes it is helping. Record all the information you receive from him, along with your own observations, to bring to the vet. The more detail you can provide, the better.

VISITING THE VET

Before you take any animal to the vet, take quiet time to explain to him in detail what is happening. Imagine suddenly being thrust into a small container, moved into a car, and having to deal with unusual noises, vibration, temperature change, and road fumes. Then you're rushed into a sterile place full of more threatening sounds and smells, and subjected to invasive, often painful tests, injections, and even surgery, with no idea of what is going on. Think of the stress such treatment would cause a human being, who could demand answers, and you can imagine how much more it would terrify an already infirm and frightened animal. If treatment is needed, explain the procedure to the animal step-by-step. You may want to ask the vet for quiet time alone, or you may feel comfortable talking to the animal in his or her presence. Reassure the animal, but don't lie and say that the shot won't hurt. Tell the truth with love and compassion. In this situation, visualization can be a very powerful tool to convey what the animal can expect.

Preparing an animal for a trip to the vet is not only humane but may also make any necessary treatment that much easier. I witnessed this firsthand when I brought my dog, Jessie, in to have a foxtail removed from her ear. When examining her, the vet found that the foxtail was lodged so deeply in the canal that he wanted to anesthetize Jessie before trying to remove it. Instead, I asked him to tell Jessie exactly what he was going to do, where he would be touching her, and what it would feel like, betting that if he did, sedation would not be necessary. Sure enough, minutes later, Jessie and the vet came into the waiting room—the doctor with a big smile on his face and Jessie with her tail wagging. The doctor told me that he couldn't believe it—Jessie had sat absolutely still while he extracted the foxtail without anesthesia. He had never before seen such a cooperative patient.

You may or may not feel comfortable asking your vet to talk with your animal. Rest assured that, with practice, your own communication with the animal can be just as effective.

THE DIAGNOSIS

Communication with your animal can be a tremendous aid in resolving the animal's problem. Many times, I've encountered animals with hard-to-detect conditions who were able to describe what ailed them well enough to me that a vet could administer proper treatment. As a loving and perceptive human, do not negate your own impressions of what may be wrong with your animal, even if you have no more evidence than "just knowing." Many vets will welcome any input you can give them. Some might be skeptical that you have obtained information directly from your animal. Don't shy away from sharing what you sense. It really doesn't matter what the vet, or anyone else, thinks. When an animal is sick, the goal is to assist the animal and help him feel better. You and your vet can work together as a team to provide care to the animal. The results will speak for themselves. Simply state the facts as you know them, to aid the doctor in his or her diagnosis and treatment. You don't need to say that you had a conversation with your dog if you don't want to. You can phrase the information in common terms, such as "I know his stomach doesn't feel very well. He is in a lot of pain and needs relief."

Hopefully, someday in the near future, veterinary schools will encompass alternative medicine and animal communication as part of their basic training. Many vets are already branching into these areas on their own.

Sometimes a person's intuition about what is wrong with an animal is as powerful a tool as the most sophisticated diagnostic tests. Brenda Bernhard, a dressage rider, called me because her horse, Corde, had been lame for an entire year. Top veterinarians had advised that Corde's trouble was in his back, but none of them had been able to correct it. When I asked Corde where he felt the problem was, he simply replied, "My shoulder."

"I knew it!" Brenda said. "That's what I've been trying to tell the vets, and they tell me it's his back." Because of her special bond and connection with her horse, she could sense where he was hurting. Corde then told me that Brenda even knew when he'd injured his shoulder—and Brenda confirmed that she did. A year earlier, she'd been taking him through some training exercises. He'd started to act tired and she wanted to stop, but she was advised by others to push him through it. She did, although it was against her better judgment, and shortly after, the horse became lame. Brenda knew Corde better than anyone, and she just needed to trust her own intuition.

Now feeling validated, Brenda took her horse to the UC-Davis School of Veterinary Medicine, where she insisted they do further testing on his shoulder. When they did, the vets confirmed that it was Corde's shoulder, not his back, that needed treatment. With the proper therapy, Corde is again enjoying his work with Brenda.

Some very common conditions, such as bladder infections in cats, are notoriously hard to diagnose. I've worked with many cats who are sent home with a clean bill of health yet complain of painful bladder irritations, for which spraying is often their only means of relief.

Jeanne Trobbe of Riverside, California called me regarding her five-year-old Himalayan cat, Capella who had been spraying in the house for two years. He had suffered from bladder infections and ulcers and was not interacting with the other cats. The spraying became so bad that they had to cage him most of the time. When I talked with Capella, he was quite uncomfortable and complained about his neck, spine, and pelvic area. He was not happy in his body, and the dry-food diet was not helping his constant bladder irritation.

Capella's bladder infections had been diagnosed, but never resolved. What went undetected by the vet in this case were Capella's structural problems. Luckily, Jeanne found a chiropractor who confirmed that the cat had problems with his neck, spine, and pelvic areas. Since he's received chiropractic adjustments, he's stopped spraying and roams the house freely once again. He is happier, more playful and active, and has become more affectionate.

Some trainers and vets may be quick to label undiagnosed ailments as psychosomatic. Behaviors such as aggressiveness, disobedience, bad attitude, or psychological imbalance can be a symptom of a body dysfunction and pain. We need to make sure we look at all possibilities.

Pauline of Albuquerque, New Mexico called me one day because her talented young Thoroughbred horse, Dash, was a physical and mental wreck. While he'd always been a joy to work with, in the last year he'd begun to bolt while being saddled, and he moved his head side to side constantly when in his stall. In Pauline's heart, she knew he was physically ailing, but the barn vet could not find the problem. The head trainer and owner of the center labeled him as a psychological problem horse.

When I tuned in to Dash, he was in such incredible discomfort and had so many aches and pains throughout his body that it was truly amazing he hadn't ever thrown a rider. He complained of pain in specific areas in his neck, shoulder, pelvis, and hips. Pauline called in two very competent and well-known vets, who were able to pinpoint these areas of pain and lameness. With chiropractic and acupuncture treatments, Dash was on his way to feeling reconnected to his body and to life again.

MONITORING PROGRESS

Once treatment has been prescribed for your animal, watch for signs to make sure that it is working. If your animal isn't getting better, the diagnosis might be incorrect. Keep checking with the animal to see how he feels. Ask him if the treatment is having a positive or negative effect, or no effect at all.

Jim, a student of mine, was concerned about his golden retriever, Sunny, named for her disposition. Lately, however, she had changed. She had stopped eating, moved very slowly, and had blood and mucus in her stools. She became lethargic, and Jim was worried about her lack of appetite. When he tuned in to Sunny, he kept getting the same message, over and over: "Parasites."

When Jim told the vet he thought his dog had parasites, she performed a routine checkup and made a diagnosis of allergies. She prescribed medication, but after continued treatment, Sunny grew worse. Jim decided to seek the opinion of a second veterinarian. When he explained about the parasites, the second vet advised Jim that the symptoms he described were usually not caused by parasites. Therefore, he also recommended treating Sunny for allergies.

With Sunny still showing no signs of improvement, Jim finally called me for help. One session with Sunny, and I confirmed Jim's original message: Sunny communicated "parasites" loud and clear. With this validation, Jim went back to the clinic and demanded the proper medication for parasites. Within one day, Sunny was back to her usual happy self, eating up a storm, and running around like a puppy. Animals know their own bodies, and we need to listen to them.

Be aware that some animals may be sensitive to prescribed medications and may suffer an overreaction.

When I was in Chicago doing a workshop, I did a house call with Kathleen Daniel and her Doberman, Sabrina. Sabrina had been very ill and under the care of four veterinarians, but none could diagnose her exact problem. Although she was on four different medications for a variety of maladies, Sabrina was extremely hyperactive, losing weight, unhappy, and unable to sleep. Kathleen was afraid that she might lose her.

Sabrina told me that she did not like her own behavior and was on so much medication that she was confused. She said she had pain in her neck and right hip. Kathleen confirmed her painful condition, showing me X rays that revealed a displaced disc and poor hips.

On her next visit to the vet, Kathleen requested that Sabrina's medication be reduced as much as possible. When asked why, she simply stated that Sabrina's behavior indicated the medication levels must be too high. Her veterinarian decided to run another battery of tests and agreed to her request. In about four weeks, Sabrina improved dramatically and is now much happier. She even looks different, with a weight gain of thirteen pounds. It seems many of her previous problems might have been induced by overmedication.

MAJOR TREATMENT DECISIONS

When it comes to making major decisions about the health care of your animals, you need to be as informed as possible. Ask the vet questions to make sure you fully understand the diagnosis, the treatment options, and the prognosis. If something does not feel right in your gut, step back from the situation, if only momentarily, to gain perspective. If you have the luxury of time, get a second opinion or do some research on the treatment options. An informed decision is always the best decision.

Involve your animals in decisions about their treatment, and ask if they even want assistance in the first place. In some cases, especially with very old or terminally ill animals, it's more humane to let them go with dignity. Whatever the situation, the animal will have definite preferences about his health care, and it will benefit him to be part of the process. Human patients who are actively involved in their own treatment—making decisions and feeling that they are not just passive "victims" of their illness—recover more quickly. Not surprisingly, the same is true of animals.

Had I not consulted with my elderly cat Scooter beforehand, it is unlikely that he would have survived surgery to remove the skin cancer he developed in one ear. When it was first diagnosed, I asked him whether he wanted to have the tumor removed, as had been suggested by most veterinarians. At the time, he said no—he just didn't feel up to it or have the energy for it. The vet's blood tests confirmed Scooter's instincts: His kidneys were functioning poorly.

Two years passed, during which time Scooter was treated with acupuncture, herbs, homeopathy, and other modes of alternative medicine. The time came to reconsider surgery for his tumor, which was growing worse. This time Scooter said, "Take it off." He had the energy to face the operation and felt optimistic about it. But he was now eighteen years old—quite aged to be undergoing surgery—so the doctor ran a series of blood tests to see if Scooter was strong enough. The results amazed her. "I should have trusted you guys," she told me. "His blood test is better than it has ever been; it's better than it was two years ago. Obviously, Scooter knows his body well!"

Scooter not only survived the operation but also surprised everyone with his speedy recovery. When I visited him after the surgery, his chief complaint about the experience was that his age seemed to be a big deal to everyone at the hospital. When I talked with the vet techs who were taking care of him, they told me how thrilled they were that Scooter was doing so well, being such an old man of eighteen. Scooter had obviously picked up on that and proved, once again, that animals do listen to our thoughts!

ALTERNATIVE MEDICINE

Western medicine is no longer the only treatment available to humans or animals. As alternative treatments gain popularity in the human population, more people are trying them with their animals. More treatments than ever, from traditional to cutting edge, are becoming available to our animals. If your vet has recommended surgery or other invasive therapies for your animal and it's not an immediate life-or-death situation, investigate the options available before going to those extremes. Know that surgery is an option, but see if other means of treatment might be successful. If not, you can always choose to go with the traditional therapy, as I did in Scooter's case. Many vets are exploring and implementing alternative treatments within their clinics. Enlightened vets are open to what works for the animal rather than simply what was taught in the classroom. Sometimes they cure animals with alternative methods when Western medicine has failed. Moreover, there is no reason in the world why all forms of medicine can't work together to provide the best solutions.

BODYWORK AND ENERGY WORK

Touch is important to everyone, including animals. The warmth, the tenderness, the love and intimacy conveyed by your touch are not only comforting but, with training, can be very healing. Several forms of bodywork are now available for animals, including massage, acupressure, and others. (Refer to the Resources section for more information.)

One method that I find works particularly well for animals is called Tellington TTouch and was derived from a human form of bodywork called Feldenkrais. Linda Tellington-Jones developed this therapy in which the practitioner gently works with the animal's body, slowly, easily, and with no pain. As Diane Stein writes in her book, *Natural Healing for Dogs & Cats: This is a method that opens new neurological pathways to the brain by use of non-habitual movements. [It] works wonders for modifying negative behaviors, taming wild or unsocialized animals gently, increasing trust and reducing aggressiveness, and for healing.*

Tellington-Jones also created a focusing technique called "labyrinth" or "ground work." By walking an animal through a series of ground poles in various patterns and asking him to perform in certain ways—"Take one step forward," "Walk backward," "Stop walking"—the animal learns to concentrate, focus, and use his mind rather than react according to old patterns. Labyrinth work is also helpful for rehabilitation after an animal has been injured or suffered neurological damage.

You may choose to find an alternative-therapy practitioner in your area if you feel that's what your animal needs. Even without training, you can do some light bodywork with your animals. For instance, if you'd like to give your animal a nurturing massage, use your intuition to guide you. He will appreciate the attention and the therapeutic benefits and will help you know where he needs your touch. While massage may be appropriate at certain times, a lighter touch or energy work might be more beneficial in another situation.

A few years ago I was called out to help a horse who had been given just about every vaccination imaginable, all at one time. The horse was so sick he couldn't tolerate being touched. I decided he needed some energy work to help his body process all of the drugs. Instead of putting my hands directly onto his body, I held my hands a few inches away from him and stroked the area above his body, always moving his energy in a downward motion to ground him. Within two hours of my leaving the barn, the horse was alert, eating, and out of his stupor.

There are some simple, basic things you can do to help balance your animal's energy flow. Obviously, it takes years of training and devotion to become a professional in this field, but try these exercises to help your animal feel a little more comfortable when he is out of sorts. I'll share with you how to feel for the energy flow of an animal's body, then how to check for imbalances, and, finally, in simplified terms, how to rebalance the energy flow.

ENERGY-BALANCING TECHNIQUE

You've already experienced the important component of this exercise when you did the Feeling Energy exercise in Chapter 4, rubbing your hands together and feeling your life energy between them.

1. Sit in a comfortable chair with your animal in the room, and relax using a meditation or simple breathing exercises. When you have found your still point, rub your hands together until you generate heat between them. When they feel hot, pull your hands about six inches apart with palms facing each other. Then pull your hands farther apart and back together without touching, like playing an accordion. Keep doing this until you feel energy between your hands. Remember, it may feel like a slight tingling sensation, a sense of warmth or heat, or as if there's a magnetic pull between your hands. You can exaggerate the feeling by cupping your hands and moving them in a circular motion like pedaling a bicycle or moving them around an imaginary ball.

2. Ask the animal for permission before you touch his body. Ask if he wants your assistance, and if so, tell him you will work with him as a true partner. You want the animal to feel that this is being done *with* his cooperation, rather than *to* him.

3. Without actually touching the animal, hold your hands a few inches away from him. Starting at his head, move down to the neck, back, and tail. Next, move down the side of the head, shoulder, and front leg. Then run your hands from the shoulder

along the side of the body to the hip and down the back leg. What do you feel under your hands? Just as you felt energy in your partner's cotton balls in the exercise in Chapter 4, you will experience your animal's energy. If you feel that nothing is happening, it can mean that the energy is blocked or stagnant in that area. If you feel extreme or excessive energy, that part of the body may have too much energy. You might even feel a cool sensation, which can mean a loss of circulation, or blocked energy in that area. When you have moved your hands over his entire body, you should have a good indication of where the energy might be blocked, where there is too much energy, and where there is a loss of circulation.

4. Now you will use similar movements to balance the animal's energy. Continue to move your hands over him, but this time with the intention of helping to balance the energy flow. Your goal is to make the energy even throughout the body. Slowly move your hands over the body, making sure that you are always moving the energy downward. Start at the head, moving to the neck, back, and tail. Next do the side of the head, the shoulder, and down the front leg; then from the shoulder, along the side of the body to the hip, and down the back leg.

Keep repeating these movements until you can feel that sense of warmth, heat, tingling, or magnetic pull you originally felt between your hands. When you feel an evenness of energy throughout the animal's body, you're done.

The animal may exhibit signs of relaxation while you are doing energy work. He might lick his lips, yawn, or fall fast asleep. If he begins to twitch, that's okay too. That's just his central nervous system realigning itself.

Work with the animal as long as you feel is appropriate—any amount of time up to one hour. It's best if the animal doesn't do any strenuous exercise afterward, which would be like having a wonderful massage and then running a 10K race. Allow the animal to relax. To reenergize yourself, wash your hands with cool water, drink plenty of water, and/or enjoy a relaxing bath or invigorating shower, depending on your own energy level.

You can also perform muscle testing on your animal to ascertain if he has food allergies, if an herb or a flower essence would be beneficial for him, or if an area of the body is uncomfortable or weak. It's a procedure as simple as the energy work described on the previous page, and if you're interested in trying it, I recommend the book *Natural Healing for Dogs & Cats* by Diane Stein. Refer to the chapter "Flower Essences & Muscle Testing for Pets." She supplies a complete description of the process and its benefits.

ACUPUNCTURE AND CHIROPRACTIC TREATMENTS

As many of my stories have already illustrated, acupuncture and chiropractic treatments work wonders on many animals, especially when they have been previously misdiagnosed or have undetected illnesses.

Karey Pohn of Encinitas, California called me regarding her nine-year-old Great Dane, Brenda, who had experienced stomach problems for almost two years and had endured two surgeries and two lavage procedures for bloat in less than a month. Now the vets were worried that she also had heart problems. After a series of X rays, an EKG, endoscopy, and blood tests, they found no problem with her heart, although she did have anemia and blood in her stools. After $4,200 and two blood transfusions, Brenda was released, although they still didn't know what was wrong with her. Brenda was listless and started having trouble going up stairs.

When I talked with Brenda, I could feel that the area around her withers was blocked and I sensed that many of her organs were not receiving the proper signals. I recommended that Karey take her to a chiropractor and an acupuncturist. The chiropractor also noticed that Brenda was sunken in the area of the withers, which governs the heart and lungs. After spinal adjustments and some acupuncture, Brenda was a different animal, with a spring in her step again, chasing and playing with the other dogs. How incredible after all the invasive procedures she had received did nothing to relieve her symptoms.

ANIMAL COMMUNICATORS IN HEALING

Some people are so perplexed by their animals' illness or behavior that they don't know where to turn. Usually, they first seek a veterinarian or trainer's help and then exhaust themselves going through a process of elimination of what it may or may not be. If no results or answers are found, many people turn to animal communicators. In the following case, no one thought this animal's problem was physical. They assumed it was all in the horse's head. Only when I learned what was actually going on with him and conveyed that information to his trainer were we able to help the animal, and his people, find success.

Nicholas, a racehorse from a well-known racetrack, was cocking his head to the left during races, causing him to lose by a nose. Obviously, his trainer and owners were anxious to fix the problem. If Nicholas could run with his head straight, he would win. They had all rallied around, guessing what could be wrong, deciding that he must be afraid of the flags and banners in the grandstand. Why else would he pull his head away?

According to Nicholas, it wasn't that at all. He wasn't afraid: He was in excruciating pain. His neck hurt so much that he had to run holding his head to the inside. In order to relieve the pain, bodywork was an essential part of the solution. When I touched the point where the pain was concentrated, he turned his head with teeth bared. I told him that I understood how bad the pain was, but that if he trusted me and allowed me to work with him, he would feel relief. As I put my hands on him again, he looked at me with great trepidation, and then slowly, as the energy began to settle into his neck, he lowered his head nearly to the ground. He was greatly relieved and thankful for the help. Everyone else was just as relieved and elated when he crossed the finish line in first place, head straight forward, making them thousands of dollars happier.

Animal communicators do not have the ability to diagnose, but we have the ability to find out exactly how the animal is feeling, which can help a veterinarian fine-tune his diagnosis and set a new course of treatment. When your animal seems ill or is acting unusual, always check with a medical professional first to rule out any physical malady. I often recommend specific veterinarians who are willing to receive information on behalf of the animal. Dr. Nancy Scanlan of Sherman Oaks, California, is this kind of vet, and she wrote to me, *Your work really helps me out with my cases. It can supply the missing information I need to round out a diagnosis and to help fine-tune a treatment.*

As you've discovered in your own hands-on experience, it is most beneficial to assume a sense of partnership with animals when it comes to the healing process. Their voices are usually the missing link. How many times have you heard vets say or said yourself, "If only animals could talk." With your telepathic skills, your animal's voice can contribute to the solution.

10

Facing Death with Animals

The relationships we share with our animal companions are often unmatched. Animals support us emotionally and spiritually—and people who are physically challenged may rely on them for physical guidance as well. Their unconditional love envelops us like a security blanket, helping us through good times and bad. The reality that seems dreadfully unfair is that their life span is shorter than ours, making it inevitable that one day we will have to cope with their death.

Let me show you how a little research, preparation, and telepathic communication can make the passing of your animal a more gentle, less fearful, and respectful transition. Some of the ideas and concepts in this chapter may be new to you; they may challenge the way you were raised, or your belief system. I like to think that there is a loving universal thread that can weave together our many points of view. My intent in this chapter is merely to share with you what the animals have revealed to me.

It is interesting that our society terms the day we take our last breath and leave our physical bodies as "death." I believe there is no death, only transition to another stage of living. However, since death is the term we are familiar with, I use it throughout the book. As Neale Donald Walsch says in his book, *Conversations with God: An Uncommon Dialogue, Book 3:*

> *Everything is always alive. There is no such thing as "dead." There is no such state of being. That which is always alive simply shapes itself into a new form—a new physical form. That form is charged with living energy, the energy of life, always.*

The death of loved ones is a natural and painful "passage" we expect to face in life, and the loss of an animal companion can present special challenges. Until the time comes, few people even know what to do with an animal's remains and what burial, cremation, or other options are available. Many of us will be confronted with the decision to end an animal's life, which is a profound responsibility. Very often, the loss of an animal will be the first death our children experience, compelling us to grapple with our own complicated feelings in order to explain and comfort them. And when animals leave their bodies, there are no established grieving rituals, leaving us without the personal and spiritual comfort and social support that we count on when we lose human companions. The death of an animal is a loss that most of us feel we will have to shoulder alone.

Fortunately, however, we don't have to—our animals can help by participating in the difficult decision-making process. Because they are more attuned than we are to the rhythms of nature, they are more accepting of the inevitability of death (which is not to suggest that death comes easily to any living creature). We owe it to them, as well as to ourselves, to prepare mindfully—overcoming denial, dealing with our grief, and making appropriate arrangements—so that we can openheartedly support them in leaving with dignity.

HOW ANIMALS VIEW DEATH

For people, death is the greatest unknown, and it is fear of this un-known that causes such pain. This pain may be especially acute for those who believe there is no life after death. Those who believe they have souls that continue to live on after death—or that even return lifetime after lifetime—often can take comfort from seeing life as an eternal cycle. As Albert Einstein said, "You cannot kill energy. Life is not the beginning nor is death the end."

Animals have no fear of death. They understand and expect the natural rhythms of life, including their own dying.

This poem was written by Patricia N. Olson, D.V.M., Ph.D., Director of Training Operations at Guide Dogs for the Blind, Inc., and was given to me by a client at one of my workshops. I believe it eloquently communicates how animals view death. (Let the word *God* in the poem refer to whatever your belief is in a higher being.)

And God asked the feline spirit
Are you ready to come home?
Oh, yes, quite so, replied the precious soul
And, as a cat, you know I am most able
To decide anything for myself

Are you coming then? asked God
Soon, replied the whiskered angel
But I must come slowly
For my human friends are troubled
For you see, they need me, quite certainly

But don't they understand? asked God
That you'll never leave them?
That your souls are intertwined? For all eternity?
That nothing is created or destroyed?
It just is . . . forever and ever and ever

Eventually they will understand,
Replied the glorious cat
For I will whisper into their hearts
That I am always with them
I just am . . . forever and ever and ever

When I talk with animals about death, it is apparent that they have souls. Among the images animals have sent me to explain death are a jacket unzipping and a sweater unbuttoning—implying that passing from one realm to the next is as easy as shedding clothes. And, just as many believe is true for humans, some animals choose to reincarnate if they have a reason for returning to the physical world.

Many of the communications I receive from animals regarding death reflect concern for their human companions. Animals take their responsibilities to their families so seriously that they often keep themselves alive, even when in great pain, until they know their people are emotionally ready to let them go.

I witnessed this intense devotion in Ozzie, Valorie Kleiman's seventeen-year-old Lhasa apso. He had back problems, could not walk, was eating very little, and was incontinent. The veterinarian warned Valorie that Ozzie's illness was degenerative and that the family should consider putting him down. Valorie then called me to help determine Ozzie's feelings in the matter. The family wanted to honor his wishes.

When I first met Ozzie, he was lying on the bed and looked as if he were already dead. I put my hand beneath his body to raise him a little and he flopped right back down, too weak to hold himself up. Valorie told me her friends thought she was being selfish, keeping Ozzie alive when he clearly needed to be put out of his misery. I was thinking the same thing, but when I asked him, "Are you ready to go?" he told me emphatically, "No, I'm not done with my job."

Using the energy-work technique described in Chapter 9, I

went over his body with my hands and discovered that his energy was profoundly imbalanced. To make him more comfortable, I showed Valorie how she could rebalance his body energy every day. Because she was so in tune with Ozzie, she caught on immediately. As she worked on him, Valorie told me that she had suffered a stroke the previous year, which had left her partially paralyzed. She'd had to learn to walk again and still dragged the left side of her body. That's why Ozzie wasn't ready to leave, I realized, and a quick check with him confirmed it. He wasn't going to abandon the person he loved until she was fully recovered. He wanted to be by her side to give her strength and encouragement, since he had been her guiding light all these years.

My visit was on a Thursday, and by Sunday Valorie called me to say that a miracle had occurred—Ozzie was running around the backyard, eating regularly, and waiting at the door, wagging his tail, every time they came home. No one could believe that this was the same Ozzie, the dog who had very nearly been euthanized— which demonstrates why it is so important to consult with an animal to determine whether his time has come. Ozzie lived for one more year, and by then he and his family were truly ready to let go with love.

PREPARING YOURSELVES

How we face death is just as important as how we face life. Every day we are faced with choices and challenges that shape our character. The transition from physical body into spirit is perhaps our toughest challenge, but in facing it, we can be transformed.

That said, it's still difficult to accept symptoms of old age or a diagnosis we don't want to hear, whether for ourselves or for our loved ones, human or animal. The most common first reaction is denial: the choice not to deal with it at all. The problem is, if you don't accept the fact that your animal is ailing, when his time comes you will not be ready. Because you haven't prepared, you will act without forethought, in a state of panic, overwhelmed by emotions and shock. There will be too much to consider, too many decisions to make in one day, and too many emotions and feelings to express.

By preparing yourself ahead of time in both emotional and practical matters surrounding the imminent passing of your animal, you can spend more quality time with your animal during his final weeks or days. You will be able to talk with your animal, get a sense of his wishes and how to honor him, and be supportive and nurturing to him. When the time comes to say good-bye, you will feel a sense of completeness and be ready to deal with your pain and grief.

Here are some ways to approach this process with open eyes and an open heart.

1. Be willing to recognize that your animal is ailing and needs help. (This issue is discussed more fully in the section "Judging Whether an Animal's Time Has Come.") Make sure you feel confident about the diagnosis and treatment you are given by your veterinarian. If not, seek a second or third opinion.

2. Discuss the situation with your family. Each of you has different needs concerning the passing of your animal friend, so it is important that each family member be heard. The death of an animal is often the first death a child will experience. Therefore, it is important that the death be treated as a natural part of life.

   You may want to develop some type of ritual for saying good-bye, including viewing old photos or movies of your animal, lighting a special candle every evening, or working as a family to create a scrapbook of the animal's life. Ask your animal for input in this matter; perhaps he'll ask that you have a party after his burial, or, be laid to rest with his favorite blanket. These suggestions and more are discussed in the section "Preparation with Your Animals."

3. Research euthanasia procedures, in case it should become necessary to help your animal leave his body. Your vet will be able to explain what is involved and what options you have (see

"Questions to Ask About Euthanasia"). With your animal's input, you may elect to have the procedure take place at the vet's clinic or at home with your family on hand. Again, it is important that each family member have the chance to share his or her feelings and preference about euthanasia.

4. Investigate your options in making the final arrangements for your animal. Discuss anything you are uncertain about with your veterinarian. In the Resources section, you'll find books and organizations to help you locate pet cemeteries and crematories, cremation information, and catalogs providing memorials and inspired gifts for your animals once they have passed on.

5. Now may be the time to come to terms with your belief system concerning death. Many organizations provide information about pet loss, grieving, and coping with euthanasia decisions. There are pet-loss support groups and even a Pet Loss Hotline. See the resources listed in the back of this book.

QUESTIONS TO ASK ABOUT EUTHANASIA

- What are the methods available for euthanasia? Most often, animals receive an injection and are gone within a few seconds. You may opt to have your animal receive a tranquilizer first, allowing additional time to say your final good-byes. This method can lessen fear and discomfort and allow for an atmosphere of dignity and gentleness for the animal and family. Ask the vet which method he or she recommends and why. Be sure to get full details—the kind of drug that might be given, the way it is administered, the animal's likely reaction—so you and your family can make an informed decision. Then choose the method that feels most comfortable to you and express your wishes to the doctor.

- Where will the procedure take place? (Know if your animal has a preference. Is she willing to go the vet's office, or would she like the vet to come to your home?) Is your vet willing to come to your home to euthanize your animal, or is there a mobile vet service in your area? Will the vet bring an assistant or come alone? If the veterinarian travels without a helper, he or she might ask for your assistance. Ask what will be needed from you, if anything.

- Can your family be present during the procedure? If this is important to you, make sure that the vet is aware of your wishes and willing to accommodate you. He might want to schedule the procedure for you after office hours, when there is more room and privacy for your family. Ask also what happens in an emergency. Some vets prefer not to have you present during lifesaving efforts or unplanned euthanasia. It is essential to make sure—ahead of time—that your vet has a policy you can accept. There is nothing more devastating than to want to be with your animal and not be allowed to when she takes her last breath.

     You may prefer not to be in the room during the procedure. While I think all beings deserve to have loved ones near them at their time of death, this is a very personal decision. You can spend time with your animal beforehand to say good-bye, then keep communicating telepathically with her after you've left the room. Send her images of the wonderful place she's going. Encircle her with a lovely white light and send her to a place of peace. Most veterinarians and their staff are dedicated to seeing that your animal experiences a peaceful death. Talk with your vet about this if you choose not to stay with the animal during euthanasia.

- What are the options for the animal's remains? They may include home burial if permitted by your city, cemetery burial, and individual or communal cremation. Ask your vet what each involves. Be sure to discuss any sanitary precautions you should be aware of. Again, ask for full details, including the means by which the animal can be transported and who will handle the arrangements. Once you have made the decision, choose whether you want to be physically in charge of handling your animal's body or have someone else, such as a family member or friend, do it.

JUDGING WHETHER AN ANIMAL'S TIME HAS COME

Death is more a process than an event, and the animal will withdraw from life in stages. How can you know when his or her time has come? Many of us find this time troubling, because while an animal may seem incapacitated, he can still be loving, emotionally alert, and seemingly happy. Or the animal may be so out of it that he seems to have one foot in the spirit world and one foot in this world. How do you know when an animal needs assistance leaving this world? You won't feel comfortable making such an important decision until you're certain it's the right one. The following information about the signs of decline in an animal were developed with advice and input from Dr. Tina Ellenbogen, a veterinarian who specializes in geriatrics and hospice care for animals.

When people perceive that an animal is in extreme pain, or can't walk, or is incontinent, they often assume the animal's quality of life is gone and that it is time to put the animal down. Dr. Ellenbogen advises us to stop at this point and get a reality check. Don't immediately assume these problems are part of the dying process. They could very well be treatable. Make sure the animal receives a thorough checkup from your vet.

For instance, Dr. Ellenbogen says that it is possible for cats with chronic renal failure to live for years. At that stage of the disease, toxin levels in the body are usually high, which makes the animal feel he is in a fog. He may exhibit signs of wobbliness or senility. He needs a gentle reminder and a soft touch to bring him back to reality. She suggests keeping these cats in a safe place so no harm comes to them.

Similarly, cats with hyperthyroidism often howl at night as if they're disoriented. If you take the time to reorient them, they're okay. Animals with chronic but not fatal diseases do require more care.

When your vet confirms that an animal is in the end stages or has an untreatable and incapacitating condition (and you've received a corroborating opinion from another vet, if that's your choice), it's time to check with the animal, telepathically, about what your next step should be. Specific questions to ask appear later in this chapter under "Preparation with Your Animals."

SIGNS OF DECLINE

Animals who are in physical decline usually sleep more. Their appetite might lessen and their body might feel cooler to the touch. Their breathing can become labored or irregular, and they can even become restless, agitated, more vocal, or confused. They have good days and bad days. When going through this transition with your animal, you will need to take each day as it comes.

In evaluating treatment and lifesaving methods, it is important to consider how much time you will gain for the animal versus the quality of that time. Consider your animal's comfort, dignity, and wishes. Is the procedure sensible and respectful to him?

As the animal's systems begin to fail, the body will eventually have to release itself from this world. Now is not the time for self-recriminations: What if I had known about that new medication? What if I had taken her to the vet sooner? What if, what if, what if? At this point, this much is certain: If it's time for your animal to leave, you do not have the power to stop what is meant to be. No medication, procedure, or magic can stop the process if your animal is ready to die. The time will come to put aside radical and invasive procedures and focus directly on making your animal as comfortable as possible with "supportive" treatment.

The best way to know whether it is an animal's time to go is to ask him. This is a time when your telepathic skills are essential, both for your own clarity and peace of mind and to help you honor your animal's wishes. You will need to ask the animal questions to determine the seriousness of her physical distress and pain level. Does the animal want further medical treatment or other assistance to feel better? Or does she feel ready to go into the spirit world? Be specific in your questioning. You want to know, in detail, how her body feels.

To provide a glimpse into what animals' thought processes are around their leaving, here are some direct messages from animals to their people, which I facilitated.

I'm mad at my body for breaking down. I'm not ready to go by any stretch of the imagination. I want to wait until my body feels like a rubber band that has been stretched to the fullest before snapping and disconnecting.

My body is failing, but I'm still so here. Take me as far as you can take me. I really won't be leaving you. I am so tied to you, like a clothespin on a clothesline. You can have a party if you'd like, but only to toast to my good life.

I feel very sleepy at times and heavy-like. I just can't get up sometimes. I need help getting up. You're used to my moans and groans. I love you dearly. We're like sisters. I won't be able to stay much longer because it's just becoming too dark and too heavy. I'd like to go on my own and know that it's okay.

Don't you still like my face and how pretty I am? We're both so soft and gentle. I do not like what's going on with my body, because I want to be with you. We're such great pals. The part I don't like is the breathing and the pressure I feel around my throat area, like I'm drowning. I don't like that. I'm willing to go through this for as long as it is doable. When it's time, I'm not sure my body will just drift off. I believe you will have to help me. I'm okay going to the vet for that.

PREPARATION WITH YOUR ANIMALS

When you have done everything you can for the animal and made him as comfortable as possible, it's time to talk with him about the inevitable—his leaving. It may well be the most difficult thing you've ever done, but by checking in with your animal about his wishes, his feelings, and his needs around dying, you honor him and the life you've had together.

Sit quietly with the animal, wherever he is most comfortable. You will feel sad, but that's okay; your animal will feel your love and concern. Take a moment to do some deep breathing or a meditation. Find your still point, then open your heart to the animal and feel that connection. Sit with that feeling for a while. When you feel ready, ask him the following questions so that you can help him through this transition gently and with love and compassion.

- I need to know when you're ready to go. What sign will you give me to let me know?
- Do you feel you will be able to leave on your own, or will you need assistance? If the animal needs assistance, then ask how the animal wants this to happen. Sometimes an animal may have very specific and definite plans for the way he wants to leave.
- Should the procedure take place at the veterinarian's clinic? If so, what can I bring along to make the setting more comfortable—your favorite blanket, toys?
- Would you prefer to be at home? And where? He might want to be outdoors under his special tree rather than indoors.
- Whom do you want to be present? He might want all the family members there, or he may request only his favorite person. Very often, animals will ask to have the chance to bid farewell to other animal friends as well as humans.

Then you will need to know what your animal's wishes are regarding the final resting place of his body. Now that you know the options available, it's time to be specific with him.

- Do you want your body left at the veterinarian's clinic? That might be okay with him. You need to ask.
- Would you prefer to be buried? Where? Be specific with your questioning. He might want to be buried under the tree near your bedroom window or near the bench where you often sit. If home burials are not permitted, would he like a place in a cemetery?

One of my clients planned to bury her cat, Mr. Whiskers, at her second home in the country, but the cat was adamantly opposed. He kept telling me that she really needed to rethink the plan, for she would feel as if he was too far away from her. He insisted she would eventually regret having buried him there. After such a persuasive argument, my client had to agree.

- Do you want to be cremated? If so, what do you want done with your ashes? Believe me, animals often have very specific preferences. One dog wanted some of her ashes sprinkled on a particular tree in the backyard, some spread around the property, but most of them put in a stuffed beanie animal that looked just like her so that her person could have her near wherever she went. Another animal wanted her person to put some of her ashes in a locket and wear it around her neck, close to her heart. A cat wanted her ashes sprinkled in the garden soil so she could be part of the colorful flowers and plants in order to remind her person of the beauty and continuity of life.

These animals recognized that they would no longer be physically present, but wanted to be there symbolically; they felt it would help their people feel happier. Even after death, animals want to help in any way they can.

Just as people do, animals fully expect to have a say in how their death occurs—so much so, as my client Sallie Dettra learned, that they go to great lengths to make their wishes known.

Sallie was worried when her eighteen-year-old long-haired tabby named Martha began to yowl in her sleep and at inexplicable times during the day. Fearing that the cat was in great pain, Sallie took her to the vet, who could find no physical cause. Still, the yowling persisted until finally Sallie, who had taken my workshop but was skeptical, decided to ask Martha straight out what was wrong. She couldn't believe what she heard.

"You're going to let me die alone!" Martha said. At first Sallie was baffled, but then she remembered talking to a friend about how much she loved Martha and how she could never face taking her to the vet if she ever had to put Martha down. Sallie realized that Martha had overheard the entire conversation and was now demanding that Sallie be present at her passing. She promised Martha that when the time came she would indeed be there, but asked Martha how she would know when that time had come. Martha assured Sallie that she would know and that she would inform her. Once Martha had made her wishes known, the yowling stopped.

Some months later, Martha announced to Sallie, "I'm tired and I want to go. Will you be okay?" After Sallie reassured her that she could manage the transition, Martha made one more request. She wanted to say good-bye to all her animal friends in the household. With Sallie holding her, Martha greeted them one by one: Matthew, the Australian shepherd, came up to present Martha with his toy and kiss her good-bye. Then Zeke, the cockatiel, flew over to Sallie's knee and gave Martha a farewell kiss, as did Daniel, the African Grey parrot. Miriam, the English black-hooded rat, stood up on her hind legs and licked Martha's nose. Then, at Martha's request, Sallie took her out to see her rabbit friend, Harvey, so they could touch noses and say their good-byes.

Then Sallie heard Martha say, "I'm ready." Cradling her in a blanket, Sallie took her to the vet's, promising to hold her as she drew her last breath. As the doctor administered the shot, Martha looked up into Sallie's eyes with serenity and peacefulness. Even Sallie's vet could feel their loving exchange and said, "Something very unusual and special has just happened here." And it had— Sallie felt completion in her relationship with Martha and was grateful that she had been able to honor the last wishes of her long-time friend.

SAYING GOOD-BYE

By now you've prepared yourself, your family, and your animal for these last moments to make the process as painless as possible. With practicalities out of the way, you can now honor this last phase of your animal's life by:

- Respecting his wishes
- Loving him enough to let him go
- Bidding him a beautiful journey as you say your last good-bye

One of the most important aspects of your good-bye will be emotionally releasing your animal, consciously freeing him from feeling obligated to stay. One of my clients says she has never had to euthanize any of her cats. She is so comfortable with the dying process that when she knows their time is nearing, she extends her gratitude for sharing their lives with her and gives them permission to leave. Her cats are then free to leave on their own when they are ready. The process is handled with grace, dignity, and gratitude.

When you tell an animal it's okay for them to go, however, you must mean it. If you do not feel it in your heart, the animal may pick up on your confusion and know that you are not ready for him to leave. He may stay on much longer than need be because he doesn't want to see you suffer. In my experience, animals would rather endure pain themselves than inflict it on their people.

My cat Soleil, who was the first animal with whom I learned to communicate, continued to teach me until the end of her life. She taught me everything I know regarding the death and dying process, including how to say good-bye. I had never experienced the death of an animal before hers, and the lessons she offered me were invaluable and will live on within me until I, too, take my last breath.

She had been ill for some time and was slowly withdrawing from this world, taking longer naps and eating less food. One night she couldn't make it up onto the bed. I knew that her time was very near, so I decided to make a bed for myself on the living room floor near her. I wanted to be as close to her as possible, physically and emotionally, until she was ready to leave.

I knew from asking her that her pain was steadily increasing and that she was going to need some assistance in leaving this world. All of the steps you have read up to this point in the chapter are the exact steps I followed in preparing for Soleil's departure. I researched the technical aspects of death, I asked what her feelings and needs were about leaving, and I asked her whether she wanted to be buried or cremated. She chose to be buried. I lived on a large ranch in the country, and she told me she wanted to be buried next to the horses' pasture where I spent a good deal of time. That way she could continue to keep an eye on the ranch. More important, she said that as she lay at rest in her favorite place, I would be reminded of the love we shared for the past sixteen years. Soleil asked to be buried wrapped in soft white cotton, strewn with fresh pink rose petals, and topped by a heart-shaped rose quartz crystal—all items that are symbols of love.

Having prepared ourselves, Soleil and I could spend our final days together saying good-bye. As we lay together on the living room floor, I reminisced about all the adventures, laughs, and tender moments we had shared. I told Soleil how my life had been enriched by being with her for all those years and how she had been such a grand teacher for me. I described all the lessons I learned about life, about myself, and about love from her. This is such an important part of the process—communicating how your animal has enriched your life—for it gives him or her a sense of satisfaction and relief. It allows your animal to think "I did a good job. Now I can go in peace, knowing that my person will be okay."

As I reminisced, I would cry and feel overwhelmed with sadness from time to time. I explained why I was so sad and that the sadness would continue to come and go for a while, assuring Soleil that I would be okay. I told her I was sad because, even though I knew her soul would live on, I wouldn't be able to stroke her or hold her anymore, or see her beautiful face, or just be with her physically.

The next step I took may not make sense to everyone, but it was important for me. I wanted to be sure that I would be able to communicate with Soleil once she was in the spirit world. To do so, I wanted to know how to feel her presence once she was out of her physical body. During our last few nights together, I sat with Soleil and felt the essence of who she was without her physical form. I would shut my eyes to feel and sense her energy as best I could, training myself to recognize her if she came back in spirit form. What did Soleil feel like? Every individual being—every flower, every tree, every human and animal—is unique and different, so each of my animals' energies feels different to me. Soleil felt light and fluffy and was surrounded by light pink energy. She even chose to be buried with rose petals and a pink, heart-shaped crystal, confirming that pink was an expression of her core essence.

Later in this chapter, I will discuss in more detail the process of contacting an animal in the spirit world or, in some cases, in his or her reincarnated form. Again, not everyone will accept this idea, but I encourage you to try it if you're curious. Wouldn't it be nice, once your animal has left his body, to feel his presence? Learning to sense your animal's unique energy will help you know for sure that the fluttering feeling around your neck is indeed your animal sending her love to you or that the thump on the bed is your little guy coming back to assure you he is okay and still looking after you.

At last, the day came when Soleil was ready to leave. As we had planned ahead of time, she was euthanized in my home. I emotionally released her so she could enter the spirit world with dignity, gracefulness, and serenity. I remained with her during the process and for a while afterward, until I sensed that her spirit had left her body. While I'm not sure that this feels the same for everyone, what I sensed with Soleil was an overall feeling of lightness. I felt her energy flow from her body and drift upward in a light and airy way. I could see a light like a rainbow move upward, and I sensed her feelings of freedom and relief as she was released from her body.

Though I grieved, I was also grateful that I had witnessed Soleil's passage into a world where she could return to wholeness. To me, an animal's passing is one of the bravest moments demanded from a human being. Learning to love your animal enough to let him go is the biggest lesson of all. Jean Foster wrote this appropriate and touching poem about this sad moment.

> I was young!
> I ran like the wind and
> The world glistened, fresh and new
> With each season.
> Colorful leaves raced across the lawn,
> Crisp and elusive.
> Snow flakes danced in howling winds,
> But winter posed no threat.
> I was young!
> Each season blended into the next,
> And each displayed its beauty.
> The years passed.
> Your joys were mine, as were your sorrows.
> Our love grew in understanding and
> I served you faithfully.
> Now, out of your love for me
> I ask your courage.
> I am old!
> My sight has dimmed.
> I no longer greet each season with joy.
> I cannot run and my body knows pain.
> So have the wisdom, dear friend, out of love,
> To bid me farewell, and send me on my way
> With dignity.

And cherish each season we shared,
For they are eternity.

DUCHESS
December 28, 1970
September 6, 1984

by Jean Foster

COMMEMORATIONS

When loved ones die, it's helpful to choose some way in which to commemorate them. This is as true with our animal companions as it is with human friends and family. One option is to keep a special memento of your animal. Remember the dog who asked that his ashes be placed in a locket for his person to wear close to her heart? Animals often suggest the keepsakes they feel their humans need to remember them. Animals might recommend their people wear their identification tags as necklaces or their collars as bracelets. One cat asked his person to have a ceremony and vow to take care of herself as he had done. She was to keep this promise by wearing a simple ring to acknowledge their special friendship.

One day a woman called me because her mare was near death and she wanted some of the horse's mane as a memento. She had been thinking about it for days but was uncomfortable clipping the mane because she feared it would be too invasive. The mare must have picked up on her thoughts. When I connected with her, she communicated that her person was welcome to snip some hair from her mane and tail. The woman now treasures her beloved horse's parting gift.

One of my dearest animal friends, a dachshund named Quackers, recently left Elaine Seamans, one of my dearest human friends, who owns a gift business.

The first time I met Quackers, I was working with her and Elaine on her howling problem when left alone. Quackers started our conversation by asking if I thought she had a pretty nose. Elaine assured me this was of great importance to her—it was the first thing most people mentioned upon meeting her. She was a dear little dog, unfortunately with a bigger problem than howling. She had liver cancer. We continued to work together because Elaine wanted to make certain she was in tune with Quackers's well-being. Elaine even attended some of my workshops, and although she was progressing with her own telepathic abilities, when Quackers's time drew near, she wanted reassurance and support. She did not want to have any regrets about decisions that might have to be made.

During this period, Quackers was very specific with me about her wishes when it came time for her to leave. She asked that Elaine make sure she smelled good and that her body be placed in a white box with beautiful white fabric. She wanted Elaine to be surrounded by white flowers and candles to symbolize the eternal flame of their love. Quackers said their communication would be stronger since Elaine would no longer be distracted by her physical body.

Quackers also kept showing me images of photographs of herself hanging side by side in Elaine's house. She said these photos would inspire Elaine to create a line of animal-related gifts that would benefit people who had lost their animals. When I told Elaine about this, she said she'd been thinking of enlarging her favorite photos of her dog.

When Quackers passed, Elaine followed all her wishes, and indeed their communication became stronger. Elaine began hearing Quackers as a gentle whisper. She listened to Quackers in utmost detail and wrote a book of poems in 1998 called Words of Quackers, a Dachshund Who Lives in Heaven. *Her life and her business have never been the same.*

Elaine expanded her business to include a line of treasured items for commemorating animals—a special memorial candle, necklaces, framed poems, and so on. To contact her regarding commemorative items, refer to the Resources section of this book.

People have suggested many ideas to me for commemorating animals, and one of the following might prove meaningful for you:

- Send announcements to those close to you.
- Write a poem, letter, or song to your animal, saying good-bye and recounting the memories of your lives together.
- Plant a tree in memory of your animal.
- Enlarge a picture and hang it in a favorite location in the house.
- Commission an artist to do a professional portrait, drawing, or sculpture.
- Make a scrapbook of your favorite photos.
- Create a collage of photos to hang in the animal's favorite room.
- Have a special photo of your animal friend imprinted on a T-shirt, mug, or set of mugs for the family.
- Have a cast made of the animal's paw print.
- Light a candle at a time of day when you would have had special time together, in the evening when you would have walked, or in the morning when you just sat together on the porch.
- Create a special box in which to keep your animal's belongings, such as his collar, leash, and favorite toy.
- Have a necklace or key ring made from your animal's identification tags.
- Clip some of your animal's fur to place in a special locket.
- Wear your animal's collar as a bracelet.
- Have a party with special friends to celebrate the life you had together; our animal friends often suggest this. They want us to celebrate the life we shared with them rather than mourn our loss.
- Using fur brushed from your animal, have a weaver or basket maker weave it through a basket.
- Make a donation to a charitable organization in memory of your animal. Choose an animal-rescue group, the Humane Society, a special veterinary school, or an animal hospital. You may choose to sponsor the care of a specific animal.

Many people who are sick, disabled, and elderly need assistance in order to keep a companion animal.

- Volunteer your services to the Humane Society or a rescue organization on behalf of your animal companion.

HANDLING GRIEF

Grief, like death itself, is a process. It may be expressed in various ways, but it is inescapable. It can begin when you first anticipate the animal's leaving and last until long after, if not forever. Tears are simply a testimonial to your love. Allow yourself to grieve throughout the process.

Grieving includes experiencing emotions such as shock, denial, anger, guilt, depression, sadness, and finally acceptance. Allow yourself to move through the pain of all these emotions. Those who don't often become stuck in their pain, as if mired in quicksand. Grieving is a personal and unique experience for each person; as you work through it, find ways that work for you to express your pain and sorrow.

When Dr. Ellenbogen and I cofacilitated a workshop on the death and dying of animals, she shared great wisdom with us. She reminded us that grief is *work*, and while it has no set time limit, it can typically take up to a year to feel a sense of recovery. Events during the year will constantly remind us of our loss: holidays, visiting places we went with our animal companions. She explained that grief is like a storm. It will happen, and we can choose to be prepared or not. Sometimes it hits us so hard because each loss in our lives brings up other losses we've experienced.

People are often surprised and confused to find that their grief over the death of an animal can be as intense as the grief of losing a human partner or family member. Why should this be so? Your grief over an animal may be deeper and last longer because it is pure, not complicated by your relationship. The animal has simply loved you unconditionally for who you are and not for what you do, or how you look, or how much money you earn. As a species, humans are not quite as evolved as animals in this regard. Animals have much to teach us about giving and receiving unconditional love. I believe one of the primary reasons they are here is to teach us how to love ourselves the way they love us.

Today, more options exist to help us resolve grief around losing an animal than there have been in the past, including specialized support groups and grief counselors specializing in animal loss. When you are mourning the death of your animal, it is important to surround yourself with people who understand. Give yourself permission to grieve. Allow yourself to have your feelings. Your sadness will ease with the passing of time. And remember, there is no right or wrong way to grieve. Allow yourself to do what most helps you.

Take the time you need to work through your grief, but keep in mind this passage from Neale Donald Walsch's book, *Conversations with God: An Uncommon Dialogue, Book 3:*

> *Mourning for them is the last thing they would want you to do. If you knew where they were, and that they were there by their own higher choice, you would celebrate their departure. If you experienced what you call the afterlife for one moment, having come to it with your grandest thought about yourself and God, you would smile the biggest smile at their funeral, and let joy fill your heart.*
>
> *We cry at funerals for our loss. It is our sadness in knowing that we will never see them again, never hold or hug or touch or be with someone we loved. And that is good crying. That honors your love and your beloved. Yet even this mourning would be short if you knew what grand realities and wondrous experiences await the joyous soul leaving the body.*

GETTING ANOTHER ANIMAL

Sometimes people who are grieving cannot stand the discomfort or loneliness they feel and want to fill that void by immediately bringing another animal into their life. Try your best to resist this impulse until you complete the cycle of grieving. Give yourself enough time to grieve for the animal you have lost. If you bring another animal into your life too soon, you risk not recognizing the animal for who he or she is and may, consciously or unconsciously, compare the animal with your last one. It is uncomfortable for an animal to come into a new environment and be the object of such mixed emotions.

This wonderful passage is from the book *Good-by My Friend: Grieving the Loss of a Pet*, by Mary and Herb Montgomery:

> *Grief is the price we pay for having loved. Through all the tears and the sadness and the pain of grief comes one thought that can make us smile again: we loved a particular animal dearly and that love was returned manyfold. When the time is right, you may feel that you have love to share with another pet. Not a pet to replace the one you had, but another animal to welcome into your home and into your heart.*

When you feel the time is right and you are ready to bring another animal into your household, avoid giving the new dog or cat the same name as the animal who passed on. That name is filled with memories and holds much emotion for you. Subconsciously, it also holds expectations of the relationship you will share with your new animal companion.

Allow this next family member to join you when you have completed your grieving process so that there can truly be a mutual sense of joy and new beginnings for all concerned. Each life is unique and irreplaceable.

THE REALM OF THE SPIRIT

As many people do, I believe that the spirit of any being lives on after death. The word *spirit* can be described in other ways, such as soul or life energy, referring to that energy you felt between your hands back in Chapter 3. It may seem subtle and intangible, but we know it to be there. If you'd like to explore communicating with your animal's spirit, or soul, or life energy, I encourage you to move forward without fear and to trust your intuitive skills. Let what we have learned through our exercises so far help you experience another aspect of the animal's world. If you're feeling skeptical, I assure you it's a normal reaction. Early in my career, I was skeptical too.

When a woman called asking me for a consultation with her late dog, Charly, I was dubious. I told her that I would certainly make the attempt on her behalf, and if I was successful she could pay me. However, if I wasn't—which I fully expected—we would consider the effort an experiment.

I was surprised when she turned up with a list of questions she had prepared for me to ask her dog. She wanted to know whether his transition had been easy. What was it like where he was? Was he with anyone? Did he have any message for her? I began the session, started going through her questions one by one, and to my amazement I started receiving answers! I had made the connection.

Charly told me, as clearly as any living being, that his transition had been easy, just as his life had been with her. He was in a place that was vast and where he could see forever. He particularly wanted to let me know about seeing a lake with ducks. When I told the woman this peculiar detail, she said they had walked daily at a nearby lake where he loved to chase the ducks. At that moment I was convinced I had actually connected to the right animal, one who was indeed in spirit form.

I asked Charly if there was a message he wanted me to give the woman. Gently and lovingly, he said, "I am surrounded by singing birds, and when she hears their song in her heart, she will know that I am near." As I relayed the message, tears began to stream down her face. She said, "Today I received his ashes and placed the urn on the mantel, and as I did, I heard the loveliest birdsong out the window. For some reason, when I heard that, I felt him in my heart. I could feel his presence with me." My communication with

Charly validated her experience, proving it wasn't just wishful thinking.

While I felt privileged to be able to offer her this confirmation and allow her to feel the presence of her dear friend, it was also a great revelation for me—proof that love need not end with death. Over the years I have continued to contact animals telepathically after death, either in their spirit or in reincarnated form, with a high degree of success. This communication came from a precious cat, Tiki, to Dorothy, her companion of an extraordinary twenty-five years.

It feels so different. My energy feels so expansive and surprising to me. I forgot what it was like not to be in a body. I can feel your empty feelings in your heart like a big hole. I try to soothe them. It will take time to heal. We were so connected. It's like our umbilical cord has been cut and the hole needs repair. You supplied me with so much energy that my way to leave was when I was not in your arms. Being in your arms was like being fed intravenously. It was like the plug finally getting pulled when I left your arms that last night. I just didn't have any more strength on my own. Oh, how we loved each other and will continue to love each other. I want you to feel warm always. I want your body to feel comforted, like you helped me to feel.

When I got here, it was like a homecoming. So many people were there to greet me. I felt like a celebrity; everybody was so concerned and there were flowers and rose petals like confetti all around me. It was like my own cheering squad. It's so beautiful here—waterfalls, as though they fall right out of the sky, billowy clouds, angels all around. It's glorious. I know you can see me here. You can visit me anytime. I miss being touched by you, but I will always remember that feeling. I'm not far, Dorothy, I'm only a breath away.

REACHING OUT TO AN ANIMAL IN SPIRIT FORM

Communication with animals in spirit form may be as simple as dreaming. You may receive messages from your animal through your dreams because this may be the most relaxed time for you to allow the communication to come through. You may also sense your animal's presence in the house, as my client did when she put the urn on the mantel. Or, of course, you may communicate directly by having a telepathic conversation.

This is where it's important to know what your animal's energy feels like. If you know that, you will be better able to recognize him when he visits in spirit form.

Communicating with an animal in spirit form is the same as communicating with an animal long distance, which we learned in Chapter 3. The method doesn't change. For some, including me, the communication seems easier, because the animal is no longer limited by a physical body.

To make a connection with an animal who has passed on, you will go through all of the steps you've learned to communicate telepathically with a live animal, summarized here:

1. Settle yourself in a quiet place within your household.
2. Do breathing exercises or a meditation to relax your mind and physical body. Let all thoughts of yesterday, today, and tomorrow drift by.
3. Allow your heart center to open and become receptive.
4. Feel the desire to make a connection with the animal in the spirit world. You can repeat your desire three times in your heart, so that your focus becomes stronger.
5. Imagine reaching out to that animal with your heart so that the connection can be made. Visualize a beam of light if you wish, or use whatever imagery works for you.
6. Then simply wait to see if the animal is available for the communication to begin. Just as in the long-distance exercise, know that animals can be busy and active in the spirit world.

They may be helping others make the transition or relaxing after their journey. Be patient. If you are unsuccessful in making a connection on a particular day, try again later or the next day.

The connection will most likely feel the same as when the animal was in a physical body. It may even feel stronger since there is no body to limit him. The process of communicating will be the same as when the animal was alive; you will still receive thoughts, feelings, impressions, and images. Now you can ask questions and share whatever information is important to you. You may want to ask if you made the right decision by assisting with his passing, or you might be curious if your animal is with another companion, animal or human, in the spirit world. You are free to talk about anything and everything. This is your opportunity to share your love, gratitude, and memories.

Communicating with an animal in spirit form can be particularly important for those who lost their animal suddenly with no chance to say good-bye. Having an opportunity to express important and tender feelings helps provide a sense of completion.

THE RETURN JOURNEY

Many of the questions I am asked to convey to animals in the spirit world are about their reincarnation, such as: Will you be coming back? If so, when? In what body? Will you still be a cat or a dog or will you be coming back in another form? How will I know it is you?

Although I truly believe in it, I will not make a case one way or another for reincarnation, but will simply pass on what thousands of animals have told me. Some choose to reincarnate, and some do not. They come back if they feel the need to return to a physical form. Animals' reasons to reincarnate may be to provide companionship or support for another animal or human, to complete unfinished business, to continue their own growth or learn lessons, or to teach lessons to others. Those who know they are coming back may even know in what body they will be returning. By telepathically contacting animals after they've left their physical body, we are able to ask what the next step is in their spiritual journey, whether they are still in spirit form or have reincarnated.

Often, when animals are ready to return, they give their people a definite sign so that they will be recognized. There may be a certain look in their eye, a mark on their body that clearly identifies them, or a certain behavior that they know will be recognizable. Even if they do not seem to know if they will reincarnate, they often tell their people to relax, assuring them they will be looking in on them from time to time. If you're interested in learning more about communicating with those in the spirit world, read the book *Talking to Heaven* by James Van Praagh, a wonderful look at this fascinating topic.

When you communicate with your animal, ask if he will come back and how you will know him. Trust that you will feel the connection you had in the past, the familiarity, the same sense of energy, and that you will continue to be able to telepathically communicate with him in his new physical body.

Rae Dellacqua asked me if a favorite horse of hers would return to her; she missed him very much. When I got in touch with him, he said he would be coming back, but wanted to return as a Border collie. When I asked him why, he said, "Because they are smart." Rae told me she had been researching the breed for quite some time, and this validated that she was on the right track.

Another client wanted to know if her horse would come back to her. He said he was thinking about being a bird since he would be able to go everywhere with her and not be left in a stall at night without her. Again, she told me she had been thinking about getting a bird as her next animal. Coincidence? You might want to think so. But, as many people believe, there are no coincidences.

This part of the book may be hard for you to contemplate, especially if this is not your belief system. Originally, it wasn't mine either, but after experiencing these things for fourteen years, I believe wholeheartedly. I am discovering that we all have the ability to return in the body that best serves our soul's purpose.

In this book, you have become acquainted with my twenty-one-year-old cat, Scooter, and his nine lives, from being lost for two months to his courageous battle with cancer for the past six years. A month after the completion of the book, the final chapter of his life in this form came to an end. As you know, a beloved animal's passing is a painful process as well as a beautiful one. Even in spirit form, Scooter continues to love me as gently as he did every single day of our twenty-one years together.

He left just four days before a workshop was to begin, and he was disappointed he couldn't stay to help me teach it. He especially liked lying in students' laps, "holding" and loving them in his own way. During the program, even though he was not with us in physical form, he certainly continued to teach us in spirit. Everyone felt his presence, listened to him intently, and gained much from his insights and wisdom.

I thank Scooter from the bottom of my heart for being my sleeping partner every night, for teaching me ever so tirelessly about patience and harmony, and for helping me write this book and bring it to a close.

I wish you a gentle good night, Scooter!

Jessie and Carol on a day off from teaching.

Carol with confident Dudley at age 13.

DIANE MOLLER

lessons
of
the heart

11

Learning to Love

This chapter holds the most important message in this book—
that animals have the power to help us transform ourselves. Animals can be our teachers as well as our healers. If we are mindful,
we can reap tremendous benefits from learning to communicate
with them.

LESSONS OF LOVE

People often say, "If only I could find a person to love me as my
dog does, I would be in heaven." Why do animals seem to love us
more fully than people do? While humans make judgments and
place conditions on others as well as on themselves, animals don't
care what job we hold, how much money we make, or what we
look like. They simply love us for who we are. Animals teach us to
love, every day, through thick and thin, even in the face of abuse
and neglect.

No words can describe the depth of our animals' love, the endless expanse of the feelings we experience in our hearts when they look into our eyes. Through animals, we learn that love is not about doing things but simply about "being." The love we have with animals is pure and uncomplicated, and all we have to do to be loved is to be there.

I learned how to give and receive that kind of love when my horse Dudley had a brush with death. Karen Martin of Phoenix, Arizona wrote my story for *The Whole Person Calendar of Los Angeles* in 1992. Here is an excerpt:

> *He had a major accident with his eye, which required stitches. All went well until he was given a shot of penicillin to which he had a severe allergic reaction, falling over on his back and thrashing about as if in an epileptic fit. Although he wanted to get up, he had absolutely no control over his body. He had always been very macho, in control. I was watching my horse die in front of me. I called to him, "Dudley, Dudley. Stay here with me, Dudley. Breathe with me." I kept breathing aloud with him so he could hear my breath. When animals are that terrified, they get lost in their fear; they have nothing to focus on. They start slipping away from you. To bring them back, you need to get them to focus on something: your voice, your words, their name, their breathing.*
>
> *I got very quiet with him, closed my eyes, and said, "Dudley, I don't know what to do for you. I'm so emotional that I don't know whether I can clearly hear something you may want to tell me . . . if you're hurting somewhere. All I know to do for you right now is to love you." At that moment, everything stopped. He gave a big sigh, put down his head, and stayed quiet.*
>
> *This was a major breakthrough in both of our lives, with profound lessons for both of us. For Dudley, it was a lesson in learning how to be vulnerable. He had never been able to let down his guard and call for help. He had always held it together for the other horses and his previous per-*

son. He was always being relied upon, depended upon. He
never had a chance to rely on a human being before. For
me, it was a major learning in what love is and how power-
ful it can be.

Love was simply about being there for him; it wasn't what I
was doing for him. With another person, we often try to prove our
love by doing things to show them we love them. With an animal,
we learn that simply being there is the essence of love. I realized
that by having Dudley breathe with me, I was making a safe environment for him, which allowed him to be vulnerable.

It's often the other way around. Animals usually protect and
comfort us, and they are consistent in their affections. Some animals have been willing to experience great pain and even give up
their lives in order to help their humans. In addition, animals often
take on our stress, sometimes resulting in physical illness.

Not surprisingly, people who have low self-esteem or are self-
critical often surround themselves with animals. They isolate from
humans and gravitate toward animals, intuitively knowing that an
animal's love will enable them to feel a sense of security and safety
in the world again. They may even restore their human relationships after healing through the animals' love.

Animals sincerely want us to see ourselves the way they see
us. In their eyes, we are beautiful and wonderful beings. Their unconditional love provides us with a feeling of safety, because they
harbor no judgment or criticism. They provide a safe environment
in which we can learn and grow.

One of the greatest gifts we can give our animals is to learn to
open our hearts to them and take that love and expand it outward to
every being—human, four-legged, two-legged, winged, finned—
and to every tree, rock, plant, and body of water. When we can do
this, we will show the animals we truly understand their message.
And when we can let go of our fears and be comfortable with who
we are, then perhaps we can stand up for our animal friends and
give them a voice. In Nelson Mandela's 1994 inaugural speech, he

eloquently said, "And as we let our own light shine, we unconsciously give other people permission to do the same. As we are liberated from our own fear, our presence automatically liberates others."

My dog, Jessie, taught me a powerful lesson about what devoted teachers animals can be.

At one of my animal communication workshop sessions, a student had brought her dog, who was uncomfortable around people. To make the dog less nervous, the two of them sat in an alcove off the main room where the rest of the group met. The group had started to practice their telepathic techniques with Jessie, when she suddenly halted communications in midstream. Baffled at first, we watched her trot over to the frightened dog in the alcove and lay her chin gently on top of the dog's head. When Jessie trotted back to the group, I asked her what had just transpired. She said she told the dog telepathically, "There is nothing to be afraid of. Just watch me and I'll show you."

Jessie came back to her place at the center of our circle, lay down with her paws crossed, and waited patiently. Suddenly the nervous dog got up and ventured into the main room. I welcomed her and telepathically reassured her that she was safe. She approached our circle, but rather than shrink in fear, she came up to each of us individually and touched her chin to our knees, just as Jessie had done at the beginning of the session. The group was speechless, moved and awed by this graphic demonstration of Jessie's healing power of love.

ANIMALS' AWARENESS

People often talk of their animal companions' sensitivities to their needs and the uncanny awareness they have of the human condition. You may experience your own animal's empathy when she tries to comfort you when you're ill or sad. I had an experience with my horse Dudley that made me realize just how sensitive animals can be.

I was doing a workshop away from home, and when I returned my landlord told me that Dudley had broken out of the pasture and a young woman had brought him back. I wanted to know what happened, so I asked Dudley about it. He said that the board came off the fence and, since the grass was higher on the other side, he decided to jump out. He assured me that he only went to eat grass.

About two weeks later, I interviewed a woman for a ranch-hand position. As soon as she walked onto the property, she told me, "I'm the one who brought your horse back." When I asked her where she'd found him, she said, "He was galloping up and down the road in front of another horse that was in pasture." She had wrapped her sweatshirt around his neck as a lead and scouted the neighborhood for his home.

You can imagine my reaction. I asked Dudley why he didn't tell me the truth. He said that if he'd told me the truth, I would have worried about him. He'd fibbed to spare me that stress.

My other horse, Tallanny, often plays with the truth to suit his own needs.

As my workshop students gathered around Tallanny one day, they asked him his age. Everyone received the same answer from him: He said he was five years old. In fact, he was twenty-three at the time. I was quite astounded that he would tell people he was five.

To help me understand his aversion to speaking the truth, he explained that if he said he was twenty-three, people would ask how long a horse lives. After learning that the average life span is in the late twenties, the students would feel melancholy, assuming that he was near the end of his life. The whole mood and energy of the workshop would change, and not in his favor. Therefore, in order to keep everyone cheerful and positive around him, Tallanny says he's only five years old. When people hear that, they think he's just a baby and emit feelings that are fun, loving, and joyful. He deliberately chooses to communicate this so he gets a favorable response rather than a negative one.

ANIMALS AS MIRRORS

REFLECTING OUR INNER SELVES

Animals' acute sensitivity to our feelings can translate into their own behavior. Very often, the way they act is a reflection of our emotions. Your animals often sense more than you do about your internal motivations and conflicted feelings. Because of their love and friendship for you, they want to help you feel balanced and happy. Should your feelings stay hidden or conflicted, they will often act them out, giving you an opportunity to look within yourself and perhaps make a change for the better.

I learned this lesson when I first started communicating with animals.

John from Alabama called me one day because his dog, Hobi, attacked people. Oddly enough, this happened only when both were in the same room with someone else. If John left the room, the dog was fine. John had been muzzling Hobi for five years.

When I contacted the dog telepathically, he was silent. I asked again, and again faced absolute silence. My first thoughts were that I had failed and lost my abilities. Because this was in the beginning of my work as an animal communicator, I immediately felt self-doubt. However, when I shared my experience with John, I was able to see the greater picture.

We were both initially perplexed until we began to talk about John's social life. Mulling his life over, John eventually told me how uncomfortable he was around people; at times, he even felt that they might in some way hurt or attack him. The light bulb went on for both of us.

This wasn't about his dog; it was about John's own fears around people. He would get so frightened that Hobi simply responded by pushing people away from John. Hobi did this because he loved him and didn't want him to get hurt.

Muzzling Hobi was only a Band-Aid solution. John needed to find out where the fear was coming from and then find ways to let

*it go. Once his fear was gone, the dog would no longer need to pro-
tect him.*

As this story demonstrates, we often want to fix the animal because we think the misbehavior is his fault, which seems much easier
than looking at our own possible involvement. My client was courageous in recognizing his responsibility to own up to his feelings.
Though it might be painful to look at our own issues, we need to be
willing to work them out—it's the only way we can grow.

I've learned over the years that when an animal has little or
nothing to say, it's often a clue to look within the family dynamic. It
can be an indication that feelings are not being expressed in the
family and the animal is simply acting them out. Interestingly
enough, I would estimate that seventy-five percent of my work involves asking my clients to examine their lives. Often, there is
something for them to learn about themselves through the animals' actions. Our animals' behavior can act as a mirror for us,
showing us aspects of ourselves that need nurturing and support.
By being aware of this, we can become motivated to change not
only for our own benefit but because we can see the direct effect it
has on them.

As Chris Griscom writes in her book, *The Healing of Emotion:*

> *Nothing happens outside ourselves that is not reflected in-
> side ourselves. . . . Healing our emotions facilitates lifting
> the emotional qualities of all human beings to the highest
> octave. We begin to feel "whole" in a completely new sense
> when we focus our attention beyond even another person,
> onto feeling a tree, a dog, the sea, a star, as part of our-
> selves.*

The old joke is that animals look like their people. What may
be closer to the truth is that animals' personalities reflect an aspect
of their guardians. People with introverted animals are often introverted themselves. Those with big, boisterous dogs often seem
loud and ebullient themselves. And, if we have ten animals, each

of those animals will be a separate aspect of ourselves: the nurturer, the clown, the explorer, the introspective one, and so on.

Maxine Berger from Sherman Oaks, California, had three animals in her household—Mr. Tibbs, an adorable buff-colored cocker spaniel; Cody, a long-haired black-and-white cat; and Samantha, a gray tabby. Maxine's situation confirmed for me that, while animals have their own distinct personalities, each animal is an aspect of our personality. Maxine called me at a time when all of her animals were experiencing some kind of upset, either behaviorally or physically.

By talking to each of them, I realized that this was a major case of "reflection." The animals were determined to show Maxine what inner changes she needed to make, and they were willing to help her make them. They were as devoted to her as she was to them.

Mr. Tibbs would frantically run from room to room, which was making everyone crazy. He said that he just wanted to make sure that everything in the household was okay. He wanted to please everyone and make sure they were all happy. Maxine identified with this trait immediately. She was a people pleaser, to a fault, and placed her own needs last on the list. As Maxine became more aware of this behavior (through the help of Mr. Tibbs's actions), she began to take better care of herself. And, as Mr. Tibbs observed Maxine's new behavior, he was pleased that he didn't have to work so hard. He would now periodically check in with everyone rather than be obsessed with his caretaking duties. He was thankful to Maxine for being so responsive to his "teaching" abilities. She was catching on quick!

Cody mirrored Maxine's physical imbalances and emotional upsets. He felt "heavy" or "weighted down" emotionally and had continual sinus problems. Maxine was again able to see herself in Cody. She saw her tendency to be too serious, allowing herself to become burdened by things. She, too, had developed frequent sinus infections. Maxine was one of the most willing clients I have ever met. Not only was she able to see the aspects of herself that needed to be nurtured and healed, but this courageous woman was willing to move forward with the changes.

Finally, Samantha was the busybody and "talker" of the household, second only to Maxine in this regard. She had the strongest personality of the animals and was extremely independent. Without hesitation, she said that Maxine needed to settle down; she was much too hyperactive. Maxine didn't have to think about this one very long. She knew she had a strong personality and loved to know everything that was going on with everyone.

Maxine took all of her animals' input to heart. She settled herself down and learned to find her still point. As soon as Maxine got quiet, all the animals became still and calm around her. Now she knows how well she's doing by watching the behavior of her animals. She uses them as a barometer. This family worked hand in hand, or perhaps paw in hand, to create balance and harmony for each other.

REFLECTING OUR RELATIONS WITH OTHERS

Animals can reflect not only what is going on within us but also in our relationships with others. However, their "reflective" behaviors cannot change a dynamic or situation. Only we can do that by being willing to make a change.

Nick and Sue, clients from Dallas, Texas, called me because their two male cats were viciously attacking the female cat. They had to keep them separated and the family was desperate. When I connected with the male cats telepathically, they confirmed that they felt driven to attack her, but gave no reason. This limited response was my clue that there was much more behind the cats' behavior, which had to do with the humans in the family.

Nick had started traveling a lot for athletic competitions. While he was on the road, Sue began to develop new friendships and a new support system, trying to keep busy and not be so lonely.

As we continued talking, Nick realized how resentful he was of

Sue's new friendships. He felt emotionally abandoned because she used to depend on him for emotional support. He was surprised at how angry he was with her. Not surprising was that the cats had been acting out the scenario. Because Nick wanted to change the situation and deal with his feelings, he had a long talk with Sue that night.

The next day I received a call from Nick telling me that he couldn't believe it. After he worked everything out with Sue, the cats had gone back to their friendly, normal selves. It can happen that fast. In this case, it did because Nick was willing to look at and deal with his feelings in order for the change to occur.

If your animals exhibit unusual behavior, consider whether it may actually be your problem. Observe the animal's action, ponder the situation, reflect on what you can learn from the situation, take responsibility, and act upon it. If you have trouble seeing a connection, ask for input from a trusted friend, or, even better, ask your animals. By observing our animals we learn to improve our own behavior. Their love truly helps us to learn and grow.

ANIMALS AS HEALERS

Animals can also help us heal the damaged aspects of ourselves. In cases where people adopt abused animals, I have found they often experience profound changes in their lives. As they nurture these animals and help them realize that not all humans are cruel and hateful, the humans often release their own walls of fear and pain. All of that nurturing and love is reflected back. As we heal them, we heal ourselves.

Some people initially feel they are "rescuing" the animal, but in time they feel the animal is rescuing them. My clients have shared countless stories in which their process of healing and rehabilitating animals allowed them to heal their own wounds of abandonment or abuse—physical, emotional, or sexual. Having these animals in their lives gives them an opportunity to deal gently with their own issues and come to peace with them.

Jeff, a client from Minnesota, came to me after he had rescued a sheltie named Suzie. Jeff told me about his problems with alcohol and that he had tried for most of his adult life to recover, without success. His family had always helped him through the difficult times, but they had decided he was now going to have to fight for himself.

Jeff said it wasn't until he adopted Suzie that he seriously came to grips with his drinking problem. When he brought her home, she began to have seizures. Jeff had to be there for Suzie, clear and sober, so he could care for her and be a source of calmness and stability. It wasn't until someone depended on him for survival that he was able to turn around his life. In adopting her, he was not only able to "rescue" Suzie from the shelter, but to "rescue" himself and bring them both to a place of harmony and health. As Jeff's life transformed, Suzie's seizures stopped. Through love, they healed together.

As the following story shows, two loving cats helped their people get over their greatest fears and resistances to change.

For years I've enjoyed working with two of my favorite clients, Mary Cordaro and Scott Davis Jones of Valley Village, California, and their two special cats, Cicely and Boston. Boston, a breed known as "rag doll" (much like a Himalayan), was mostly Mary's cat, and Cicely, a Zen-like Abyssinian, had a close bond with Scott. Most recently, we all worked together as first Cicely and then Boston passed on into the realm of the spirit.

One of Scott's biggest fears in life was death. When the cats suffered from kidney failure, Scott (a screenwriter who works from home) took care of administering subcutaneous fluids daily—for eight months with Cicely, and later for two years with Boston. When Boston required this treatment, Scott found himself uncomfortable with the process, even though he was familiar with it by then. Boston was so old and frail, and Scott was afraid he might hurt him. Boston, however, accepted the treatment with no problems, and Scott said it was as if he knew he was just trying to help. The daily ritual forged a special bond between the two.

Scott cherished having the responsibility for these wonderful creatures, who were so forgiving of his blunders. He was able to take what he learned from them—their sensitivity and acceptance—and model it in his other relationships. Scott experienced an epiphany as he realized that all beings are connected. He was grateful to Boston and Cicely for teaching him this lesson.

As Cicely grew increasingly ill despite the treatments, Scott and Mary knew her time had come and made arrangements to have a vet come to their home to assist with her transition. This would be Scott's first experience with death, and he had no idea what to expect. When the vet arrived, the cat leapt from Scott's lap and ran into the bedroom. This burst of energy confused Scott, leaving him bereft and guilt-ridden. If she had so much energy all of a sudden, was it really time to put her down? He didn't realize that this is often the case; when animals know they are leaving, they exhibit a sudden burst of energy, often in celebration of their leaving, a confirmation that it is indeed time for them to move on. Cicely's death would bother Scott for a long time, resolved only after Boston, too, passed away four years later.

Boston's passing was a healing experience for Scott. In the past, Boston shook with fear whenever the vet came, but Scott said that on this day, the cat met the vet with a demeanor of absolute calm and a sense of great dignity and courage. He lay his head in Mary's hands and slipped into the spirit realm in peace. Scott found inspiration and meaning in watching death unfold this way and realized that the journey could be courageous and graceful.

Shortly thereafter, as Scott drove along the 405 Freeway, a John Lennon song came on the radio: "Across the Universe." As he listened to the lyrics, Scott felt Cicely's presence and knew she was telling him that she was okay. He felt so comforted by this communication that it set him free of his anguish over her dying. He began to see that death did not have to be about fear, or judgment, or danger. It was simply a passage and could be a beautiful experience. Both Cicely and Boston had healed Scott of his biggest fear in life, a fear he'd carried with him always. Scott's hope now is that when it's his time to make the journey, he can leave with the same graciousness as Boston.

Mary's experience with the two cats' transitions were as differ-

*ent as her lessons were. A "Bau-Biologist," or healthy-home spe-
cialist, Mary's work required that she be out in the field, and she
often worked long, hard hours. The cats did not like how hard she
worked and felt it was their job to slow her down. Boston, in particular, helped her by being her "rag doll." Although he wouldn't
let anyone else touch him in this way, he let Mary squish him, roll
him over—very much like a dog instead of a cat. He was gentle in
his demeanor and slowed Mary down, bringing childlike behavior
back into her life by letting her play with him endlessly.*

*Cicely, on the other hand, demanded awareness from Mary.
She would sit and stare at her, and Mary knew she was insisting
that she stop, settle down, and get quiet. She also knew that there
was something to be learned from these moments, and she worked
through her workaholic tendencies as a result.*

*When Cicely passed on, Boston disengaged from Mary for a
time and comforted Scott. While Mary felt abandoned, she knew
the cat was helping Scott with his grief. Mary chose to view this
time as a healthy period of detachment from Boston before his inevitable passing. The two had always been so close that she knew it
would eventually be helpful to her. And it was; when he took his
last breath, Mary had a healthy perspective as she held him and
eased him through his journey.*

*Scott and Mary were grateful students of Boston and Cicely,
who were of tremendous service in helping them overcome their
fears and blockages.*

Just as these precious cats helped their people heal, so did a
feisty little Chihuahua named Marco, whose behavior might have
been cause for a much less happy ending had his person not been
so open-minded and spiritually aware.

*Two years ago, I had the pleasure of meeting Marsha Malamet,
an accomplished songwriter who has written songs for world-
famous artists, including Barbra Streisand, Faith Hill, and Luther
Vandross. She called me because she was having a problem with
Marco, one of her two Chihuahuas.*

When I arrived at Marsha's home, I met both dogs, Marco and Monte. While Monte was a happy guy, enjoying his dog life, Marco was obviously in distress. Marsha said she felt that Marco was like a mini-human being. He wore his emotions on his face—you could see them in his eyes. He was very responsive to Marsha and her every emotion. Marco even got sick when Marsha was grieving over the loss of a friend. But Marco was also moody and went crazy, barking every time Marsha left the house. Now he was beginning to bite her, and Marsha was afraid he'd keep getting more and more out of control.

Because Marsha is so aware, astute, and spiritually evolved, she knew something was going on that needed to be addressed and that she had something to learn from Marco. She knew that when parents have unresolved issues, children often act them out; she was pretty certain that animals played the same role in acting out their people's unconscious issues.

When I listened to Marco, he told me how dreadful it had been for him at the pet store before Marsha bought him. He said he had been there for a very long time and that people would come into the store and pick him up, but they would always leave him there. He had so much pain from being repeatedly abandoned that he became frantic whenever Marsha left the house. When he struck out at her, it was his way of begging her not to leave him alone again. As I told her this, Marsha recognized her own abandonment issues from childhood and realized they were both dealing with the same trauma. Marco said he was also angry with Marsha for bringing Monte into his life. He didn't want a relationship with another dog, just with Marsha.

Marsha now understood why he was behaving this way, and every time she left the house, she told Marco how long she'd be gone and showed him a mental image of her returning, excited to see him. She also greeted him first when arriving home, since she now knew his true feelings about Monte.

When Marsha saw Marco for who he was and realized he was her mirror, and when she was truly in the moment with him, his *biting stopped. Unfortunately, however, he would bite her one more time, and the biggest lesson would be learned.*

One day Marco was biting his paw. He'd been doing it a lot lately, so Marsha tried to look at it to see if anything was wrong. To her great surprise and disappointment, Marco bit her. She became enraged and hurt. Seemingly out of the blue, memories of her childhood flashed before her. As a child, she had been caretaker to her sickly mother and never felt any appreciation in return. Now, as she wondered how Marco could do this to her when she was just trying to be the best possible caretaker, it all sounded a bit too familiar.

Allowing herself to get in touch with her pent-up feelings of anger as a child was worth two years of therapy, Marsha said. Marco mirrored Marsha's own dance of anger and resentment. He was able to express anger, and she was able to learn from his demonstration—a deeply needed healing for Marsha. And now Marsha needed to learn to be the best caretaker possible for herself, to let go of the past and her anger and to move forward with life.

Marsha loves Marco now more than ever, for being her teacher and healer. She says that it's not about the bite; it's about what happens afterward and the choices we make. Rather than believe that he was a mean or bad dog, she chose to take the opportunity to learn about herself. Many people would have given up on Marco, but Marsha saw it as her moment of grace. She accepts Marco's imperfections, which helps her to accept her own imperfections. To learn to love her own imperfections is to love herself—the biggest lesson for all of us.

As long as we can see the reflections our animals lovingly share, we're on our way to healing not only others but, most important, ourselves. As Ralph Waldo Emerson said: "It is one of the most beautiful compensations of this life that no man can sincerely try to help another without helping himself."

ANIMALS AS TEACHERS

As you helped your animal adapt to his new home, trained him, played with him, cared for him, did you ever suspect that he would be your teacher? Animals are the most gentle, loving, and wise teachers you will ever know. Just when you least expect it, they can present you with powerful lessons. Their methods may range from subtle to bold, funny to serious, behavioral or physical—whatever it takes to get your attention and help you learn.

How simply this is said in a poem written by my uncle, William Curran, who loved and cherished his dog until the end of his days.

> I want my boy to have a dog, or maybe two or three.
> He'll learn from them much easier than he would learn
>   from me.
>
> A dog will show him how to love and bear no grudge or
>   hate.
> I'm not so good at that myself, but dogs will do it straight.
>
> I want my boy to have a dog to be his pal and friend
> So he may learn that friendship is faithful to the end.
>
> There never yet has been a dog who learned to double-
>   cross
> Nor catered to you when you won, then dropped you
>   when you lost.

THEY TEACH US TO BE IN THE MOMENT

Marsha Burns from Sherman Oaks, California called me one day, worried about her nine-year-young golden retriever, Mattie. Mattie's left leg and shoulder had been removed six months previously due to cancer. The cancer had spread, and tumors now invaded her heart, neck, and lung. Marsha wanted me to check in with her to see if she was ready to go, since the vets were suggesting it was time. She didn't want Mattie to suffer.

Marsha had always lived a busy, on-the-go lifestyle. "During Mattie's nine years, occasionally I would notice I just wasn't present with her," she said. "It's not that I didn't love her, but I've always been so busy, so nervous, so driven. I just didn't know how to take the time to be in the moment." Mattie's illness and surgery changed all that. Marsha spent more quality time with Mattie, and the two developed a close bond.

When I checked in with her, Mattie told me that she was not ready to go. She wanted Marsha to know she was not afraid to die, but that she was scared for her. She didn't want to leave Marsha, because she didn't know who would care for her the way she did. She helped to keep her focused, in the moment, and who else would do that?

She still wanted to go for her walks with Marsha and still loved having her company. She didn't mind if Marsha had to cry—she could handle it. She wasn't going to leave Marsha until the time was absolutely right for both of them, and she even described how Marsha would know when it was time for her to go.

Marsha decided to try slowing down, to be in the moment for Mattie's sake, since she'd never been able to do that for herself. Even physically, Marsha had to slow her walks with Mattie, since the dog was growing increasingly weaker. They'd take longer rest breaks, sitting on the curb, providing even more quiet time to be together and express their love for each other. Marsha says she will always treasure these memories. When Mattie passed on, she gave Marsha the exact sign she'd promised, and Marsha, while sad, finally felt prepared.

Mattie gave Marsha an extraordinary gift, but Marsha also gave Mattie the greatest gift of her life. She learned the lesson Mattie was here to teach her, to be in the moment.

If we observe animals' behavior—they eat when they want to, sleep when they want to, play when they want to, and love unconditionally—what better role model could we have? We need to adopt these same ways of being in our own lives. Animals do not worry about the past or think only of the future. They are present in every precious moment.

THEY TEACH US WHAT IS MISSING WITHIN OURSELVES

As we've learned, animals reflect what is going on within our lives and in our relationships with others. They can also teach us the missing links we need to change our lives.

Fern Marks of Burbank, California called me because her Black Smoke Persian cat, Melissa, was in the hospital, seriously ill with kidney failure. She wasn't eating or responding. Fern wanted to know if Melissa wanted to be released from this life. She didn't want to keep the cat here if she wanted to leave.

Recently, Fern had started her own business, which she found extremely stressful, overwhelming, and time-consuming. She had always felt that Melissa was a difficult cat because she didn't get along with the two male cats in the household and wouldn't eat by herself unless Fern was standing right next to her. Even when Melissa was at her water bowl, she would dart away if the other cats approached her. Now, stressed by her life, Fern was beginning to get short-tempered and angry with Melissa, wanting her to "snap out of" her fearful behavior and take care of herself.

When Fern and I talked, I told her how animals sometimes reflect what is going on within us. When Fern thought about it for a moment, she recognized herself in Melissa. She admitted she was not taking care of herself.

When I spoke with Melissa, she said she wanted to stay, but she needed Fern to love herself. She also needed Fern's love and for her to understand that the other cats were often aggressive with her. Fern felt so strongly about Melissa's communication that she gave up her business and went to work for someone else. She immediately felt the burden lift from her shoulders and became more attuned to herself and to Melissa's longing to be loved. Fern real-

ized that Melissa had taken on her negativity, which had made her sick. From that moment on, the two had a bond that could not be broken.

The day after our session, the vet called Fern, saying he wasn't quite sure what had happened or how, but that Melissa was ready to go home. She returned to the loving and understanding arms of Fern and began to play for the first time in her life.

The next story shows us just how much animals have to teach us about life, our relationship with ourselves, our relations with others, and the importance of our spiritual connection. Pam Putch, the proud guardian of these two precious cats, wrote the touching story of Angeli and Miele.

Last October my fourteen-year-old kitty, Miele, started to show signs of illness. She had been diagnosed with melanoma cancer two years earlier. I was inexperienced with the dying process and needed advice and guidance. I heard about an animal communicator named Carol Gurney and wanted to have a session with her as I prepared for Miele's transition.

Miele was bold, full of moxie, charm, and affection. Angeli, her younger sister by a year, was the polar opposite—small, delicate, and quiet. To me, Angeli was a mirror of all the things that I was shy about in myself. Miele was the mirror of all the things that I was proud of. As Carol began speaking over the phone, I knew instantly that she had connected with Miele. The thoughts were humorous, matter-of-fact, and a little prideful. Miele talked about her beauty, her food desires, and when asked about the dying process, she seemed completely calm. She was more concerned about me than herself. The notion that this dear little creature had focused on caring for me through her ordeal lifted my fear of what was ahead.

A couple of weeks later, Miele became more uncomfortable and I sensed that we were getting close. Carol encouraged me to talk more to Miele. In the time we had left, I began talking to her about everything. During this period, I became a hermit, spending every nonworking moment with Miele. It was a big change, because I had always been the type to load my free time with friends, meals, and activities. The solitude of the healing work that we did every day felt as close to meditation as I ever had come. Miele and I had a deep, wordless, loving connection and I savored every single moment I had left with her.

During those three months, I paid little attention to Angeli. When I did think about the future, I wondered dubiously what our relationship would be like without Miele. The family dynamic was so defined. Miele was my cat and Angeli was Miele's cat. In hindsight, I realize that Angeli watched lovingly over both of us. Even though Miele was getting weaker, Angeli never tried to eat the baby food from Miele's bowl, she allowed Miele the pick of the sleeping spots, and she would never interrupt a healing session.

The time to ease Miele's pain came, and I knew that I needed to help her. One week after Miele left the planet, Angeli stopped eating. This went on for days, and after visits to different vets and a night in the animal hospital, the diagnosis was still unclear. I sought medical treatment with Dr. Roger Valentine, who practices alternative as well as traditional veterinary medicine. Instinctively, I knew that he was the right person to help. His commitment to Angeli's health was beyond what I had ever experienced from a vet. Despite our efforts to pinpoint the problem, Angeli's fast continued. I knew that she couldn't live much longer by force-feeding, and as I watched her sit in the closet day by day, I feared the worst. I needed a different kind of help, so I called Carol. The communication confirmed my fears. Angeli did not know how to "be" without Miele. She felt abandoned and wanted to be with Miele. She was feeling the grief more deeply than I was. I had never had a great connection with Angeli, and if that was her desire, it felt right to let her go, even though it was heartbreaking.

Through my tears, I resolved to accept her wishes. As part of this process of letting go, Carol encouraged me to talk to Angeli about all the wonderful times we had shared, and she comforted me by telling me what Angeli felt she had given me. Her gift was "music." Carol used the illustration of me as the violinist being given a bow by Angeli in order to make "music." It was a beautiful image from a precious heart, and I felt my own heart beginning to open. Then I asked Carol to tell Angeli things that I had always felt about her. Angeli taught me to find the soft and gentle places in my heart; she reminded me that the quality of grace was within me. Carol communicated this to Angeli. After a quiet moment, Carol said, "Wow, fireworks just went off in your cat." Angeli said, "Wow, I did that? I can't believe I did something so big for her." My heart leapt, and I asked if that meant Angeli wanted to stay with me. The answer was a timid "I'll think about it." This was an incredibly moving and big experience between Angeli and me. It felt as if we were a married couple who had lived together for thirteen years and had never really said how much we loved each other. The emotion and love reverberated throughout the house.

Ten minutes after Carol left, Angeli went to her food bowl and, for the first time in four weeks, ate on her own. From that moment on, things changed between us. We stared into each other's eyes for long periods of time; she let me hold her indefinitely. These things were never part of our relationship before. After a few days, I had the feeling that she had decided to stay. And from that moment, I committed myself to the healing of her body.

A month later, however, Angeli was continuing to lose weight and strength. I prepared a list of questions—most of which were a laundry list of her ailments—to try to gain some insight for the vet. Carol came to the house, and together we sat with Angeli in the walk-in closet. As I began the questions, Carol interrupted. "Angeli does not want us to focus so much attention on her shrinking body. She sees herself as growing huge in a spiritual way." The simplicity and profoundness of that idea astounded me. I realized that I had been so focused on her physical health that I had missed the greatest event of all: The timid, introverted cat I had known for thirteen years had grown to be a spiritual giant.

Carol continued, "Angeli wants you to know that you gave her the courage to stay. And even if she is not around physically at some point, she will still be connected to you. She says, 'I will still exist.' I was awestruck by this session. The love that I felt from this creature was completely unconditional. I realized that the last six months had been about love, not death. It was hard for me to give Angeli up, but I knew that I had done everything I could for her body. I turned my energies toward making the moments that we had left as full of love as I could.

In the last few weeks of her life, I talked to Angeli constantly. I said her name over and over, as Carol said Angeli wanted to hear. I told her in as many ways as I could what she had meant to me and what she had given me. I told her how I saw her essence: spring flowers and sunlight and violin music and grace. These moments together lifted my spirit and lifted the sadness of what was coming. And I will never forget how her soulful gaze filled my heart.

Now that both Miele and Angeli are gone, I feel them in me; Miele sits on my shoulders and Angeli lies near my heart. Such love lifts and supports and keeps on going even after the body is no longer there. And there have been changes in my life. Violin music has never been as beautiful to me. Those quiet and alone moments that used to feel empty and scary to me are now full, and I crave them.

The last time Carol came to my house, she used the image of an umbilical cord or a kite to describe how Angeli and I would always be connected. I am in the process of making two kites. They are in the shapes of giant hearts, and one will have Angeli's face on it and the other will have Miele's. I will take the kites to the beach and fly them as a celebration of our special relationship.

This story is so special because without Pam's openness, sensitivity, and willingness to honor and respect life and its lessons, none of the learning would have been possible for her or for Miele and Angeli. I have the utmost respect for people who are willing to have that heart to heart connection, and I applaud Pam for her willingness to listen to her animals' inner wisdom and apply the Lessons of Love.

THEY TEACH US TO ACCEPT AND RESPECT WHO THEY ARE

Just as people do, animals have distinct personalities and desires. Some may want to be house dogs, or some may enjoy the show ring, while others simply want to play the role of caretaker. Some animals are happiest in a large family, and others want to be the only animal. It's important to let them express exactly who they are, without limitations.

Alice Abdullah sent her five-month-old female Doberman, Channing, to be trained for competition by one of the country's top handlers. Channing came from a long line of champions, and Alice thought she would fit in beautifully with her family of three other show Dobermans. When Channing returned, Alice was able to position her properly for competition, but the dog would not allow the judges to touch her. At shows, she would jump, spin, and do anything it took not to be handled. Alice said it was as if she was saying, "I don't want to do this." Alice couldn't understand why she was behaving this way.

When I arrived on the scene, Channing wouldn't let me in the door. She growled and showed aggressive behavior. When I asked her why she was acting that way, she said she was frustrated that she wasn't liked by her family for who she was. She did not want to be a show dog, and she was unhappy trying to fit in with the other show dogs in the family.

Once Alice heard this, she changed her attitude and accepted Channing's wishes. The dog then changed her behavior and settled down. In Alice's heart, however, she knew that Channing would be better off being the only dog in a family. Even though she was committed to keeping her and believed strongly in keeping animals for life, Alice could see how much things had changed just by accepting Channing's desires, so eventually she became brave enough to let the dog go to another family, where she could truly be content.

We often think that we must have our animals for a lifetime, but sometimes that's not what is meant to be. Sometimes our animals are merely visitors. They may not be the right fit for your family; if so, love them enough to let them go. When my horse Dudley needed to move on, it would have been selfish of me to keep him and expect him to do what I wanted to do. The day Alice let Channing go was one of the hardest she had to face, but she did the right thing. She now gets reports about how happy Channing is as the only dog in her new family.

THEY TEACH US TO TRUST OURSELVES

Throughout this book and in the stories I have shared with you, trust has been the essential lesson. By having faith in us, animals teach us to trust ourselves at a core level. As you can see from the experiences of Maxine, Fern, Jeff, and others, each was able to have faith in the relationship with their animals and trust their guidance. However, they each took it a step farther. They allowed themselves to trust their own inner wisdom to make major changes in their lives—a journey of moving from self-doubt to self-trust.

THEY TEACH US TO FIND THE JOY IN LIFE

Every day, animals reward us with their never-ending enthusiasm and unconditional love. They magically appear on our laps or by our side when we're tired, weak, or ill. Their comforting warmth and reassuring presence gives us the energy and strength to heal. You may remember times when you've felt lonely, sad, or discouraged—and a gentle but persistent nudge wouldn't let you give up.

We often forget how to play and enjoy ourselves. We are so caught up with jobs and responsibilities that we forget to take the time to enjoy life. Setting aside time to play with our animals is a wondrous antidote. By simply being who they are, they help us balance our lives.

Animals bring laughter back into our lives. So many people tell me that when they are in the middle of an argument, one of their animals will come right between them, performing crazy antics that bring the arguing humans to laughter and shift the mood of the conversation.

Our animal friends bring us such lightness and joy, and I truly believe this is their purpose here with us.

Barbara from Tampa, Florida called regarding her terrier, Jenni. Both of them had been suffering from long-term health problems, and they had become isolated in their home. Barbara wanted to know how Jenni was feeling about her health and the overall situation and if there was anything she could do to help her.

The first thing Jenni told me was that she didn't want Barbara to worry about her. She felt that Barbara had enough stress in her life and didn't need any more worries. She had lots of advice for what Barbara could do to help herself: take her for more walks so they could both get some exercise, keep flowers around the house, and listen to more music. Apparently, these were things Barbara used to do for herself, but had not done in some time. Jenni desperately wanted Barbara to bring the fun and laughter back into her life—she was adamant about it.

Barbara started acting on Jenni's suggestions. When they went for walks in the park, Barbara found herself surrounded by people wanting to pet Jenni, and she naturally started to meet them. She watched kids play in the park, something she'd always loved to do but had forgotten about. After the long isolation, she was finally able to bring herself back out into the world.

THEY TEACH US TO RECONNECT WITH OUR PLACE IN THE NATURAL WORLD

While many people acknowledge that language can exist between machines and humans, they have a hard time acknowledging that language (in the form of telepathic communication) can exist between animals and humans. Amazing amounts of time and money are spent on computers, classes, and consultants in order to communicate with inanimate objects, yet many people still are unwilling to learn this natural and relevant language. Thanks to all of you, however, things are changing in our society. We are finally recognizing ourselves as intuitive beings, and when we acknowledge that within ourselves we can acknowledge it with animals.

We tend to see our lives as separate from the world of nature. We live so much in the material world that we forget our place of origin. Indigenous people are more in tune with the rhythms of nature and how people fit into the ecology of the world. In our so-called "civilized" societies, we lose that. Even the animals living with us remain more aware than we do. By having animals in our lives, we can keep in touch with the primitive and instinctual part of ourselves that we have forgotten.

I received this message from an animal who was at the point of death. He felt compelled to relay it very explicitly and concretely to his humans.

> *They need to go for walks away from home, in the country. They need to get away from routine, to go by the water, to the gardens, places where thinking doesn't matter but where "being" is all there is. There's no music or magic in routine chores. Make me a promise that you will partake of the magic in nature—listen to the bees, the butterflies, surround yourself with the little things in life that hold all meaning.*

Chris Griscom makes this point beautifully in her book, *The Healing of Emotion*, when she writes:

> *The world around us is not, after all, separate or detached from us. Every being we see on the street, every life situation we perceive outside of ourselves, is within us. Instead of resisting this, we simply need to let our consciousness expand so far that we can try out this way of viewing things. The power lies in healing internal energies and seeing their transmutation reflected in the world.*

Nature can live without us, but we cannot live without nature. Increasingly, people are being spiritually drawn into the country, the hills, the forests, to commune with nature. I have theories as to why this might be. I think we have finally gotten to the place where we know our lives are not working for us and we want to change our ways. By going into nature, we allow ourselves to be quiet and listen. We start by listening to the birds, the wind, and the flow of the creek. This allows us to still our bodies and minds so we can connect again with our spiritual selves, returning to our natural place within the world. It's like going home.

We need to acknowledge, honor, and respect all the aspects of ourselves in order to recognize and respect all other human and nonhuman beings. By connecting heart to heart with ourselves, we are able to see and nurture all of who we are: emotional, spiritual, physical, and mental beings. We regain the balance we so desperately seek to feel whole, at peace, and abundant within. The connection brings us back to our center and allows us to get back in touch with a sense of sacredness, enabling us to return "home."

And to my surprise, I was now going to find my path back home through the most challenging period of my life. When I finished the book in June 2000, not only did I lose my father, but my two lifetime companion cats left this world, one after the other: first Scooter of 21 years, then Joy Boy, the joy of my life for fourteen years. It was a year of great loss, but as we know, with loss comes changes and blessings.

Joy Boy's leaving gave me the courage to go deeper within myself in silence. Because I missed his physical presence, it forced me to spend that quiet time with myself to reconnect with both Scooter and Joy Boy. Not one day has passed since Joy Boy left that I haven't sat quietly, allowing myself to make that connection. Strangely enough, even though I've always made time to help others achieve this, I would not have taken this time with myself had Joy Boy still been in physical form. Both cats are guiding me back to my center, enabling me to return to my real home, deep within my heart.

I believe Joy Boy knew it was time to leave in order to teach me the lessons of true self-care. I sincerely hope that your journey with your animals takes you to that place called trust. We can all strive to keep the hearts of humanity alive by connecting heart to heart. Let your animals give you the courage to make that connection.

In closing, I'd like to share a meditation with you that I do with students at my training programs to help us stay connected at a heart level. Do this meditation with another person or in a group. Sit in chairs or on the floor. Extend your hands outward to a partner (or those on either side of you in a circle) and hold each other's hands, the palm of your left hand facing up and the palm of your right hand facing down. Your left side represents your female energy (receptivity), so having your palm face upward allows you to receive the energy from your partner or the person on your left. Your right side represents your male energy (action/sending), so having your palm facing downward allows you to send energy to your partner or the person on your right. Once you have gathered in this position, begin the meditation:

♥ Close your eyes and take some deep breaths, scanning your body for any tension that you are holding. Breathe into those areas, and on the exhale, allow all of that tension to release.

♥ Imagine that roots from a very wise and old tree are growing from the bottoms of your feet and extending deep into the earth. These roots will help keep you grounded and connected to the earth throughout the entire day.

♥ Now imagine that you have two doors on the top of your head, and above your head is a most wondrous light that comes to you from the highest spiritual plane. Gently and easily, allow these doors to open, and let the light flow effortlessly into and throughout your entire body, allowing every aspect of your being to relax. With each breath you take, your body becomes more and more relaxed, and your mind becomes more and more quiet. Allow yourself to expand into this light, feeling peaceful. Let all thoughts of yesterday, today, and tomorrow just drift by.

❤️ Let every atom, molecule, and cell in your body be filled and nurtured by this light, allowing it to fill every part of your being.

❤️ Once you feel relaxed, begin to gather and focus your energy in your heart center, allowing a lovely pink light to emerge and surround that area. Let yourself feel nurtured and at peace. Most important, allow yourself to feel all the love and compassion you have for yourself—to recognize and accept how beautiful you are. Allow this pink energy to serve as a mirror for you so you can see and feel how beautiful and magnificent you are. Remember, this loving aspect of yourself is who the animals see all the time.

❤️ Now allow that pink energy to move outward, spiraling from your body into the middle of the circle to connect with the group's energy. Then let that energy flow outward to those animals and people who are in need of assistance at this time. Allow their hearts to be touched and as open as yours is, so that all of humankind can see the beauty within their own hearts, so that they may see that animals are truly our brothers and sisters.

❤️ After a few minutes, send that loving pink light from your heart to the heart center of the person to your right. You are connected heart to heart. Remember that this is the place from which we speak and listen to each other and to the animals. Take a few moments to feel that connection with each other and the tremendous loving energy you have created together. And then slowly begin to take deep breaths, and with each breath you take, become more and more aware of your physical body and your environment. When you feel complete, open your eyes.

May this light guide you, comfort you, and protect you on this wonderful journey we call life. And may this light help you love yourself the way your animal loves you—unconditionally. I dedicate this poem, "The Bridge" by Rachelle Hasnas, to all of you who have read my book. Thank you for having the courage to recognize who you are and who your animals are, and to bridge the gap between humans and animals.

THE BRIDGE

I have been searching seeking,
Restless in the constant knowing that all that is
Is not what it seems.
A wisdom within, yearning to be free,
Will not let me sleep one more life away.
That inner voice will be still no longer,
For my time has come to hear
What my Soul has known since the beginning of time.

I have finally chosen the path back home;
No longer do I wander aimlessly on.
There is purpose to my steps,
For the light has come and fills me
With its love and sense of divinity.
All fears recede as I take on the awareness,
Knowing that I am God
Joyfully I take my power back,
Though a bit hesitantly as I understand
That with this Truth comes responsibility.

Am I ready to be who I am?
Yet, do I have a choice any longer
To remain who I thought I was?
For yesterday's dream fades fast
Nothing left to hold on to
I stand on the brink of tomorrow.
It comes to me now, so strong and so sure.
I am a Bridge from what was, to what comes;
A link from the old to the new.
The choice has been made
There's no turning back
In freedom I walk proudly in Light!

BIBLIOGRAPHY AND SUGGESTED READING LIST

ANIMAL COMMUNICATION AND SPIRITUAL

Boone, J. Allen. *Kinship with All Life*. New York: HarperCollins Publications, 1954.

Gallegos, Eligio Stephen. *The Personal Totem Pole: Animal Imagery, the Chakras and Psychotherapy*. Santa Fe: Moon Bear Press, 1990.

Griscom, Chris. *The Healing of Emotion: Awakening the Fearless Self*. Galisteo, NM: Light Institute Press, 1999.

Masson, Jeffrey Moussaieff, and McCarthy, Susan. *When Elephants Weep: The Emotional Lives of Animals*. New York: Delacorte Press, 1995.

McElroy, Susan Chernak. *Animals as Teachers & Healers: True Stories & Reflections*. Troutdale, OR: New Sage Press, 1996.

Morgan, Marlo. *Mutant Message Down Under*. Lees Summit, MO: MM Co., 1991.

Myers, Arthur. *Communicating with Animals: Unleashing The Spiritual Connection Between People and Animals*. Chicago: Contemporary Books, 1997.

Randour, Mary Lou. *Animal Grace: Entering a Spiritual Relationship with Our Fellow Creatures*. Novato, CA: New World Library, 2000.

Roads, Michael J. *Talking with Nature*. Tiburon, CA: H. J. Kramer Inc., 1987.

Smith, Penelope. *Animal Talk, Interspecies Telepathic Communication, Second Edition*. Hillsboro, OR: Beyond Words Publishing, Inc., 1999.

Walsch, Neale Donald. *Conversations with God: An Uncommon Dialogue, Book 3*. Charlottesville, VA: Hampton Roads Publishing Company, Inc., 1998.

DEATH AND DYING

Kübler-Ross, Elisabeth. *On Death and Dying*. New York: Macmillan Publishing Co., Inc., 1969.

Montgomery, Mary and Herb. *A Final Act of Caring: Ending the Life of an Animal Friend*. Minneapolis: Montgomery Press, 1993.

Sibbitt, Sally. *"Oh, Where Has My Pet Gone?" A Pet Loss Memory Book, Ages 3–103*. Wayzata, MN: Libby Press, 1991.

Van Praagh, James. *Talking to Heaven: A Medium's Message of Life After Death*. New York: Signet, 1999.

ALTERNATIVE HEALTH CARE

Billinghurst, Dr. Ian. *Give Your Dog a Bone: The Practical Commonsense Way to Feed Dogs For a Long Healthy Life*. N.S.W. Australia: Ian Billinghurst, 1996.

Brennan, Barbara Ann. *Hands of Light: A Guide to Healing Through the Human Energy Field*. New York: Bantam Books, 1987.

Fox, Dr. Michael W. *The Healing Touch*. New York: Newmarket Press, 1990.

Frazier, Anitra, with Eckroate, Norma. *The New Natural Cat: A Complete Guide for Finicky Owners*. New York: Plume Books, 1990.

Goldstein, Martin, D.V.M. *The Nature of Animal Healing*. New York: Alfred A. Knopf, 1999.

McKay, Pat. *Reigning Cats and Dogs: Good Nutrition, Healthy Happy Animals.* South Pasadena, CA: Oscar Publications, 1992.

Pitcairn, Richard H., D.V.M., and Pitcairn, Susan Hubble. *Dr. Pitcairn's Complete Guide to Natural Health for Dogs & Cats.* Emmaus, PA: Rodale Press, 1995.

Schoen, Allen, D.V.M., and Proctor, Pam. *Love, Miracles and Animal Healing.* New York: Simon & Schuster, 1995.

Stein, Diane. *Natural Healing for Dogs & Cats.* Freedom, CA: The Crossing Press, 1993.

Tellington-Jones, Linda, with Taylor, Sybil. *The Tellington TTouch: A Breakthrough Technique to Train and Care for Your Favorite Animal.* New York: Viking Press, 1992.

ANIMALS' UNDERSTANDING OF TIME

Feuerstein, Georg. *Structures of Consciousness: The Genius of Jean Gebser.* Lower Lake, CA: Integral Publishing, 1987.

Sheldrake, Rupert. *Dogs That Know When Their Owners Are Coming Home and Other Unexplained Powers of Animals: An Investigation.* New York: Crown Publishing, 1999.

Wilbur, Ken. *A Brief History of Everything.* Boston: Shambhala Publications, 1996.

RESOURCES

ALTERNATIVE HEALTH CARE
Nelson Bach USA Ltd.
Wilmington Technology Park
100 Research Drive
Wilmington, MA 01887
978-988-3833
Fax: 978-988-0233
Bach Flower Remedies
Brochure: Pets Have Emotions Too
Bach Flower Essences for Pets

Tellington TTouch
TTEAM Training USA
Linda Tellington-Jones
P.O. Box 3793
Santa Fe, NM 87501-0793
800-854-8326
www.Lindatellingtonjones.com

DEATH AND DYING
Products
Elaine Seamans for AT-CHOO
577 N. Kenmore, #2
Los Angeles, CA 90004
323-644-2745
Animal Memorial Gifts

Services and Organizations
AVMA
American Veterinary Medical Association
1931 N. Meacham Road
Suite 100
Schaumburg, IL 60173-4360
800-248-AVMA
www.avma.org
Information on pet-loss support groups, allied groups, on-line grief
and loss brochures

IAPC
International Association of Pet Cemeteries and Crematories
5055 Route 11
P.O. Box 163
Ellenburg Depot, NY 12935
800-952-5541
Listing of U.S. and Canadian Animal Crematories and Cemeteries

Delta Society
289 Perimeter Road East
Renton, WA 98055-1329
800-869-6898
425-226-7357
www.deltasociety.org
Promoting the Human/Animal Bond

Nikki Hospice Foundation for Pets
Rosemoor House
400 New Bedford Drive
Vallejo, CA 94591
707-557-8595
www.csum.edu/pethospice/
Database of veterinarians interested in hospice work

Pet Loss Hotline
Department of Family Practice
c/o School of Veterinary Medicine
University of California
Davis, CA 95616
530-752-1011

Pet Loss websites:
www.petloss.com
www.dogheaven.com

ANIMAL CARE
AAHABV
American Association of Human/Animal Bond Veterinarians
Dr. Sally Walshaw
4550 Comanche Drive
Okemos, MI 48864
www.members.aol.com/guyh7/aahabv.htm
Involved in hospice work

AAHV
American Association of House-Call Veterinarians
Schaumburg, IL
www.avma.org
Follow links to allied groups or call
800-248-AVMA

AHVMA
American Holistic Veterinary Medical Association
2214 Old Emmorton Road
Bel Air, MD 21014
410-569-0795
AHVMA@cs.com

Dr. Tina Ellenbogen
Mobile Veterinary Services
Animal Home Care and Hospice
425-485-PETS
P.O. Box 1744
Bothell, WA 90841
Dr.TinaVet@aol.com
Packets and resource lists available

LOST AND FOUND
AKC
American Kennel Club
800-252-7894
www.akc.org
Recovery for purebreds

Animal Recovery
www.pmia.com
Offers free listings

The Humane Society Animal Rescue Team
H.A.R.T. Rescue Line
P. O. Box 920
Fillmore, CA 93016
805-524-4542
Fax: 805-524-5738
www.hartrescuelines.org

National Pet Recovery
800-984-8638
www.petrecovery.com

Pet Finders
800-274-2556
www.petfindersalert.com

Sherlock Bones
800-942-6637
www.sherlockbones.com
Tracer of missing pets

MISCELLANEOUS PRODUCTS AND SERVICES
Animal Portraits
Custom Oil Paintings
By Karrel Christopher
19 Fairbanks Street, #11
Brookline, MA 02446
www.Karrelart@cs.com

Cat Fence-In
P.O. Box 795
Sparks, NV 88432
888-738-9099
www.catfencein.com

ABOUT THE AUTHOR

Carol Gurney teaches workshops in animal communication, from beginning to advanced levels, as well as bodywork for animals. She is also available for private tutoring and animal communication consultations. For more information on her workshops or any of her products, please e-mail her at: cgurney@earthlink.net or visit her website: www.animalcommunicator.net.